9-9-25

Perspectives on
CHARISMATIC RENEWAL

Perspectives on
CHARISMATIC RENEWAL
EDITOR: EDWARD D. O'CONNOR, C.S.C.

UNIVERSITY OF NOTRE DAME PRESS
NOTRE DAME/LONDON

NIHIL OBSTAT: Robert Nogosek, C.S.C.
Censor Deputatus
IMPRIMATUR: Leo A. Pursley, D.D.
Bishop of Fort Wayne-South Bend
Feast of Pentecost, May 18, 1975

ɩ

Library of Congress Cataloging in Publication Data
Main entry under title:

Perspectives on charismatic renewal.

Includes bibliographical references and index.
1. Pentecostalism—History—Addresses, essays,
lectures.   2. Holy Spirit—Addresses, essays,
lectures.   3. Pentecostalism—Bibliography.
I. O'Connor, Edward Dennis.
BX8762.P47   260   75–19875
ISBN 0–268–01516–3
ISBN 0–268–01517–1 pbk.

1890121

To Margie, Ben, Allee, Bill,
Kathleen, Eileen and Joe;
and in memory of Paul

CONTENTS

ACKNOWLEDGMENT

The preparation of this book was facilitated by a release from part of my teaching duties at the University of Notre Dame, thanks to generous subsidies from the Congregation of Holy Cross and the Catholic Charismatic Renewal Service Committee. To all three of these organizations I am profoundly grateful.

The manuscript of this book was typed by Shirley Schneck, with assists from Bernice Hegedus, Monica Markley, Marie Meilner, Carmela Rulli and Ryan Welsh, of the Faculty Stenographic Pool at Notre Dame. Anyone who has ever had to prepare his own manuscript knows what a great help it is to be able to have recourse to devoted and generous typists, as these were. For this I am sincerely grateful.

Finally, I must thank Thomas Bonaiuto, who drew up the index with his usual care and accuracy; and Cae Esworthy, who, in mediating between the manuscript and the printer, added a breath of the Spirit to trustworthy professional competence.

Edward D. O'Connor, C.S.C
February 10, 1975

CONTRIBUTORS

CARROLL STUHLMUELLER, C.P., born in Hamilton, Ohio, in 1923, made his religious profession in the Congregation of Passionist Fathers in 1943. After studying in Passionist seminaries in Detroit and Louisville, he was ordained a priest in 1950. He did graduate studies in theology at Catholic University, Washington (1951–1952), and at the Biblical Institute in Rome (1953–1954), receiving his doctorate there in 1968. He has taught Scripture at the Passionist Theologate in Louisville (1954–1965), at St. Meinrad Seminary, Saint Meinrad (1965–1968), at St. John's University, New York (1970–1974), and at the Catholic Theological Union of Chicago (1968–) where he is currently Professor of Scripture. During the fall and winter of 1973, he was visiting professor at the Ecole Biblique et Archéologique of Jerusalem.

Principal publications: *The Gospel of St. Luke* (Collegeville: Liturgical Press, 1960); *The Book of Isaiah, Ch. 40–66* (Collegeville: Liturgical Press, 1965); *The Prophets and the Word of God* (Notre Dame: Fides, 1966); *Creative Redemption in Deutero-Isaiah, Analecta Biblica* 43 (Rome: Pontifical Biblical Institute, 1970). Besides contributing numerous articles to *The New Catholic Encyclopedia* (New York: McGraw-Hill, 1966), *The Jerome Biblical Commentary* (New York: Prentice-Hall, 1968), and various journals, he is associate editor of the *Catholic Biblical Quarterly* (since 1973) and *The Bible Today* (since 1965).

He is now at work on a study of "Biblical theology and the problem of synthesis," as well as a popular book on "Religious life in Biblical focus."

ANTON-HERMANN CHROUST, born in Würzburg, Germany, in 1907, studied at the universities of Würzburg, Erlangen, Heidelberg, Munich, Bologna, Paris (the Sorbonne), London, and Harvard, receiving doctorates in law from Erlangen and Harvard, and in Philosophy from Munich. He has taught law, history, and the history of philosophy at Harvard Law School (1935–1941), Yale Law School (1961–1962, 1966–1967), and the University of Notre Dame (1946–1972), where he still resides, lecturing and writing.

Besides over 200 learned articles, he has published the following books: *Socrates: Man and Myth, the Two Socratic Apologies of Xenophon* (London: 1957); *Aristotle: Protrepticus, a reconstruction* (University of Notre Dame Press, 1964); *The Rise of the Legal Profession in America* 2 vols. (University of Oklahoma Press, 1965); and *Aristotle: New Light on His Life and on Some of His Lost Works* 2 vols. (University of Notre Dame Press, and London: Routledge, 1973).

JEAN LAPORTE was born in 1924 at St-Satur (Cher), France. After fifteen years spent in pastoral work and religious teaching, and in the preparation and publication, conjointly with E. Jarry, of the series, *Témoins de la Foi* (Paris: Bloud & Gay), in 1966 he joined the faculty of the University of Notre Dame, where he is now an Associate Professor, teaching Greek and Latin Patristics. He has also taught summer courses at St. Joseph's College (Orange, California), Siena Heights (Adrian, Michigan), and St. John's University (Collegeville, Minnesota).

Principal publications: French translation of Quasten's *Patrology* (Paris: Cerf, 1956 and 1962); *Lacordaire* (Paris: Bloud & Gay, 1961); *De Josepho* in the series, *Les Oeuvres de Philon d'Alexandrie* (Paris: 1965); *L'Eucharistie chez Philon d'Alexandrie* (doctoral thesis, Paris: Beauchesne, 1972). Other works, published or in preparation, have to do with Philo, Origen, the ministry and ordination of women, the Roman See, and an introduction to patristic literature.

JAMES KRITZECK, born in St. Cloud, Minnesota, in 1930, studied at the universities of Minnesota, Princeton, and Harvard, receiving his Ph.D. from Princeton in 1954. He taught at Princeton from 1954 until 1965, when he became a member of the Princeton Institute for Advanced Study (1965–1967). Since 1965, he has been on the faculty of the University of Notre Dame as professor of oriental languages and history, and as director and fellow of the Institute for Advanced Religious Studies. He was consulting editor of *The New Catholic Encyclopedia* 1963–1967, and editor for the section on non-christian religions for *The Catholic Theological Encyclopedia* 1969–1970.

Besides numerous scholarly articles, Dr. Kritzeck has published the following books: *Peter the Venerable and Islam* (Princeton: University Press, 1964); *Anthology of Islamic Literature* (New York: Holt, Rinehart, and Winston, 1964); *Sons of Abraham* (Baltimore: Helicon, 1965), and *Modern Islamic Literature* (New York: Holt, Rinehart and Winston, 1970), besides collaborating on several others.

He is at present preparing the following works: *Islam in Southeast Asia, The Islamic Manuscripts in the Bibliotheca Ambrosiana of Milan, Ibn Hazm of Cordova: A Biography,* and *Sons of Abraham: Jews, Christians and Moslems* (an expansion of the work published in 1965).

LOUIS BOUYER of the Oratory was born in Paris in

1913. After studies at the universities of Paris and Strasbourg, he served as minister in the Lutheran Church of France until the Second World War, when he entered the Roman Catholic Church. He studied for the priesthood at the Institut Catholique in Paris, and entered the Oratory. From 1944 he was professor of Church History and Spiritual Theology at the Institut Catholique, until he resigned in 1961 to work on various Roman Commissions (the Consilium for Liturgical Reform, the Sacred Congregation for Divine Worship, the Secretariat for Promoting Christian Unity, the International Theological Commission, etc.). Meanwhile he lectured extensively as a visiting theologian in the United States, England, Spain, and Africa.

He is author of some 40 books, not to speak of innumerable articles. Among the more important of his writings are: *L'Incarnation et l'Eglise: Corps du Christ dans la Théologie de Saint Athanase* (Paris: Cerf, 1943); *Liturgical Piety* (Notre Dame: University Press, 1955); *Newman: His Life and Spirituality* (London: Burns and Oates, 1958); *The Spirit and Forms of Protestantism* (London: Collins, 1963); *Rite and Man* (Notre Dame: University Press, 1963); *Dictionary of Theology* (New York: Desclee, 1965); *Eucharist* (Notre Dame: University Press, 1968); *The Decomposition of Catholicism* (Chiacgo: Franciscan Herald Press, 1969); and *L'Eglise de Dieu: Corps du Christ et Temple de l'Esprit* (Paris: Cerf, 1970). Father Bouyer has also contributed volumes 1 and 3 to *The History of Christian Spirituality* published in collaboration with Jean Leclercq, François Vandenbroucke and Louis Cognet which is still in the process of translation (New York: Desclee, 1970ff.).

Father Bouyer is now working on a book dealing with the Holy Spirit.

EDWARD D. O'CONNOR, C.S.C., born in Denver, Colorado, in 1922, entered the congregation of Holy Cross in 1939. After studies at the University of Notre Dame and Holy Cross College (Washington, D.C.), he was ordained a priest in 1948. He did his doctoral studies in theology at the Institut Catholique of Paris and Le Saulchoir, receiving the S.T.D. from the Angelicum (Rome) in 1962. In 1952 he joined the faculty of the University of Notre Dame, where he is now associate professor of theology. Since 1967 he has also been involved in activities associated with the Charismatic Renewal.

Principal publications: *The Dogma of the Immaculate Conception: History and Significance* (Notre Dame: University Press, 1958); *Faith in the Synoptic Gospels* (Notre Dame: University Press, 1961); *The Pentecostal Movement in the Catholic Church* (Notre Dame: Ave Maria Press, 1971). Present projects: a series of volumes on the theology, historical background and spirituality of the Charismatic Renewal.

INTRODUCTION
EDWARD D. O'CONNOR, C.S.C.

The aim of this volume, and of the others which are projected in this series, is to draw upon the resources of the university in shedding light on the significance of the charismatic renewal or Pentecostal movement. *University* here refers not only to Notre Dame, the publisher of the present volume, but to the whole world of academic institutions and disciplines.

The University and the Charismatic Renewal

Ten or twenty years ago it would have seemed incongruous for a modern American university to devote serious attention to such bizarre phenomena as glossolalia, faith healing and prophecy, which, for better or for worse, have come to be taken as emblematic of the charismatic renewal. But there is no eluding the fact that the Pentecostal movement originated in the heartland of America, right at the beginning of the twentieth century.[1] Although it largely ignored and was ignored by the great religious thinkers of the century—the Barths, Bultmanns and Tillichs, as well as the Blondels, Sertillanges and Rahners—and rudely violates some of their most honored dicta about the religious needs of contemporary man, it is proving to be perhaps the most vigorous religious movement of this century.

For six decades, if the academic disciplines took any notice of the Pentecostal movement at all, it was usually with annoyance or amusement as at an embarassing

1

anachronism. Instead of withering under this scorn, the movement flourished, even while more conventional religious observance began to go into serious decline. Now, in the seventies, the academics seem to be retooling in preparation for an explanation of the movement as a predictable result of psychological, social and economic factors of our culture. Since Mohammed did not go to the mountain, the mountain is going after Mohammed.

In any case, it is obviously not in academic circles that the charismatic renewal was conceived, engendered, or nurtured. There was even a common assumption that such a movement could flourish only among the un-educated. It was depicted as a defense mechanism whereby the dispossessed of the world comforted themselves for the lack of earthly goods by fantasies of spiritual power.[2] But this view proved untenable when the renewal broke out among socially and economically well established Episcopalians, Lutherans, and Pres-byterians, and especially when, in the Catholic Church, it appeared first in predominantly university ambients: at Duquesne, Notre Dame, Michigan State and Michigan (to say nothing of subsequent developments elsewhere). When the latter development became publicized, some people regarded it as just one more instance of college students off on an adventure. Others learnedly analyzed it as an anti-intellectual reaction to the pressures and tensions of academic life. People looking on from a certain distance began to speak of the "intellectual" character of the Catholic charismatic renewal.

The vanity of the first two explanations has been demonstrated both by the fact that this renewal had several beginnings not connected with college campuses, e.g. in St. Louis, Missouri, in Orange County, California, and elsewhere, and above all by the fact that after the initial outburst, the renewal has developed more among settled adults than among young students.

No doubt, the atmosphere of a university as well as its physical equipment facilitates the dissemination of new ideas and movements; and it is to be expected that in a Catholic university, more than in most other locales, people will be found who are relatively well educated in their faith and seriously concerned about deepening and renewing it. But there are negative factors also. Besides the basic sociological fact that the constantly changing student body makes a stable movement difficult to maintain, universities are prone to sophistry, academic unrealism, and brash rationalism, all of which are seriously inimical to the growth of faith.

In sum, the charismatic renewal is neither an intellectual nor anti-intellectual movement. It germinated, not out of an idea, but out of experience of the action of the Holy Spirit in loving fellowship, and this continues to be the source of its vigor. This movement vindicates for itself the statement of St. Paul, "My speech and my message were not in plausible words of wisdom, but in demonstrations of the Spirit and power" (I Cor. 2:4).

But the fact that it is not the offspring of the university does not imply that the charismatic renewal has nothing to gain from academic studies. Its well-being requires that it be understood as accurately as possible both by those who take part in it and by those who don't. And while it is true that things of the Spirit can only be understood spiritually (I Cor. 2:14)—an inviolable principle which academics must take particular care not to forget—it is also true that the charismatic renewal has roots, attachments and analogs in the nature of the human psyche, in the dynamics of social interaction, in the cultural matrix in which the renewal occurs, in non-Christian religions, and in para-religious rituals, all of which are proper subjects of the academic disciplines. The Spirit of God may be the ultimate source of energy for this movement, but His work is not a creation *ex nihilo:* it is a recreation, a regeneration, a radical renewal of materials already provided by human nature and human history. Neither the charismatic outburst of the first century, nor that of the twentieth, occurred in utter

discontinuity with the world that preceded and paralleled them. Their background, without adequately
explaining them, does illumine their significance and
helps to define their distinctive character.

The purpose of the series here introduced is to put
this movement in perspective, not precisely to promote it.
Most of the contributors to the present volume are
neither committed to nor involved in the charismatic
renewal; some may even be quite unsympathetic to its
motifs. But they are all competent in disciplines which
from one angle or another can shed light on it. Also, this
volume is not designed to be a coherent whole; it is a
collection of papers, as the subsequent volumes will also
be. The *Perspectives* series is meant to provide a vehicle for
serious academic studies on the charismatic renewal,
somewhat in the style of a yearbook, although not
committed to appear at regular intervals.[3]

The Uniqueness of the Christian Gift of the Spirit.

It is an axiom of Christian faith that the Holy Spirit
cannot be received except as a gift from Christ. The third
person of the Holy Trinity is not an *anima mundi,* a kind
of great world spirit that can be tapped by means of some
ascetic discipline or yoga, or attained by persons of
'mystical' temperament. In Himself He is divinity,
transcending the range of our powers, inaccessible even
to our minds. For us men, He has become the Spirit of
Christ, who was operative in Jesus when He worked
miracles and cast out devils, and was poured out by the
risen Lord upon His disciples. In fact, the Holy Spirit is
the principal and distinctive gift of Christ, to which all
His other gifts and works are subordinate. Christianity in
essence is nothing other than being filled with the Holy
Spirit: "Anyone who does not have the Spirit of Christ,
does not belong to Him" (Rom. 8:9).

Nevertheless, Christian faith itself recognizes that the Spirit was clearly operative in the world before that gift which occurred on the great Pentecost. Not only did He inspire the people of Israel in preparation for the coming of Christ, but He is also at work in the world outside the Judeo-Christian sphere.[4] Regardless of how *ruach* is interpreted by the translators of Genesis 1:2, there is an obscure truth in the lyric of Gerard Manley Hopkins that compellingly demands assent:

> There lives the dearest freshness deep down
>   things;
> And though the last lights off the black West
>   went
> Oh, morning, on the brown brink eastward,
>   springs—
> Because the Holy Ghost over the bent world
> Broods with warm breast and with ah! bright
>   wings![5]

At the very least, these lines are a harmonious echo of Psalm 104:30: "When you send forth your Spirit, they are created, and you renew the face of the earth."

On the other hand, the comparative study of religions makes it evident that both the concept of *Holy Spirit,* and charismatic works such as prophecy and healing, have analogs in non-Christian religions. Furthermore, reflection on the charisms themselves has led many to the view that, at least in some cases or to some extent, they have a natural basis which is activated by the Spirit, rather than being conferred *de novo* in a wholly supernatural way. Finally, the notion of spirits who enter into, inspire, and even take possession of men is common to many religious traditions. Even those psychologists who regard the entire realm of good and evil spirits as fundamentally delusional are obliged to recognize that such 'delusions' are sizeable factors in human life with which every adequate anthropology has got to reckon.

Hence there arises inevitably the question, which

will, however, have a different meaning for believers and
non-believers: what is distinctive about the Christian gift
of the Spirit? What characterizes it by contrast with its
pagan, pre-Christian and natural analogs? While the
essays published here do not furnish adequate material
for a definitive reply to this question, they do suggest
some hypotheses that may be worthy of further investigation. A comparison of the place occupied by the Holy
Spirit in Christian thought and life with that of the
parallels registered in Israel, Greece and Islam brings out
two obvious contrasts. First, in Christianity the Spirit is
given to everyone instead of being reserved to a few
extraordinary prophets, shamans, or mystics. Second,
the activity ascribed to the Holy Spirit in Christianity is
incomparably more abundant, diverse, and specific than
in the other religions.

The idea that a man can be introduced into a
personal and intimate relationship with the divine
spirit—as Moses, for example, spoke with God face to
face (Exod. 33:18–23)—is commonplace in diverse religious traditions. But this is not usually regarded as the
common lot of men; it is reserved for a privileged few,
who by that fact become intermediaries between the
spirit world and their commonplace brethren. Christianity, however, proclaims the outpouring of the Spirit of
God "on all flesh"—not just on kings and prophets, but
even on slaves (and what is more, women slaves!)—as Joel
foretold (2:28f.) and St. Peter proclaimed (Acts 2:17).
They shall all become prophets, it is said, seeing visions
and dreaming heavenly dreams. All of God's children are
led by the Spirit of God (Rom. 18:14).

Paradoxically, however, this universal outpouring of
the Spirit does not suppress the distinction between those
who have special gifts and those who do not. Not all are
prophets in the narrower sense,[6] not all are workers of
miracles, not all are glossolalics or interpreters, any more
than all are apostles or teachers, says St. Paul (I Cor.
12:29–30) in writing to a community that was not lacking

in any spiritual gift (I Cor. 1:7). Far from abolishing the
notion of intermediaries with God, Christianity gives all
believers the role of interceding for one another (I Tim.
2:1) not by reducing all to a common function, but by
conferring distinct offices and ministries on different
persons, organically interrelated and interdependent in
the structure of the Body (I Cor. 12; Eph. 4:4–16) for the
ministry of the Spirit (II Cor. 3:8).

Hence, even if we compare Christianity with other
religions on the basis of what we may call extraordinary
pneumatic manifestations, the contrast is noteworthy.
But before going into that, we must note the preliminary
difficulty of assessing the wonder stories with which
almost every popular tradition abounds.

Even when one can deal with the evidence at first
hand, it is hard to get to the truth of such reports. In spite
of all the means of communication and testing made
available by modern technology, many people today are
perplexed as to what to make of Kathryn Kuhlman, Yuri
Geller, Jeanne Dixon or the miracle-healers of the
Philippines; how much more difficult it is to evalute
legends that have come down from ancient and un-
familiar civilizations! To what extent do they transmit
real experiences, and to what extent are they the product
of hallucination, fantasy, poetry, and prevarication?
Because of the staggering difficulties involved in dealing
with this question, we will have to prescind from it; but we
do not do so in the spirit so often encountered in such
studies, that attribute an equal reality to all of these
legends simply because they are there. If you are serious
in trying to evaluate a religious tradition that lays claim to
healing, prophecy, levitation and the like, it surely makes
a fundamental difference whether these things occurred
in reality or only in imagination. Where you are not in a
position to decide such a question, the weight of your
conclusions is drastically curtailed. (To argue that what
matters is not the factual truth of the legend, but what it
meant for those who transmitted it, is grossly specious.

To know the beliefs and ideals of a people is indeed already something important; but it doesn't take the moment out of the question, whether what that people clung to was imagination or reality.)

But even prescinding from the question of realism, it would seem that we can observe a remarkable difference between the charismatic experiences claimed by Christians and the pneumatic phenomena of other religious traditions. In Greece and Islam we read of enthusiasm and ecstasy, inspiration and visions; but these notions are vague and indistinct, and the references are usually quite general. The Old Testament is much more specific in its accounts of prophets and judges; but apart from them not many other works of significance are ascribed to the Spirit of Yahweh.

In turning to the Christian tradition, we are struck first of all by the rich diversity of functions attributed to the Holy Spirit; secondly, by the definite, distinct character of at least many of them; and thirdly, by the fundamental importance of the Spirit's activity for the Christian life. He cleanses, regenerates, and enlightens; He imparts wisdom and filial piety; He appoints bishops, equips pastors, inspires virgins and fortifies martyrs; He is the source of healing and deliverance, of prophecy, miracles, tongues, interpretation and discernment; He imparts love to all, and by His power those who have been His faithful temples will one day be raised from the dead. In addition to what He does for individuals, He is the link that binds the entire community together in a living, organic union: He is the soul that vivifies it as the Body of Christ.

In sum, the works of the Spirit seem to play a far more important, abundant and definite role in Christian tradition than their analogs elsewhere. This hypothesis will need to be tested from many angles, for instance, by comparison with the complex angelology of later Judaism or the polymorphous divinities and fakirs of Hinduism; but that is a task to be left to specialists.

The Uniqueness of the Christian Revelation of the Holy Spirit

A third question raised by these studies has to do with the very idea of the Holy Spirit. According to some of the best exponents of Christian theology,[7] the Holy Spirit, just as He can only be received from Christ, can only be known through Christ's revelation. The trinity of persons in God is the mystery of mysteries, which nothing in nature can disclose to the inquiring intellect of man. As no one knows the Father unless the Son reveals Him, so likewise no one knows the Holy Spirit except by this same revelation. In fact the two are revealed together, for only the Holy Spirit enables us to cry *"Abba, Father"* (Rom. 8:15).

But when he looks abroad at other religions, the Christian may be somewhat startled to find in many of them an impulse towards the recognition of a quasi-divine figure remarkably similar to the Holy Spirit. It may not surprise him that in the Old Testament the Spirit of God gradually takes on a more definite character and undergoes a kind of personification that prepares the way for the New Testament revelation, even receiving the very name, *Holy Spirit,* in the wisdom literature. But when Islam too, despite its conscious and passionate rejection of Trinitarianism, is found, at least in certain circles such as that of the sufis (who are of no inconsiderable importance!), developing the concept of a Holy Spirit scarcely distinguishable from Allah Himself, the problem becomes more serious.

The "world soul" elaborated in various schools of Greek thought had such an obvious affinity with the Christian Holy Spirit that the two were identified by some of the Greek Fathers and medieval scholastics. Likewise Zoroaster speaks of a "Most Holy Spirit" of God, opposed to the Evil Spirit. Other analogs for the Holy Spirit that have been suggested are the Ka of early

Egyptian religion, and the Hindu Atman in its relationship with Brahman.

One must beware of being fascinated by superficial similarities between notions belonging to radically disparate patterns of thought;[8] nevertheless, we can hardly avoid at least posing the question: is there something in the very nature or structure of the world that tends to suggest to the soul of man the idea of a divine spirit? If so, how are the uniqueness of the Christian revelation and the intrinsic mystery of the Holy Spirit to be safeguarded? May it be that wind and breath are natural religious symbols prepared by Providence in view of their ultimate elucidation by the prophetic Word?

There does not seem to exist any general study of the notion of spirit as applied to the divinity in the diverse religious traditions of mankind. Perhaps the elucidation of the particular traditions has not yet sufficiently advanced to make such a study feasible. The present volume in any case does not propose to achieve such a work, but only to pose some of the questions, to suggest possible answers, and to provide in an accessible form some of the necessary materials.

The Christian charisms must be studied against the background of those of the Old Testament, among which prophecy was by far predominant. In fact, by the time of Christ the prophets had come to be equated with "men of the Spirit." When St. Peter on Pentecost cites (Acts 2:17–21) the prophecy of Joel, the statements, "I will pour out my Spirit upon all flesh," and "they shall prophesy," are apparently meant as synonyms.

However, the forms of prophecy were much more variegated than is generally realized, and the very style of prophecy underwent considerable evolution between its primitive beginnings and its sublime literary achievements. And even though we acknowledge divine inspiration as the ultimate root and benchmark of Biblical prophecy, we must nevertheless reckon with strong affinities between the early Hebrew prophets and their orgiastic pagan counterparts.

—The Editor

PROPHECY IN ISRAEL

CARROLL STUHLMUELLER

"Prophecy," wrote Bernhard Duhm as far back as 1916, "has its history. . . . [Its nature and manifestation are] not a timeless revelation."[1] This observation, the quintessence of a lifetime of study, was inscribed in the last book to be written by this patriarch of modern scientific investigation into the biblical prophets. It is still being repeated.[2]

It seems impossible to arrive at a definition of prophecy so clear and specific that people of any age can thereby discern quickly what is a true prophet and how to become one. Prophecy, rightly states Rolf Rendtorff, "embraces such [widely] different phenomena."[3] According to Ivan Engnell, "it occurs in different cultures and religions, both in the highly developed cultures of antiquity and in different peoples of our day, with very diverse meanings and in widely different contexts."[4] Yet, because of the importance of this question—what is a prophet and how do we react, if we or someone else turn out to be prophetic?—we must plunge ahead in our discussion.

Prophecy: A Divine Enrichment of Traditional Religion

From all this uncertainty among the masters, one certain conclusion can still be drawn: through the power of His spirit, God has continuously exploded the restric-

13

tive confines of human definitions of prophecy, even
those of any particular age of the Bible. We will find some
biblical norms for spotting false prophets, yet we must
obediently look to God for the *positive* signs of prophecy.
No one makes himself a prophet; each prophet sur-
renders to a divine initiative and is called by God: "Go!
Prophesy!"

The first of the 'classical' or 'writing' prophets,
Amos, rejected the high priest Amaziah's definition of
the prophetic office. This tough, desert-trained
shepherd spat back his words disdainfully before
pompous authority:

> I am no prophet, nor a member of any
> prophetic group! . . .
> The Lord took me . . . and declared:
> *"Go! Prophesy to my people!"* (Amos 7:14–15)

Amos rejected the noun 'prophet'[5] but was willing to
accept the verb, to make of prophesying what God willed.
A noun is always more static and determined in meaning;
a verb is always more open to living adaptation. Amos
asserted that God would make him into his own special
kind of prophet. Amos was to be a shock to false
institutionalization and rigid human standards. Yet
when Amos' ministry was completed, the people Israel
through their institutional authority called this extraordinary man by the very title he once rejected. And as
such he is introduced to us in the Bible.

The office of prophet somehow remains divine
property, whose secret qualities must be learned anew by
each succeeding generation. Nonetheless, the person
with a faith obedient to God's surprises can, like the Bible
itself, look across the long series of prophets—from
Samuel before 1050 BC till Malachi around 450
BC—and discern a continuity and a tradition. From this
long history of prophecy, we hope to discover a few
crucial moments of evolutionary leaps in its development

and so to isolate some of the more important aspects. Although each new manifestation of prophecy strikes *foudroyant,* still this surprise will not consist in anything totally new but rather in the marvelous ways God can still combine the diverse qualities of the old.

Within Biblical tradition prophecy appeared in two principal manifestations. The representatives of the first group are often called the 'charismatic' or the 'ecstatic' prophet. Sometimes the Hebrew word *nabî'* (in the plural, *nebî'îm*) is applied to them. In the Bible they feature prominently in those books which the Jewish canon entitles 'the early prophets' (Joshua, Judges, 1–2 Samuel, 1–2 Kings). Since these books appear to be historical, an important feature of prophecy comes to our attention at once. Prophets address themselves to God's presence within history, that is, within the continuity and institutions of human events. The second group are designated somewhat improperly the 'writing prophets' (we have books under their name, yet their principal duty did not lie in writing but in preaching) or more correctly the 'classical prophets' (the word 'prophet' usually evokes the name of such classical figures as Isaiah or Jeremiah).[6] In the Hebrew Bible they are grouped together as the 'latter prophets,' i.e., the three major (Isaiah, Jeremiah and Ezekiel)[7] and the twelve minor (Hosea to Malachi).

These opening remarks about biblical prophecy speak an important message for the charismatic movement and its own contemporary form of prophecy. Touching the more traditional styles of religion and its basic institutions, prophecy presumes their existence, even while it challenges and seemingly disrupts their orderly arrangements. Amos, we saw, rejected the high priest Amaziah's concept of prophecy. Yet Amos' new kind of prophecy eventually enriched tradition and so ensured its continuity. The very community which the prophet threatened later edited the prophet's words and placed them within its institutional expression of faith, the word of God in the Bible.[8] Prophets must persevere loyally within the traditional covenant for their words ever to become part of the Bible.[9]

At the same time, institutional authority within established religion must humbly take a warning from its past history and avoid any quick execution of its troublesome challengers. Prophets, in particular, are very difficult to judge during their lifetime. While the Bible provides various ways in which the prophetic qualities unite and express themselves, still the Bible does not exhaust the possible varieties within prophecy. In Old Testament and New Testament times, each new series of prophets took the community by surprise, up to and including the prophet Jesus.[10]

Ecstatic Prophecy and Charismatic Communities

Appearance

When prophecy first appeared in the Bible, it seemed like a swift invasion of divine power into the more normal handling of human life.[11] This abruptness almost contradicts our opening remark that "prophecy has a history," but we will mention later how ecstatic prophecy, like many other institutional forms within early Israel, developed out of the land and culture of Canaan and the ancient Near East.

Such a sudden manifestation, however, ought to stir little wonder in a religion based on the *mirabilia Dei,* the marvelous interventions of God at the Red Sea, Mount Sinai, and the Jordan River (Exodus 14–15; 19–24; and Joshua 1–6), interventions continuously celebrated in the liturgy (Psalms 105, 114, 136).[12]

Prophecy not only showed up unannounced,[13] but it was also rather solidly established and highly revered. In the text of I Sam. 10, Samuel has "poured oil on Saul's head . . . saying: 'The Lord anoints you commander over his heritage.' "This passage is clearly favorable to a transition from Israel's more democratic style of independent, tribal government to the unified monarchy, and we note the sense of *change within continuity,* always a hallmark of prophetic action. Samuel proceeded to offer Saul several signs of God's choice of him as Israel's leader. Emphasis lay with the third sign: the band of ecstatic prophets.

> After that you will come to Gibeath-elohim, where there is a garrison of the Philistines. As you enter the city, you will meet a band of prophets (*nebî'îm*) coming down from the high place preceded by lyres, tambourines, flutes and harps. They will be prophesying ecstatically. The spirit of the Lord will rush upon you and you will ecstatically prophesy with them and you will be changed into another person. (I Sam. 10:5–6)

The key words in this passage are variously translated, and this difference leads us into a discussion of the ecstatic or charismatic prophet. Just to mention a couple instances where modern bibles vary:

New American Bible (NAB)	*New English Bible (NEB)*
Gibeath-elohim	Hill of God
in a prophetic state	with prophetic rapture
spirit of the Lord	spirit of the Lord
rush upon you	suddenly take possession of you
in their prophetic state	rapt like a prophet
changed into another man	become another man

La Bible de Jérusalem (BdJ)	*Revised Standard Version (RSV)*
Gibéa de Dieu	Gibeath-elohim
seront en délire	prophesying
l'esprit de Yahvé	spirit of the Lord
fondra sur toi	come mightily upon you
en délire	prophesy with them
changé en un autre homme	turned into another man

Jerusalem Bible (JB)

Gibeah of God
in an ecstasy
spirit of the Lord
will seize you
go into an ecstasy
changed into another man

The *RSV* is the least sensational and probably the least exact—not incorrect, simply too vague with its bland translation "prophesying." The *NEB, JB* and *BdJ* at once draw the reader into a place of mystery as they indicate *God's* rights over Gibeah and its sanctuary; the *NAB* and *RSV* make the entire phrase into a proper name, *Gibeath-elohim*.[14] The act of prophesying (*RSV*) is more vividly described in all the other translations in accord with the *hithpael* or intensive-reflexive state of the Hebrew verb: "prophetic state" (*NAB*), "rapture" (*NEB*), "ecstasy" (*JB*), "delirium or frenzy" (*BdJ*). "The spirit of the Lord" overpowers Saul, "rushing upon him" (*NAB*), "mightily" (*RSV*), "seizing him" (*JB*), "suddenly taking possession of him" (*NEB*), changing him into a *different* person. The Hebrew word *'aḥēr* can even mean a "strange" or "alien"[15] type of person.

Prophetic Titles

Names or titles of these early prophetic or ecstatic groups then can tell us much about them. The most popular word is *nābî*, a noun which migrated out of Mesopotamia, perhaps very early with Abraham, and represents a form of the Akkadian *nabu*, 'to announce or call.' The Hebrew noun *nābî'* with *ā-î* combination of vowels, at once indicates passivity, as other examples indicate: *māshîah*, *'anointed* messiah,' *nāzîr*, *'consecrated* nazirite' (see Num. 6:1–20), *'anî*, 'made poor' (hence the *'anawîm*).[16] This passivity to an outside force becomes all the more pronounced in the verbs derived from the noun.[17] Although the verb is translated in a transitive or at least in an active sense, the Hebrew form is either passive or intensive-reflexive. In each case the one who prophesies has been subjected to an overwhelming interior experience.

Other Hebrew titles for prophecy, like *rō'eh* and *hōzeh,* 'seer,' properly indicate an extraordinary ability to perceive *secret* or *hidden details* in an object which everyone else concurrently sees only superficially.[18] The Hebrew verb *rā'āh* developed into a technical word for divine revelation.[19] For the seer, as Abraham Heschel remarked, "prophecy . . . is not a quiet insight . . . It is a startling insight: a thunder in the world and a lightning in the soul."[20] Another title for prophet, 'a man of God' (*'îsh 'elōhîm*) at once bespeaks a special relationship to the divine, a person possessed or owned by the Spirit!

Without a doubt, then, the Hebrew words for prophet stress human passivity before an overwhelming experience of God. Prophets, thereby, are endowed with a keen perceptive vision, to peer deeply beneath the surface where others see only in a myopic way. Prophets seem to be caught in a trance and become overwhelmed by God and transformed into a different type of person. They sing and dance—"with lyres, tambourines, flutes and harps"—in a joy beyond rational explanation. They announce a divine message and enable the deep mysteries of everyone's life to come to the surface for all to see. Prophecy, therefore, is contagious and Saul himself upon encountering the *nebî'îm* fell into an ecstatic trance or delirium (I Sam. 10:6; 19:18–24).

True, ecstatic prophecy at times degenerated into orgies of irrational behavior (I Kings 18:20–40; Isa. 28:7), but these excesses must not blind us to the many instances where the Bible represents ecstatic behavior very favorably.

Total Consistency

Ecstatic or charismatic groups shock the rest of us into a profound realization of what miracles God can perform through and in human beings. Because extraordinary divine intervention in human history is at the heart of biblical religion, the Spirit must continue to rush upon his servants and transform them—so that the martyr sings while marching to death, the pain-wracked body carries a peaceful smile into eternity, the rejected person responds with loving smile, and the most stereotyped greeting from us brings a response as spontaneous as a child's from the 'charismatic' stranger. No more than poets can suppress poetry can persons of the spirit silence the joy, peace and song of God's heart within them.

> I say to myself, I will not mention him,
>   I will speak in his name no more.
> But then it becomes like fire burning in my
>   heart,
>   imprisoned in my bones;
> I grow weary holding it in,
>   I cannot endure it. (Jer. 20:9)

And so the prophet Jeremiah's confession of sorrow not only must be written, but the cursing of his birth must be interrupted with ecstatic joy:

> Sing to the Lord,
>   praise the Lord,
> For he has rescued the life of the poor
>   from the power of the wicked. (Jer. 20:13)

Because ecstatic prophecy entails such tensions, stretching a person taut in extreme directions of anger and peace, pain and joy, saintliness and sinfulness, the prophet cannot compromise in the least way. Because the prophet is *in extremis,* in a condition far exceeding human control, seized by the Spirit and wrapped in a trance, he must *totally* surrender to the Spirit of God. Otherwise the ecstatic prophet, lacking normal inhibitions, will collapse suddenly into weird excesses and even into horrendous debauchery. The saint cannot tolerate the type of dishonest and secretive compromises which the rest of us can get by with. Could Jesus have committed a slight, deliberate sin? Would not even a minor misdemeanor have precipitated a total, mortal collapse of Himself? The ecstatic understands the expectations of Jesus as obligatory: "Say, 'Yes' when you mean 'Yes' and 'No' when you mean 'No.' Anything beyond that is from the evil one." (Matt. 5:37) as well as the injunction in the Epistle to the Ephesians as necessary: As for lewd conduct or promiscuousness or lust of any sort, let them not even be mentioned among you; your holiness forbids this. (Eph. 5:3)

For still another reason the ecstatic must live by a complete openness to God and without hesitation allow the entire person and all its vitality to move spontaneously towards God. Otherwise the prophet becomes a god to himself or herself, and confuses human eccentricities with ecstatic manifestations. The extraordinary is then used to manipulate others who stand in wonder of the ecstatic.

The dangers of ecstasy point out, as was mentioned already, that the charismatic person cannot live independently of Israel or the Church and its stabilizing traditions. Prophecy which enriched Israel and seemed most responsible for Israel's survival in the two to three hundred years after Moses, could not have been borne, much less have remained alive, without the more normative institutions of the people, such as judges, levitical priesthood, elders and tribal organization.[21]

Charismatic Communities

Granted the extraordinary nature of their call, ecstatic prophets tended to move away from Israelite settlements and to form separate communities. These confraternities existed near Jericho (II Kings 2:5–7), Gibeah (I Sam. 10:10), Rama (I Sam. 19:23), Bethel (II Kings 2:3), Gilgal (II Kings 4:38), and other cities. It seems that others could join who were attracted by the fervor of the ecstatics, but were not necessarily gifted by the Spirit with any unusual charisms. It is not a rare occurrence for disciples to attach themselves to masters, hoping to learn by a slow human process what may have been given in an extraordinary way to the master.

The charismatic communities set up a viable religious life, with a distinctive kind of dress and hair style,[22] a common table,[23] a dependency on alms,[24] probably in poverty,[25] in a cluster of cells under a leader,[26] yet loosely organized, some being married[27] while others apparently remained celibate.[28] Moreover, some would wander through the countryside, while others stayed more permanently in a single place. They celebrated the liturgy, probably in a more enthusiastic way than the levitical priests.[29]

As already noted, these charismatic communities preserved the fervor and the purity of Israelite religion during the *Sturm und Drang* period after Moses, a time of violence as well as syncretization and absorption of Canaanite ways. These changes were necessary for Israel to survive in an agricultural land, vastly different from the semi-nomadic existence of Moses in the desert. Even the prophets absorbed Canaanite and Mesopotamian ways of announcing the divine will. But for the most part, the communities of ecstatic prophets preserved a pure Mosaic intuition of Yahweh, Israel's Savior who chose this people as His very own. Perhaps because the foreign threats were so mighty and the ways of human survival at times so turbulent, Israel weathered the storm only because of the extraordinary reaction of these prophets rapt in God, peering far beyond and far more deeply than all their brothers and sisters.

In other words, it might be that God's call to ecstatic prophecy is conditioned by the needs of the time. Like all other divine gifts, this one too is to be judged in terms of its pastoral effectiveness. Within the larger community of God's people, each individual must locate the larger ambient where balance and purpose and the overriding virtue of charity are achieved. When charismatic communities declined and became corrupt, it might have been due principally to the fact that the times changed and *they* did not! And so God summoned a new set of prophets.

Classical Prophets

When the prophet Amos stood before the assembly of Israel and declared:
hear this word! (3:1–5:6)
hear this! (5:4–14)
woe to you! (5:7–17, 18–27; 6:1–14)

everyone knew instinctively that this man had been summoned by God. He must have seen a vision (7:1–9; 8:1–3). Yet, he worked no miracle nor did he stand before them in a trance. What he saw, they saw— pampered, obese women (4:1–3) and the perfumed, supine, fleshy bodies of the male population (6:4–6). They hated this leather-skinned shepherd who would reach his unwashed hands into the secret areas of their conscience and lay their embarrassment before the public eye, so crudely and sarcastically and yet with more artistic aplomb than their most sophisticated poets ever displayed.

Continuity with Evolutionary Leap

So different was Amos from the ecstatic prophets! The people preferred the marvelous manifestations of the latter who titillated them with thaumaturgic excitement and surrounded their insensate hearts with pompous robes of pietistic splendor. They rejected Amos, yet he was still responsible for an evolutionary leap in biblical religion, being the first of that most extraordinary series of religious leaders known in world history. With Amos 'classical' prophesy at once achieved perfection, and for that reason it seemed as explosive as the first appearance of ecstatic prophecy in Israel.

The issues between the two styles of prophecy as well as the confrontation between institutional authority and prophetic word are forcefully presented in Amos 7:10–17. With a style logically arranged to the Semitic mind, this biographical account is attached to the vision in 7:9. It begins where the latter ends—with the mention of the prosperous and popular Jeroboam II, King of Israel (786–746 BC).

> 7:9 ... I will attack the dynasty of Jeroboam with sword.

> 7:10ff... Amaziah, the priest of Bethel, sent word to Jeroboam, king of Israel: "Amos has conspired against you within Israel; the country cannot endure all his words...."

> To Amos, Amaziah said: "Off with you, visionary, flee to the land of Judah! There earn your bread by prophesying, but never again prophesy in Bethel [in Hebrew, *beth-'el* = house (of) God]; for it is the king's sanctuary and a royal temple [in Hebrew, *beth mamlekah* = house (of) royalty—]."

> Amos answered Amaziah, "I am no prophet nor do I belong to any prophetic [or ecstatic] group. I am a shepherd and a dresser of sycamores.[30] The Lord took me[31] and said to me, '*Go! Prophesy to my people, Israel!*' "

This biographical interlude within the collection of Amos' speeches was drafted by a friendly disciple, convinced that Yahweh had commissioned this uncouth man to announce the divine word.[32] Skillfully contrasting words, the biographer indicated how the divine sanctuary, *Beth-'el*, 'the house of God,' had been profaned by high priest and king into a *beth mamlekah,* 'the house [subservient] to human royalty.' This same writer was convinced that his master Amos was a genuine spokesman for God, and if he also composed the opening verse to the entire collection of Amos' words (1:1), he even declared that Amos acted as a 'seer' (*ḥāzāh*).

In both cases (1:1 & 7:12–15) the biographer deliberately rejected the noun, 'seer' or 'prophet,' and thereby adamantly refused to identify Amos with the institution of ecstatic prophet then in existence. He made use of verbs, 'to see in vision' and 'to prophesy,' indicating how Amos was transforming the nouns and the institution into something new. Amos disdainfully repudiated the insinuation of Amaziah that he belonged to the degenerate form of prophecy then in Israel. While the high priest considered prophecy, like priesthood, a livelihood ("earn your bread by prophesying"—v. 12), Amos spat back that he "worked" for his living, sweating overtime on a second job to make ends meet. He had nothing to gain or lose by prophesying. Abraham Heschel incisively drew the line between the two forms of prophecy: "the paradox is that while the ecstatic disregards consciousness in order to enrich self, the prophet disregards the self and enriches his consciousness."[33]

Amos, nonetheless, was not cutting all contact with the past nor dynamiting Israel's institutions.[34] He spoke favorably of ecstatic prophets and Nazirites in 2:11–12; he incorporated a liturgical refrain about the exodus (2:10; 3:1; 9:7) and modeled an important speech upon covenant worship.[35] In fact, most of his preaching adhered almost rigidly to accepted literary styles within Israel's institutions.[36] Finally, the editor of his sermons found no contradiction between the prophet's words and the great institutions of the Jerusalem temple (1:2) and the Davidic royalty (9:11).

Amos, we maintain, never intended to create new institutions: he dealt with spirit and conscience. But it so happened, accidentally so far as his intentions were concerned, that a new style of prophet emerged which not only replaced the ecstatic but even with time appropriated the name *nābî'*.[37] If Amos became the first of the 'classical prophets,' it was by divine design, not his own planning. This newness emerged, therefore, as a continuation of the old institution.

A few conclusions can be drawn about the life-style and goals of the classical prophets.[38] To begin with, they did not base their mission upon any professional status, miraculous manifestations, or group pressure. In their appeal to conscience, they stood on their own two feet and spoke in the name of a personal God. Such a response was demanded by the times when religion had degenerated into false, flimsy externals (Isa. 1:10–17; Jer. 7; Hos. 6), into material attitudes, social injustices and gross sensuality (Amos 2:6–16; 8:4–6; Hos. 1–3), with superstitious confidence in divine promises (Amos 5:18–20; Jer. 28:2–4). Furthermore, the prophetic message was woven out of the threads of the prophet's daily life, his or her character, problems, hopes, prejudices and viewpoint. God's hand was clearly observed in daily events (Isa. 10:1; Hab. 2:4). But unlike the ecstatic prophets, they did not indulge in revolutionary activity nor crusade for the holy war (I Kings 20; II Kings 3:11–19).

In view of these facts some serious questions can be addressed to the contemporary scene. Can one set out to be a classical prophet? Amos was seized by God, who said, "Go! Prophesy to my people!" Is the self-styled prophet to be trusted? Amos denied the title. Is the quitter a prophet? Amos was engaged in prophecy, not for livelihood nor external achievement, but to speak the word of God. Is the revolutionary or extreme leftist prophetic? Amos did not manipulate nor act with any hidden agenda. How does one maintain like Amos the taut tension between loyalty to institutions and challenge to their rigid externalism?

The Secular Revolution

The words 'secular' and 'sacred' are foreign to biblical culture, but they speak both to our contemporary society and to the discussion of biblical prophecy itself.[39] By 'secular' we mean an honest attempt to make use of human forms to express and thereby interact with the mysterious presence and expectations of God within life. But by 'sacred' we understand a continuous awareness of God, personally addressing us in each human moment and thereby leading us to form a liturgical community of worship in which earthly objects become translucently symbolic of unearthly expectations already in our midst. When the sacred seemed to lose all contact with Israel's earthly existence—with social injustices and sensual self-satisfaction—and so was separated from the God of Israel, the God daily present in human life, the sacred became an idol, competing with God. It was thus rightly condemned as superstitious human attempts to mimic God, and so to control all the mysterious areas of human existence.[40]

The classical prophets reexerted the truly secular sphere of salvation history, where God was truly present, personally challenging his people to decency, kindness and humble prayer.

> You have been told, o man, what is good,
>   and what the Lord requires of you:
> Only to do the right and to love goodness,
>   and to walk humbly with your God. (Micah
>   6:8)

The classical prophets rightly insisted upon their unique call by God, in some extraordinary, albeit interior summons (Amos declared, "The Lord *took* me . . .")[41] and they spoke with divine authority, self-confidently feeling no need for miracles or professional status to support their authority. For this very reason they used the

market-place language of the people, seemingly so
secular, to shock Israelites into the realization that God
was present, threatening, judging and condemning
them. James D. G. Dunn has summed up this sacred-in-
origin and secular-in-style approach of the classical
prophets: "non-rational in its stimulus as rational in its
content."[42]

In discussing the secular revolution of the classical
prophets, we cannot delay over such technical yet highly
important questions as their employment of 'prophetic',
'messenger,' or 'law court' styles common at the time in
the culture inside and especially outside Israel.[43] We
draw attention to details more immediately obvious in
the biblical text.

Amos and the classical prophets after him appear so
human that we can almost draw their portrait and we can
certainly psychoanalyze their character.[44] The secular
revolution shows up as well in the very fact that their
preaching survives in written form. What they proclaimed as the word of God is enclosed within human
expressions, Hebrew grammar and Canaanite alphabet.
Alphabetical writing is far more humanly manageable
than the very complicated, extensive forms of
hieroglyphics—or 'sacred [picture] writings' as that word
means. Alphabets were invented in Canaan to make
communication easier between less educated or more
commercially minded people.[45] Alphabet is far more
secular than hieroglyphics. Because the words of the
classical prophets were recorded, we today can argue
over what they meant much more vigorously and con-
fidently than we can over the meaning of the prophets
Elijah or Elisha.[46]

The humanity of the classical prophets shows up as
well in their hesitations, frustrations, agonies and doubts.
Rather than a bolt of lightning out of the heavens
enabling him to be overcome by celestial visions and rapt
in a trance, a bleak moment of absence forced the
classical prophet to cry out in agony, "Oh, that you would

rend the heavens and come down!" and "Return [O absent God] for the sake of your servants" (Is. 63:19, 17). Jeremiah in desperation even called God a "liar" (15:18) in a diary of his confessions never intended to be made public. Strangely enough, Jeremiah's poignant questions *to* God are now preserved in the Bible as the word *of* God to us!

The 'secular' or the 'human' stance of the classical prophet actually introduces us to the greatest mystery about God, what Abraham Heschel called his "pathos." God participated so thoroughly in the fabric of human existence—He is not present "as an onlooker"[47]—that by suffering the burden of human rejection the prophet is experiencing God's concern for his wayward people. For God then, Israel was not an idea but a loving anxiety. And so it happened that in this secular revolution of the classical prophets the transcendent God became so close to Israel that nothing thereafter was more transcendent—more baffling and more mysterious and therefore more divine—than God's total immersion and absolute, immanent presence among his people.

The idea can be expressed by way of this example. The hand of another person, held at a distance from us, is difficult to discern; it may be but a speck in the distance and its movements vague and mysterious. One is rapt almost in trance, fixing one's gaze upon it. Here we locate the ecstatic prophet, lost in wonder at the distant and awesome God. Or again that hand can be so close as to wrap itself around one's eyes. Now there is total darkness. One no longer experiences difficulty in seeing, but an absolute impossibility in seeing anything at all. In the agony of this painful blindness, the classical prophet found God.

Dealing with secular details and feeling within himself the agony of the seeming absence of God, the prophet faced the serious problem of credibility. Who would believe him when he himself questioned God? Yet the prophet's question never doubted God's presence nor God's goodness. Jeremiah began his first confession with firm faith: *"You are just,* O Lord, but I must argue against you! . . . Why does the way of the godless prosper?"* (Jer. 12:1) The prophet, therefore, was convinced of God's goodness and fidelity, yet was baffled by the absence of its manifestation in human life. At the heart of the prophetic message was the weight of God's sorrow over the indifference and the injustice corrupting his people. *The prophet's authority then consisted in that indescribable yet palpable conviction: God is present as a loving person, concerned and even in agony over his people.* The secular experience was necessary to feel the weight of this divine revelation.

The Purpose of Unfulfilled Dreams

In our unguarded moments we think of prophets as soothsayers announcing the future. Actually, they lived the future in the demands they made upon the present moment. The prophet's experience of God's goodness or fidelity could be so overwhelming, especially when by contrast that same prophet was caught in the selfish, proud manoeuvering of the people, that for a moment he was swept away from the present into the distant future. We notice here the interaction of past, present and future. The prophet's continuous experience of God causes the past to crash into the present moment with aspirations so vast that the present moment disintegrates and the prophet is thrust into the future.

The way by which the prophet's past experience of God impregnated the present moment with future life put a serious challenge upon each contemporary audience. The Bible's purpose, accordingly,

> was not simply to provide a description of what religion was, but to establish a witness as to what that religion should have been. The Old Testament continually transcends the con-

> temporary religion of Israel, for, whilst it arose out of it, it points to a purity of faith, and a standard of morality, which that religion as a whole never attained.[48]

One of the most important roles of the prophet, therefore, lay in sustaining unfulfilled hopes, that these might be transmitted to the next generation.

This prophetic role is rooted deeply in biblical tradition. Moses never set foot in the promised land and Jesus never saw the Church. Each performed his role, like the prophet, leaving a legacy of ideals for the future to implement. For this reason too the most important image of the Bible is that of the exodus.[49] The human experience is that the way forward is more significant than the final stage of arrival. Even Jesus was destined to progress "steadily in wisdom and age and grace" (Luke 2:52).

When the prophet spoke about the future, his language was caught within the limited vision of his own lifetime. He spoke primarily to bring an ever greater awareness of God's goodness into the lives of his contemporaries. He was not concerned with the future for its own sake,[50] but for the way it could pull a discouraged and dismayed people out of their frustration, in order to look forward to forgiveness and peace.[51] By sharpening the contrast, this hope for the future made the burden of present sinfulness all the more painful. Hope would not allow the luxury of giving up, as the people wanted it in the time of Jeremiah: "Let us lie down in our shame, let our disgrace cover us" (Jer. 3:25).

In his confidence and at times enthusiasm for the possibilities of the present moment, the prophet could even express the goodness and forgiveness of God in terms never fulfilled. In other words, his language combined vaulting hopes within the limited structures of an historical moment.

A case at point appears in Jeremiah 30–31. These

chapters represent some of the first preaching of the prophet, between 627 and 621 BC. The foreign tyrant Assyria was collapsing into smoke and chaos, and an independence movement was sweeping through the subjugated states of the once colossal empire. Babylon had already revolted and set up her own monarchy and in a few years would march her army north to level Assyria's capital, Nineveh, to the ground. Jeremiah not only exulted over the independence of his own people, the former northern kingdom of Israel, but also announced the return of the northern tribes deported by Assyria a hundred years previously. He tells Rachel, the mother of these tribes, as she "mourns . . . because her children are no more":

> Cease your cries of mourning,
>   wipe the tears from your eyes.
> The sorrow you have shown shall have its
>   reward,
>   says the Lord,
>   they shall return from the enemy's land.
> There is hope for your future, says the Lord.
>   (Jer. 31:16–17)

In the reconstruction of the devastated land and the reassembly of the people he foresaw "a new covenant" (Jer. 31:31–34)!

The northern tribes never returned![52] Matthew's Gospel sees the text fulfilled in the martyrdom of God's innocent saints who will rise with Jesus from the abode of death and so return to their promised land (Matt. 2:17–18). Christian theology applies the new covenant passage to the Eucharist, the blood of the new covenant (Luke 22:20). The New Testament grants a fulfillment so vast to these prophetical texts, that even the Christian interpretation awaits the distant future for their realization!

Prophecies, therefore, are intended to sustain hope

within the present moment for a future beyond one's dreams. "Those who *wait* upon the Lord," wrote Second Isaiah, "renew their strength" (Isa. 40:31). Prophecies are encouragement for now, not a set of blueprints for the future. God's history can be different from what we anticipate.

Prophecies, in fact, tended to undergo frequent adaptations and editing. One of the most startling examples occurred in the book of Joel, where Isaiah's idyllic picture of world peace (Isa. 2:4; Micah 4:3) was dramatically reversed and the very text of the earlier prophet was turned around. Joel wrote:

> Declare this among the nations:
> > proclaim a war,
> > rouse the warriors to arms!
> Let all the soldiers
> > report and march!
> *Beat the plowshares into swords,*
> > *and your pruning hooks into spears;*
> > let the weak man say, "I am a warrior!"
> > > (Joel 4:9–10)

Each prophet was rooted in his own age, spoke from his own temperament, and was primarily concerned with the welfare of his contemporary Israel.

Once again, as earlier in the case of the ecstatic prophet, the stability of Israel and her continuous tradition were rooted in the priesthood (and at times the royalty). The classical prophets presumed the existence of this basic organization, worked for its enrichment and purification, and eventually submitted what they had spoken or written to this authority for preservation and interpretation.[53]

Prophecy, accordingly, comforts, challenges and sustains faith in God as a personal savior, now present, to lead his people into the future beyond the limited terms of the original prophecy. There is continuity of tradition, but always the possibility of evolutionary leaps. In its inception as well as in its fulfillment, prophecy is a summons from God to which we must respond with obedient surrender. "The Lord *took* me . . . and said to me, 'Go! Prophesy to my people!'"

In Conclusion

Prophecy is the challenging thrust from Israel's savior God, preventing his people from stopping along the way of their exodus. Their promised land lay always in the future; they must not make into an idol any achievement, however holy and even divine in origin. The danger of such idolatry always lurked around Israel's institutions, whose purpose was to provide enough unity and security to enable each Israelite to undertake the business of the moment with full energy. Prophets, therefore, tended to be gadflies to priesthood and royalty.

As God's instruments to purify, enrich and continue the onward pilgrimage of Israel and her institutions, prophets had to modulate and to adapt to the various ages of Israel and her organizational leadership. "Prophecy has its history."

In the first centuries after Moses, a time of heroic endeavors and chaotic failures, the prophet's mantle had to be cut to the same heroic size. The *ecstatic prophet* dealt with miracles, trances, music, total dedication within separate communities, with the strength to say only yea or nay and never to compromise.

In a later, more sophisticated age the *classical prophet* tackled the serious social, governmental, and cultic problems and kept the people's attention fixed upon the immediate pressing secular necessities. They must not camouflage current moral depravity with ancient promises about divine election and brilliant days of the

Lord. This new series of individual prophets, with no other authority but their stinging rebuke to conscience, seemed to be rebels championing a secular revolution. As we look more closely, we detect the hidden God, burdened with Israel's injustices and crying out for reform and a return to goodness and humility. No present moment was ever so depraved that a prophet could not find God, burdened with that same concern. A happy future was always possible. The future, however, was never limited to the immediate perspective of the prophet.

The many models of prophecy in the Bible do not exhaust God's power. Prophecy continues to have its history. If each of us not only seeks to do the work at hand as energetically as possible but also submits to possibilities known only to God; and if each of us never prejudges God's infinite response in the neighbor—then there will be people whom God in divine freedom summons to "Go! Prophesy to my people!"

II. ▬ ▬▬ ▬

When the Christians at Corinth and elsewhere laid claim to such spiritual gifts as prophecy and glossolalia, their hearers would not have been altogether astounded. The notion of pneumatic powers and divine inspiration was familiar to the Greeks. The problem for Christians was not to establish credence in such things, but to distinguish the authentic inspirations of the Holy Spirit from those which came from other sources, as we can perceive from St. John's warning, "Do not believe every spirit, but test the spirits to see whether they are of God" (I John 4:1), as well as from the criteria offered by St. Paul (I Cor. 12:1–3). The following essay presents some of the Greek notions about divine inspiration.

–The Editor

INSPIRATION IN ANCIENT GREECE

ANTON-HERMANN CHROUST

Ancient Hellenic tradition in general has it that man's notion of the gods, the divine or things supernatural, originated with the inspired powers of the human soul. Such inspirations come to man either while in a state of trance, a state of madness or commerce with the divine, or while asleep through his dreams, that is, while the soul is temporarily freed from its incarceration in the body and thus realizes its true nature. When the soul is isolated in this trance or sleep, it assumes its true nature and foresees and foretells the future, remembers the past, and understands the present. And it is in this state of the soul that men came to assume the existence of some deities or of something divine.[1] For the early Greek philosophers it is inspiration (and hence revelation) which enables man to know truth by supplying him with the ultimate premises on which all truth rests.

There are two major forms of mystical inspiration or inspired powers: the enthusiastic and the shamanic inspiration.[2] In the enthusiastic inspiration man is possessed or *entheos,* 'full of the god.'[3] He abandons his identity and thus opens himself completely to the divine and its influence. Hence his state is one of *pathein* in which the active intellect is completely eliminated: the inspired man is possessed. In this state, he becomes an instrument or mouthpiece through which the deity speaks. The best known example of this enthusiastic inspiration is probably the Delphic priestess. An example among the ancient philosophers would be Heraclitus of

37

Ephesus, who insisted that we should not heed him but solely the *logos* speaking through him. It might also be worthwhile to point out that Plato refers to this enthusiastic inspiration in the *Ion*[4], the *Menexenus*[5], and in the *Phaedrus*[6].

The shamanic inspiration refers to the following: in contrast to the body, the human soul is something divine. As such it can and may leave the body under certain circumstances, as when man is asleep, fainting, gravely ill[7], on the threshold of death, or in a state of ecstatic exaltation or frenzied trance. In other words, whenever the body is inactive the soul may by itself throw off the fetters of the body and unfold its truest and fullest capabilities without being influenced by some external factors or forces. After throwing off these fetters, the soul travels to the world beyond where it sees things unseen by ordinary man or receives information denied ordinary people. This shamanic inspiration, which is actually a travel inspiration, is reflected for example in the Cretan king Minos, who regularly visits the Idean Cave to receive instructions from Zeus. Among philosophers, it is exemplified by Parmenides and Pythagoras. Among others, it is referred to in Xenophon[8] and Plato[9]. It has been conjectured that the shamanic inspiration theory came to Greece from the northeast, probably Asia via Thrace. It is still believed in by certain Siberian tribes, and is reflected, for instance, in the *Arabian Nights* (the flying horse, the flying chariot or the magic carpet). In the traditional lore of these Siberian tribes the soul or spirit of the *shaman,* the 'wise man,' when in an exalted state leaves his body, mounts a raven, wild goose or some other bird, travels to the seat of the deity and receives certain information which he divulges when his soul returns to his body, that is, when he awakens from his trance.

At a later date the enthusiastic inspiration and the shamanic inspiration were occasionally combined. This seems to follow from Cicero's *De Divinatione,*[10] where we are told that when temporarily separated from the body, the soul of man is capable of prophesying future events. And this is also the case with seers and other men when they are dreaming. In *De Divinatione,* Cicero insists that

> when sleep has freed the mind or soul from its association or contact with the body, it re-members the past, discerns the present, and foresees the future. For the body of a sleeping man lies like that of a dead man, but his mind or soul is active and alive.[11]

And Plato states that in sleep the soul "is free to reach out, in pure and independent thought, after some new knowledge of things past, present or future," especially, when man had previously quieted two of the three elements or parts in his soul (namely, the passionate and appetitive parts) and has awakened the third element or part wherein wisdom resides." Then he is in a fair way to grasp in his dreams the truth of things, and the visions of his dreams will not be unlawful."[12] Those whose souls escape the bondage of the body and are capable of rising above and of travelling beyond the body also receive enthusiastic inspirations. In this state they actually see and hear things which they subsequently divulge. Those souls which are capable of leaving the body temporarily are also enthusiastically inspired or inflamed by many things. It might be noted here that in a unique or mystical way the notion of travel inspiration is somewhat akin to the popular saying that "travel broadens the mind." In any event, it might explain the curiosity which impelled a Solon or a Hecataeus to undertake distant travels and "to see the world."[13]

There also exists a third type of inspiration which likewise is a kind of combination of the enthusiastic with the shamanic inspiration: dreams sent by the gods. The fact that these dreams come from without qualifies them as enthusiastic inspirations, while the fact that in these particular dreams the soul so to speak 'transcends' empirical reality and visualizes future events, would classify them as shamanic inspirations. This third type can be found, for instance, in Homer[14], Herodotus[15], Plato[16], and in Aristotle's lost work entitled *Eudemus* or *On the Soul*.

In ancient Hellenic lore the shamanic inspiration is also referred to, for instance, in the story of Hermotimus of Clazomenae. According to Greek tradition, as reported by Tertullian[17], and Al-Kindi[18], when Hermotimus fell asleep, his soul left the body which for the time being remained as if dead. In this state of freedom from incarceration in the body the soul acquired visionary powers. It visualized the ultimate truths and hence attained the most perfect knowledge or *theoria*.

Al-Kindi likewise relates the story of a Greek king, in my opinion Hermotimus of Clazomenae, "whose soul was caught up in ecstacy and who for days remained neither alive nor dead." When this king, Hermotimus, again came to himself, "he told about the many things he had seen in the invisible world, namely, souls, forms and angels." He gave the proofs of all this by foretelling how long people would live, and he prophesied future disasters. "And everything happened as he had told." The reason for all this was that his soul had acquired such knowledge because in the state of ecstacy it had travelled to the world beyond and had been near leaving the body.[19] Al-Kindi refers here to the shamanic inspiration through which certain people acquire a kind of knowledge that is denied ordinary men. Still more will the soul or spirit possess a knowledge of future events or supernatural things on the threshold of death. For here the soul, which is about to shed its contact with the body, apparently travels into the 'beyond' in an anticipatory mood. In this state the soul, perhaps due to inspiration, apparently anticipates things or events it will soon envision more perfectly or events which will occur in the future. Thus Socrates informs his judges that he would prophesy to them, for he "was already in that state when men are most prophetic, namely, when they are about to die."[20] And according to Homer the dying Patroclus prophesied the death of Hector,[21] and the dying Hector foretells the death of Achilles.[22]

The traditional Hellenic explanation of how man's belief in the divine and in the existence of the divine originated is in fact one of mystical revelation which assumes two major forms: direct inspiration in which the deity seeks out certain people, takes possession of them, and reveals itself through this possessed person; and shamanic inspiration where in a state of trance man seeks out the deity which reveals certain matters to him. In any event, man is always in the state of a recipient or *pathein*. This is also brought out by Synesius of Cyrene (born 370 A.D.) who, in his *Dio* 7, points out that those who are initiated into the mysteries experience a sudden change rather than go through a gradual learning process: they are fitted for a certain purpose whenever they are ready. This sudden change is completely irrational, it is a leap, a manifestation of outright ecstatic mysticism. Essentially the same notion can be found in Michael Psellus. In his *Scholion ad Johannem Climacum*[23] Psellus relates:

> I have promised to teach you what I myself have learned, not what I have experienced within myself . . . The former is a matter of instruction, the latter is the result of mystical experience. The first one comes to men by hearing actually spoken words, the second one has its origin when the mind itself has experienced or received direct inner illumination . . . The latter is related to the mysteries and is akin to the Eleusian rites.

In these rites he who was initiated into the mysteries was molded rather than taught. Psellus continues by illustrating his second point:

> He who on the strength of the self-moving faculty of the soul arrives at the conclusion that the soul is immortal receives a didactic form of

instruction rather than an insight based on inspired initiation. But he who through an immediate vision of the spirit visualizes the soul in its true essence—or he who, even without contemplation is convinced of this immortality directly and without any intervening rationalization or reasoning [and without any formal instruction]... such a person is acting from an 'impact' [*pathein*] or inspiration, and hence, is an initiated person.

He is inspired and thus knows the truth about the soul. In his *Olympic Discourse or On Man's First Conceptions of God*[24], Dio Chrysostom (Dio of Prusa) maintains that

the notion of a rule of the universe ... arises ... without the aid of a teacher.... The earlier men ... were illuminated on every side by the divine as well as by the magnificent glories of the heavens and the stars, of the sun and by night of the moon ... seeing wondrous sights and hearing the varied voices of the winds, the forests, the rivers and the sea.... How, then, could they have remained ignorant and have had no inkling of Him Who had sowed and planted and now is preserving and nourishing them, when on every side they are filled with the divine nature through both sight and hearing, and in fact through every sense? ... So it is very much the same if anyone were to place a man ... in some mysterious shrine of extraordinary beauty in order to be initiated, where he would see many mystic sights and hear many mysterious voices ... where light and darkness would appear to him alternately, and a thousand other things would occur.... Is it not possible that the whole human race receives the complete and truly perfect initiation, not in a little building erected by the Athenians for the reception of a

small company [this is definitely an allusion to
the initiation rites of the Eleusian mysteries] but
in this universe . . . in which countless marvels
become manifest at every moment and,
furthermore, where the initiation rites are
performed not by human beings . . . but by the
immortal gods themselves. . . . This influence
reaches even senseless [and uneducated] brutes,
so that even they recognize and honor
God. . . ."[24]

What Dio Chrysostom expresses here is simply that
the wondrously beautiful and orderly universe is in fact
the voice of God through which He speaks to all men,
through which He reveals Himself and thus takes hold of
men by a kind of inspiration.

In his *De Tranquillitate Animi* 20,[25] Plutarch maintains that:

the universe is a most sacred temple most
worthy of God [incidentally, a Stoic notion].
Man is initiated into his temple by being born
into it . . . and by becoming an awed spectator
of this resplendent reality which proclaims the
existence of God. Human life, being itself the
most perfect initiation, should therefore be full
of tranquility and joy . . . [During the ordinary
(human) initiation rites such as the initiation
rites of the Eleusian mysteries] we sit in reverent
silence and dignified posture . . . In the initiation rites over which God Himself presides and
in which He initiates us [into this world], however, men actually shun these festivals [that is,
the joy of living their lives in this wondrous
universe or temple of God] by lamentations,
heaviness of heart and crushing worries.

This analogy between the particular rites accompanying
the initiation into some particular mystery cult, and
man's general initiation into God's world at birth indi-

cates Plutarch's belief that throughout man's earthly life
God reveals Himself gradually by progressively taking
hold of him and by constantly inspiring him.

In his *Eudemian Ethics*,[26] commonly considered a
fairly early work of Aristotle, the Stagirite admits that:

> the starting point of reasoning is not reason
> itself but something greater [than human
> reason]. What, then, could be greater than
> rational knowledge or the human intellect but
> God? . . . For this reason those are called
> fortunate who, whatever they start on, succeed
> in it without being good at reasoning. And
> rational deliberation is of no advantage to them,
> for they have in themselves a principle which is
> better than intellect and deliberation. . . . They
> have inspiration, but they cannot deliberate.
> Though lacking reason, they attain the attribute
> of the prudent or wise man, and their divination
> is speedy. And we must include in this all
> knowledge except the knowledge which comes
> from reasoning. In some instances this
> knowledge is due to some [inner] experience.
> And inner experience . . . makes use of God. . . .
> These are the men in whom the reasoning
> powers are relaxed. . . .

All this would indicate that Aristotle too, at least the early
Aristotle, believed in divine inspiration which he calls
"irrational" or, to be more exact, should have called
'meta-rational.'

The essential affinity of the statements made in Dio
Chrysostom's *Olympic Discourse* (27 ff.), Michael Psellus'
Scholion ad Johannem Climacum, Synesius' *Dio* 7, and
Aristotle's *Eudemian Ethics* (1248 a 23 ff.), is rather obvious. They insist or imply that an immediate and direct
awareness of the supernatural or of God is possible and
real without such intermediary factors as a distinct
worldly teacher or, perhaps, a rational—inferential,

inductive or deductive—process. This immediate and direct awareness is the effect of enthusiastic inspiration which results in infused wisdom or visionary knowledge.

All this calls to mind the story about the minstrel Phemius, who had never been taught how to sing, and who could not sing until he had received the gift of song and poetry in a dream.[27] Demodocus, instructed by the Muses or by Apollo himself, suddenly could tell all that the Achaeans had done and suffered at Troy, as if he himself had been present at these events. He could sing any song whatever, for the Muses or Apollo had implanted the gift of song in his heart, had given him the word on his tongue without him having to seek it. He had learned none of his songs; all had sprung from his inner self. When asked by Odysseus to relate the story of the Trojan horse, Demodocus was impelled by the god and began to speak forth.[28] Thus the inspired poet suddenly knows what takes place, has taken place or will take place above, beneath or on the earth.[29] This knowledge is inspiration, characterized by Plato as divinely inspired or infused madness which is actually a blessing in that it is allied with prophecy (*mantike* and *manike*).[30] The Muses, daughters of Memory, in the case of Demodocus, and in that of other minstrels and poets, have freed his soul from the limitations of time as well as those of space. According to Plato,[31] mantic inspiration is also the gift of Apollo who, as Homer tells us,[32] endowed the seer Calchas with a knowledge of the past, the present and the future. Hence, inspired divination is quite as much concerned with the past and the hidden present as it is with the future. Augury, on the other hand, is mainly confined to the forecasting of coming events.

The *Meno* and *Phaedo* of Plato as well as some of the other Platonic dialogues attempt to prove that the human soul already existed before it became incarnate. In its pre-incarnation state the soul visualized directly the perfect Ideas: it possessed a "beatific vision" of the Ideas, a vision of which it carries a blurred 'recollection' (*anamnesis*) into its state of incarnate existence. This vision, which is the beginning as well as the foundation of all true knowledge, in the final analysis constitutes the most perfect form of inspiration or revelation. Hence true knowledge comes out of the inspired mind itself. 'Learning' in the Platonic sense is the process of acquiring knowledge through proper recollection, that is, ultimately through inspiration rather than through a formal transferal of information from the teacher to the pupil. This being so, all knowledge worthy of the name is actually recovered out of man's inspired mind, and the truth on which all philosophic virtue depends is gained by recollection (*anamnesis*) of "things once visualized." Truly wise men, Plato insists, are guided not by ordinary knowledge or wisdom, but by inspiration. In this wise men are like seers or poets "who in their rapt condition say many true things but do not know what they mean."[33] They have no intelligence (*nous*), but are possessed by divine inspiration which is a gift of God.[34]

The Pythagorean school of philosophy, it must be kept in mind, was no mere succession of master and pupil, but a sort of fraternity or "monastic order"[35] which was subdivided into a novitiate, a probationary stage and full admission.[36] It was modelled on certain mystical cult-societies into which admission was gained by solemn initiation rites. In the process of initiation there were two distinct stages: a preliminary ceremonial purification which fitted the candidate to proceed to the second stage in which symbolic cult-objects and ritual performances were revealed to the postulant. To participate in these rites assured the participant of a better lot in the other world. The revelation of these cult-objects and rituals, which was meant to make the postulant accessible to inspirations, was accompanied by some instructions in the meaning of sacred things seen and enacted. The entire initiation procedure was based on the belief that there is another world, an invisible world of gods and spirits, where the initiated individual soul will have its place after death. Revelation and inspiration are the only means of access to a knowledge of this 'world beyond.' The initiate claimed to be one of those who know about this 'world beyond' and, hence, to be the only truly 'wise man' (*sophos*). In the *Phaedo*[37] as well as in other works[38] Plato developed the more profound significance of the Pythagorean notion of purification followed by revelation and inspiration. This particular significance consists in the deliverance of the soul, which by its nature and origin is divine, from its imprisonment in the mortal body—or to be more exact, in the partial deliverance of the soul during this life, to be completed after death. The knowledge whereby the soul is delivered is the constant contemplation of the eternal truths. In this sense Pythagoreanism was both a philosophy and a religion. Philosophically, the truth contemplated is the ultimate nature of all things, while religiously the truth contemplated constitutes that knowledge which enables man to advance to spiritual perfection by assimilating his own nature to the unseen order of the 'world beyond.' In the *Republic* Plato expressed the fundamental Pythagorean religious and philosophic outlook when he states that

> a man whose thoughts are fixed on true reality has no leisure to look down upon the affairs of worldly men . . . He contemplates the world of unchanging and harmonious order and being, where reason alone governs. . . . This he imitates and to this he will, as far as he can, conform himself. So also the philosopher, who is in constant companionship with the divine order of the universe, will reproduce within his soul this order and conform to this order and thus may become godlike as far as this is possible for man.[39]

We should not dismiss as wonder-working charlatans or fraudulent magicians such figures from early Greek mythology as the Hyperborean Abaris who flew through the air on his arrow, or Aristeas of Proconnesus and Hermotimus of Clazonemae who travelled in spirit from their bodies, or Salmoxis who, like King Minos of Crete or Epimenides, retired to an underground cavern to seek inspired wisdom and information. The cloud of legendary miracles surrounding Orpheus, Epimenides or Pythagoras should not detract from their significance for the history of Greek religion and Greek philosophy. This is brought out, for instance, by Parmenides of Elea whose didactic-philosophic poem begins with the account that he travelled on the Sun's chariot beyond the gates of night and day—in a way a mythical doublet of Phaeton's or Elias' performance—to the throne of the goddess[40] who told him that "being is one. . . ." Heraclitus of Ephesus said of himself that when he was young he knew nothing, but when full-grown he had come to know everything. He was no man's pupil, but claimed that he had "searched himself" and had learned everything from himself.[41] When he says that people should not listen to him but to the *logos* which speaks through him, he admits that he is the prophet of a wisdom which he found within himself.[42] In this sense he is the mouth-piece of the deity which speaks through him: he is possessed by the deity. Lucretius compares the pronouncements of the pre-socratic philosophers to the oracles of Apollo. He hails the sayings or poetry of Empedocles as the voice of an inspired genius "who had been divinely inspired to discover many truths, and who has given, from his heart's innermost shrine, responses with more sanctity and more certainty than any delivered by the Pythian prophetess."[43]

In the final analysis, poetic genius, intuitive divination and the second vision manifest in dreams or the inspirations received at the threshold of death are manifestations of the mystic's commerce with the divine. The wise man of Greek lore includes poets and seers as well as sages and philosophers. Socrates confesses in Plato's *Apology* "I know that poets do write poems not by wisdom, but by a sort of genius and inspiration. They are like diviners or soothsayers who also say many fine things, but do not understand their meaning."[44] In the *Phaedrus*, Plato insists that

> he who knocks at the gates of poetry untouched by the madness of the Muses, believing that art alone will make him an accomplished poet, will be denied access to the mysteries, and his sober compositions will be eclipsed by the creations of inspired madness.[45]

And Clement of Alexandria has preserved Democritus' statement that "truly noble poetry is that which is written with the breath of divine inspiration."[46] For "God takes away the minds of poets and uses them as his ministers, as He uses diviners and prophets, in order that we may know . . . that God Himself is the speaker and that through them He is conversing with us."[47]

The identity or common quality of the divinely inspired poet and the divinely inspired prophet or seer is obvious with one exception. The business of the poet or minstrel is to entertain by relating the glories of old, while the business of the prophet or seer is to interpret the intentions of the gods or to foretell future events. Poetry, the ancients believed, is the exalted language of prophecy, and throughout its history true poetry has resisted, until our own time, every effort to bring it down to the level of everyday speech. Because it expresses a more or less exalted mood, it cannot dispense with an exalted language. It is this exaltation which the ancients had in mind when they insisted that the true poet is inspired by the Muses—when they maintained that the poet is akin to, or identical with, the inspired prophet.

Our original assumption was that all true knowledge lies beyond the reach of the senses in everyday experience: it is a knowledge which, by way of inspiration, has been revealed to persons endowed with exceptional intellectual and artistic gifts. Such persons have often undergone a special training and have mastered a special technique, frequently by way of inspiration. They have direct access to the unseen world, and they have direct communion with the gods or spirits, whose existence they proclaim and whose will they interpret. They are able to survey the whole course of temporal events: the past, the hidden present and the future. Originally, this power is claimed in identical terms for the prophet or seer, who is inspired by Apollo, and for the poet who is inspired by the Muses. With these forms of 'divine madness' Plato ranks the 'madness' of the philosopher, rapt by his passion for truth. Behind Plato's myth lies the heaven-journey of Parmenides who first declared that the truth revealed to him was not that of the past or of the future, but the truth of a timeless and unchanging reality.

In the *Phaedrus* (265B ff.), Plato describes a second form of prophetic inspiration or madness which is the gift of Dionysius rather than that of Apollo. Here divination is concerned with the past and the present, but not with the future. It reveals some ancient wrath of offended gods or spirits whose vengeance is the cause of hereditary afflictions. This particular prophetic inspiration reveals not only the cause of this wrath, but also the means of deliverance and absolution from present evils. According to Aeschylus, *Eumenides* 62, Orestes, driven mad by the ancient wrath which has haunted his ancestry, is purified and absolved by Loxias, the "physician-seer, reader of portents and purifier of houses." The Cretan mystic Epimenides, above all, was a purifier, and his task was to discover those forgotten errors or sins of which present evils and misfortunes were the consequences.

As late as the fourth century B.C., Plato insisted that "the poets are divine and divinely inspired people. With the aid of the Muses or Graces they frequently tell the truth of what has happened."[49] In any event, the poets who like Hesiod composed theogonies or cosmogonies—those 'theologians' whom Aristotle calls the precursors of the natural philosophers—all claimed they were uttering revealed or inspired truths.[50] In this they call to mind "the words of Amos, who was among the herdsmen of Tekoa, which he saw concerning Israel,"[51] "the vision of Obadiah: Thus said the Lord,"[52] and "the word of the Lord which came to Micah . . . which he saw concerning Samaria."[53] The term 'divine,' frequently applied in Greek antiquity to prophets, seers, poets and philosophers (in the course of time the philosopher became the successor of the prophet, poet and sage of earlier days) signifies a 'divinely inspired person'. This term also recognizes the existence of a class of people whose wisdom or knowledge is not derived from ordinary human experience, but has been acquired by direct access to the world of the gods or spirits, to a timeless reality, or through direct divine revelation or inspiration.

When in the course of time the poet and prophet (or seer) became distinct persons, the prophet's concern was to foresee the future, while that of the poet was to focus on the imaginative vision of the past. The poet's visions, which are a blend of myth and history, reach back to the very beginning. In his *Theogony,* Theognis relates stories concerning the generation of the gods, the succession of divine dynasties, and the war of the Olympian gods with the Titanic gods. Beyond the theogonies there were the cosmogonies which dealt with the original formation of an ordered universe. So long as this field was monopolized by the inspired poets, there was no clear distinction between fact and fiction, history and myth. In ancient Greece it was Homer who secured for the poets following him an authority which was reserved in other civilizations to the priestly caste. The priest was an official charged with conducting public worship and offering sacrifices, acts which the gods demanded in exchange for the gifts they could grant or withhold. The seer or prophet was preoccupied with the interpretation of omens declaring the intentions of the gods. The origin of the gods or that of the world, however, remained the concern of the poet and at a later date, that of the philosopher.

According to Sextus Empiricus,[54] who credits

Aristotle with the observation, men's thoughts of the gods originated not only from the inspired powers of the soul, but also from the phenomena of the heavens. He also attributes to Aristotle the opinion that the heavenly bodies contributed to man's belief in the existence of gods or God, particularly when he observed the wonders of the heavens and their perfect and orderly movements. Thus they came to think that there is a God Who is the cause of all this wondrous beauty and orderliness. They reasoned simply from the perfect artifact to the perfect Artificer.

There are similar passages in Sextus Empiricus' *Adversus Mathematicos*[55], and Philo of Alexandria's *Legum Allegoriarum Libri Tres*,[56] *De Praemiis et Poenis*,[57] and *De Specialibus Legibus*,[58] and Cicero's *De Natura Deorum*.[59] Recognized as fragments of Aristotle's lost work, *On Philosophy*,[60] these passages clearly distinguish between a knowledge of the supernatural based on 'inspiration' (*pathein*), and a knowledge grounded in 'inferential reasoning' (*mathein*).

Cicero's statement in *De Natura Deorum* is worthy of being cited:

> Suppose there were men who had always lived underground, in good and well-constructed and well-lighted dwellings, adorned with statues and pictures, and furnished with everything in which those who are thought to be happy abound. Suppose, however, that they had never gone above ground, but had learned by report and hearsay [here Cicero seems to allude to divine inspiration] that there is a divine authority and power. Suppose, then, at some time, the jaws of the earth should open, and they were able to escape and make their way from those hidden dwellings into the regions which we inhabit. When they suddenly saw the earth and the seas and the sky—when they learned the grandeur of the clouds and the

power of the winds; when they saw the sun and learned its grandeur and beauty and the power shown in its filling the sky with light and making the day; when, again, night darkened the lands and they saw the whole sky spangled and adorned with stars, and the changing light of the moon, now waxing now waning; and the risings and settings of all these celestial bodies, their courses settled and immutable throughout all eternity—when they saw all those things, most certainly they would have come to the conclusion both that there are gods and that these great works are the works of gods.

The reports of Cicero, Philo of Alexandria and Sextus Empiricus would indicate that Aristotle may properly be called the founder of rational theology, and that he is the first known philosopher-theologian who articulated the cosmological proof for the existence of God. It should be borne in mind, however, that in the Laws[61] a work which was composed at approximately the same time as Aristotle's *On Philosophy,* Plato insists that of the two things which lead men to believe in the gods, "one is the argument from the order and movement of the stars and of all things under the dominion of the 'Mind' which ordered the universe," while the other is "poetic inspiration." It may be maintained, moreover, that Aristotle based his arguments in support of the existence of God, the gods or of the divine, both on direct 'mystic illumination' and 'inspiration' (*pathein*), and on deductive, inductive or inferential 'reasoning' (*mathein*). This becomes quite clear from the statement of Sextus Empiricus,[62] that, according to Aristotle, men's thought of the gods or of the divine originated from two sources: the experiences of the soul, that is, 'mystical inspiration,' and the phenomena of the heavens.

Philo of Alexandria also maintains[63] that philosophers are awed by the wonders of the visible universe and, because of their philosophic inclination,

they conclude that such wondrous beauties and orderliness could not be the result of mere accident but must
rather be the deliberate handiwork of a supreme artificer. Philo[64] insists that people who proceed along
these lines of reasoning (*mathein*) have chosen the "second best road," for they know of God and of His existence only through His "shadow"—His creation. He
insists that the best way of knowing God and of His
existence is through God Himself: through divine and
direct revelation and personal inspiration (*pathein*).

In conclusion it may be stated that a close study of
early Greek intellectual history divulges that rational
philosophy, in which the Greek philosophers put their
trust, ultimately derived its impetus from inspiration:
sages, prophets and poets. It is illuminating also to note
that the inspired prophet-poet-sage was the prototype of
the first philosopher, a point modern philosophers and
historians of ancient philosophy do not always seem to
cherish. The example of mediaeval scholasticism,
however, should furnish persuasive proof that
philosophy may be eminently rational and yet be completely open to revelation and inspiration.

III. ▬▬▬

The coming of the Holy Spirit had a powerful impact on every aspect of the Church's life. The citation of the innumerable and amazingly diverse effects of the Spirit's action, which begins in the New Testament writings, is carried forward by the Fathers of the Church, especially in the Greek-speaking world, who also made the first embryonic attempts to classify them. The following essay is a survey of this impossibly rich material.

—The Editor

THE HOLY SPIRIT, SOURCE OF LIFE AND ACTIVITY ACCORDING TO THE EARLY CHURCH

JEAN LAPORTE

Introduction

The object of this inquiry is the notion of the Holy Spirit as life and energy in the early Church. The speculations and controversies of the post-Nicene Church about the person and divine nature of the Spirit are not included in the present study for two reasons: first, because they belong to a later period; second, and more importantly because to consider them as basic or as a criterion makes it much more difficult to understand the way in which the early Church perceived the Spirit. By "life and energy" is meant what classical theology referred to as the 'operations' of the Spirit. These operations include the work of the Spirit in a Christian or in the Church, and by extension, in the life of man not limited to Israel or the Church. They also include the 'manifestations' of the Spirit—His gifts and charisms— which are obvious to the believer and often strike the attention of the unbeliever.

It is immediately apparent that the Spirit had great importance especially in the life of the early Church: prophecy, martyrdom, and leadership. The work of the Spirit is of first importance in anthropology and ethics as the agent of the creation and resurrection of man, his purification and sanctification. The Spirit permeates the history of redemption: the sin of man, the prophets, the incarnation, death and resurrection of Christ, Pentecost, the mission to the Gentiles, judgment and reward. The Spirit is active in the word of God and the sacraments, and in the struggle against evil spirits and supernatural powers.

Research[1] in the field of the operations of the Spirit is still embryonic, and is vitiated by controversial or systematic approaches, especially as regards the ante-Nicene Fathers. Theologians have been more interested in the post-Nicene theology of the Spirit. They were concerned with defining His place in the blessed Trinity, His divinity, and His procession from the Father and the Son. On these points, they considered the ante-Nicene pneumatology as imperfect, or as a mere source of references for or against post-Nicene theses. Some historians of the institutions and doctrines of the early Church laid the emphasis on charismatic leadership in the early Church, and on Montanism as a renewal of charismatic leadership over against the institution. They treat Montanism as holding a monopoly on Christian prophecy and literature about the Spirit. Hence they tended to blame the Church of the Apologists and of the so-called orthodoxy for being contaminated by Greek patterns and doctrines (such as the concept of leadership as office) and by Stoic pneumatology, in addition to rejecting Montanism, which for these historians was genuine Christianity relying on prophecy.

Many texts wrongly ascribed to Montanism, such as *Didache, Hermas, Irenaeus,* the *Passion of Perpetua,* the *Odes of Solomon,* should be freed from this artificial monopoly. Once gathered together, the scattered elements of prophecy and the other manifestations of the Spirit offer a new view of prophecy and other forms of charismatic life in the context of a Church already aware of the presence of the Spirit in all its true members. Interesting texts from post-Nicene Fathers such as Basil, Gregory Nazianzen and even Augustine, repeat and continue the

tradition of the ante-Nicene pneumatology. One of
Basil's texts particularly led me to inquire into the development of ante-Nicene pneumatology because it
presented a synthesis, the coherence and the detail of
which called for an explanation:

> And His operations, what are they? . . . If you
> think of the creation, the powers of the heavens
> were established by the Spirit, the establishment
> being understood to refer to disability to fall
> away from good. For it is from the Spirit that the
> powers derive their close relationship to God,
> their inability to change to evil, and their
> continuance in blessedness. Is it Christ's advent?
> The Spirit is forerunner. Is there the Incarnate
> presence? The Spirit is inseparable. Working of
> miracles and gifts of healing are through the
> Holy Spirit. Demons were driven out by the
> Spirit of God. The devil was brought to naught
> by the presence of the Spirit, for "you were
> washed, you were sanctified, in the name of the
> Lord Jesus Christ, and in the Holy Spirit of our
> God" (I Cor. 6:11). There is close relationship
> with God through the Spirit, for "God has sent
> forth the Spirit of His Son into your hearts,
> crying Abba, Father" (Gal. 4:6). The resurrec-
> tion from the dead is effected by the operation
> of the Spirit, for "You send forth your Spirit;
> they are created; and You renew the face of the
> earth" (Ps. 104:30). If here creation may be
> taken to mean the bringing of the departed to
> life again, how mighty is not the operation of the
> Spirit, Who is to us the dispenser of the life that
> follows on the resurrection, and attunes our
> souls to the spiritual life beyond? Or if here by
> creation is meant the change to a better condi-
> tion of those who in this life have fallen into sin,
> the renewal which takes place in this life, and

the transmutation from our earthly and sensuous life to the heavenly conversation, which takes place in us through the Spirit, then our souls are exalted to the highest pitch of admiration.[2]

The recent developments of Pentecostalism, with its ecumenical aspects, its supernatural manifestations, its powerful effects on those involved, its orientations, and its supposed antecedents, especially in Montanism and other sectarian groups of the Middle Ages and of our times, challenge the patrologist. I hope that my inquiry[3] will clarify some aspects of the theology of the Spirit in the early Church, and open to those interested in the life and prayer in the Spirit today the wonderful and helpful experience of the early Church.

I shall first discuss briefly the pneumatology of the apologists, which seems to depend very much on the Greeks, and that of Jewish Christianity which uses the images of angelology. I shall not venture into the field of Old Testament or New Testament pneumatology, except to point out the Fathers' use of biblical sources such as the narratives of creation, the vision of the dry bones in Ezekiel, texts of Paul, etc. It should be noted that the Fathers of the Church have their own way of interpreting scripture, which does not correspond to the methods of modern exegesis.

Then I shall study the role of the Spirit in Christian anthropology. Here I shall try to ascertain the common doctrine of the early Church. There is a danger here as elsewhere in building a system out of scattered components derived from different origins and artificially combined. However, we can in fact speak of a common teaching; particular opinions will be pointed out when necessary. But the several usages of the term 'spirit' must be carefully distinguished in order to avoid ambiguity and confusion, and to determine the specific role of the Holy Spirit, or Spirit of God, which is not the same thing as the spirit which belongs to the structure of man or of the world. A particular aspect of this doctrine will be the role of the Spirit in the purification of the soul from sin and its sanctification.

For a complete development of this subject, we must turn to the consideration of Christology, or better, to the history of redemption which includes the prophets, Christ, and the apostles. The Spirit is the spirit of the pre-existing Word of God who spoke through the prophets as well as the spirit of Christ, working in the incarnate Jesus. At Pentecost, Christ sent the Spirit from His Father to His Church, or to "all flesh," according to the prophecy of Joel.

The spiritual interpretation of scripture, that is, its understanding by the prophets of the Old Testament and by Christians endowed with the gift of wisdom, is closely related to the role of the Spirit in the history of redemption. The general theme of prophecy in scripture, as the early Fathers saw it, was Christ's coming and our membership in Christ. We can reach this understanding if our senses are purified and, from being carnal, become spiritual. Therefore the Spirit works in both the prophets who wrote the scriptures, and in the disciples of Christ who read and interpret them. Of course, Paul and the Apostles who are directly or indirectly the authors of the books of the New Testament, were inspired by the Spirit.

The Spirit works in us, not only when we interpret the word of God in scripture, but also through baptism and the eucharist. The sacraments are efficacious because the Spirit of God grants the elements and rites a specific power, or because He himself performs in us the works which they figure. The Spirit inspires our prayer when we use the hymns of scripture, or write new hymns, or simply pray in the Spirit.

Charisms are frequent in the early Church, where charismatic forms of Christian life developed. The first form, of course, is prophecy. Montanism is a very interesting test case for the theology of the Spirit. I would give it a positive evaluation, although it turned into a sect. Even in this regard, it is a precious witness to the freedom of the Spirit of God, who may inspire sectarians, as we see in the case of Tertullian.*

The orthodox Church seems to have overreacted to Montanism, and failed to acknowledge its positive values. We should not, however, overemphasize Montanism. The texts wrongly ascribed to its influence are a witness, along with other information, to the existence of charismatic activities in the early Church everywhere. For instance, the prophets of the *Didache*, the servants of God living according to the ideals of the kingdom of heaven, the widows of pastoral epistles and of the *Didascalia Apostolorum*, the holy members of the communities seen through Clement of Alexandria, the reflections on the discernment of spirits in Hermas, the narratives of visions experienced by Hermas, Perpetua and others, reveal to us the forms adopted in the second and third century by Christian prophecy and charismatic life. These forms are rooted in the New Testament, both in the Gospels and in the Epistles of Paul, and are in the line of the counsels more than of the commandments of Jesus.

In the last section I shall distinguish three types of spiritual life involving the charisms of prophecy, wisdom and heroism: the martyr, the 'didascale' in possession of the gift of wisdom, and the monk engaged in spiritual warfare against passions and evil spirits on the battlefield of inner life.

The Divine Spirit in the Apologists

The Apologists use the Stoic doctrine of the spirit but oppose its radical materialism, and affirm the

---

* In a somewhat different appraisal of Montanism, see chapter V, p. 119. (Editor)

transcendence of God. According to Athenagoras,[4] Christians are not atheists since they distinguish God from matter and acknowledge one God, the maker of the universe who is Himself uncreated but has made all things by the Logos which is from Him.

In a synthetic formula, Athenagoras associates the creator in Plato's *Timaeus* with the Spirit holding all things together, in order to show that Greek philosophy also affirms the unity of God. "God has framed all things by the Logos, and holds them together by His Spirit." He refers to other philosophers who confirm this view. He says that Aristotle and his followers see the ethereal space and stars as a body quickened by a soul which is itself not subject to motion. The Stoics hold a theory of the artistic fire, of seminal principles, and of a spirit permeating the whole world: but God is this artistic fire, and therefore He is one (5–6).

Tatian[5] distinguishes between the spirit operating in matter and the divine Spirit: God is a spirit, not pervading matter, but the maker of material spirits and of the forms that are in matter; He is invisible, impalpable, being Himself the father of both sensible and invisible things. There is a spirit which is called the soul, and another spirit which is greater than the soul, and can be identified as the image and likeness of God in man. Tatian distinguishes other kinds of spirits: a material spirit, a spirit in the waters, a spirit in animals, a spirit in men, a spirit in angels, a spirit in the stars. The idea that God is spirit, which is a statement of scripture, reappears later on as the affirmation that God is incorporeal (in Origen and Augustine) or on the contrary, that God is corporeal (in Tertullian who is more deeply influenced by the Stoics). According to Tertullian, the Spirit is God's body, a body of its own kind, and the Word of God also is corporeal, thereby able to pervade and influence lower bodily natures as does the Logos in man.[6]

According to the Apologists, not only is God spirit, but there is in the Godhead a Spirit of God who comes third after the Father and the Word, thus completing the divine Trinity. Theophilus of Antioch is the first to use the term 'triad', or 'trinity', in this sense.[7] Justin praises Plato for giving the second place to the Logos and the third to the Spirit, and seems to parallel this Platonic doctrine with the Christian notion of God: "We reasonably worship Jesus Christ, having learned that He is the Son of the true God Himself, and holding Him in the second place, and the prophetic Spirit in the third."[8]

Athenagoras affirms their unity: "We acknowledge a God, and a Son His Logos, and a Holy Spirit, because the Son is the Intelligence, Reason, Wisdom of the Father, and the Spirit an effluence, as light from fire."[9] He also distinguishes them from the angels.

Irenaeus compares the Son and the Spirit to the two hands of God, i.e. His helpers in all His works.[10] Tertullian offers a specific teaching on the Trinity:

> The Father, the Son, and the Holy Spirit are three, however, not in condition, but in degree; not in substance, but in form; not in power, but in aspect, yet of one substance, and of one condition, and of one power, inasmuch as He is one God, from whom these degrees and forms and aspects are reckoned, under the name of the Father, and of the Son, and of the Holy Spirit.[11]

In the third century, with Tertullian, Clement, and Origen, we find a well developed theology of the Son and of the Spirit.[12] But we will not dwell, in the present study, on the deity or personality of the Spirit.

What is the source of this theology? As we have seen, the Apologists acknowledge some dependence on the Greeks, and their pneumatology is obviously inspired by the Stoics, who granted a very large importance to the notion of spirit.[13] The same will reappear in their anthropology and in their doctrine of inspiration. But they correct the Stoic pneumatology, and affirm a transcendent God. And they rely on other sources, properly Christian (Paul and the New Testament) or Jewish (the Old Testament, the extra-biblical Apocrypha, and Philo of Alexandria). As a matter of fact, even the pneumatology of Paul and Philo at times assimilated, and at times diverged from, that of the Stoics, while also relying on the Old Testament.

In Paul, the Spirit of God works in the creation of the world and of man, and is the agent of inspiration, spiritual life, and bodily resurrection.[14] In the extra-biblical Apocrypha also, which were written, corrected, or used by Christians, we find a theology of the Spirit. For instance, in the *Ascension of Isaiah* the Spirit is represented by the 'angel of the Spirit'.[15] This theology, which is typical of Jewish Christianity, reappears in Hermas.[16] Its theological aspects became obsolete, but such other aspects as its angelology, its doctrine of good and the evil spirits, and the conception of the transformation of the body after the resurrection as the putting on of a new garment,[17] already found in Paul, survive in the early Church.[18] In the Old Testament the Spirit appears in the narratives of the creation of man in Genesis, some sentences of the Psalms, some texts of the Wisdom of Solomon,[19] the chapter about the resurrection of the dry bones in Ezekiel, the statements about the inspiration of Moses and the Prophets.[20]

The references to spirit in the Gospels and in Acts are particularly important for the sections dealing with charismatic life. Philo[21] offers a parallel context of thought in the Judaism of the Diaspora. He distinguishes between the Spirit of God and all other spirits, which are understood in the sense of Stoicism. The Spirit of God has an important part in his anthropology as a divine energy and a partner of man, and in prophetic inspiration. And although we can affirm the reality of the divine Spirit, we cannot speak of the Spirit as personal in Philo. In this regard, the Apologists make a step forward.

The Spirit in Christian Anthropology

The Spirit has an important part in the anthropology of the early Christian Church, especially with regard to the creation and the resurrection of man, and to the purification and sanctification of the soul. Basically, this is an anthropology of the Image of God in man—sometimes of the image of the Image of God. Man can lose the likeness of God—the participation of God—by passion and sin.[22] Insofar as the image of God is pure, the Spirit of God can accomplish His work of sanctification or deification.[23] The Spirit is also the physician of the soul,[24] strengthening the spirit in man and weakening the flesh.[25] But the flesh itself is involved in sanctification, even on earth, according to Clement of Alexandria.[26] And according to *Didascalia Apostolorum,* marriage is holy: lawful intercourse does not preclude the presence of the Spirit.[27]

Insofar as the flesh means an inclination to sin, there is in man an antagonism between flesh and spirit, as we find in the Gospels and in Paul: "The desires of the flesh are against the Spirit, and the desires of the Spirit are against the flesh; for these are opposed to each other, to prevent you from doing what you would" (Gal. 5:17). This teaching of Paul underlies all patristic anthropology, and survives in a more complex form even when other distinctions are added, such as the Greek body-soul distinction, or the distinction between the spirit of man and the Spirit of God. The conflict between the spirit and the flesh goes back to the sin of our first forefather. Since we share in Adam, we must put off the old man in order to put on Christ, the new man created according to the image of God in justice and holiness.[28] Tatian says:

> In the beginning, the spirit was a constant companion of the soul, but forsook it because the latter was not willing to follow . . . The soul is not immortal, but mortal; but, if it acquires the

> knowledge of God, it dies not, although for a
> time it be dissolved ... If the soul continues
> solitary, it tends downward toward matter, and
> dies with the flesh; but if it enters into union
> with the Divine Spirit, it is no longer helpless,
> but ascends to the regions to which the Spirit
> guides it: for the dwelling place of the Spirit is
> above, but the soul comes from below.[29]

Here we find the schema, flesh-soul-spirit.

Sometimes the soul is dropped, and we find only flesh and spirit. But we should not therefore suppose that there is no soul, since the flesh or the spirit perform the functions of the soul.[30] We find the schema body-soul-spirit of man-Spirit of God, for instance, in Tertullian, who distinguishes between *afflatus* and *spiritus:* man was given a "living soul" by the inbreathing of God,[31] so that the soul is like an hydraulic organ[32] in which the operations of the senses and of the mind can be performed, but the soul does not become spirit. The spirit is given to man by God as an addition in order to perform a particular function, corresponding to a spiritual nature: salvation and sanctification.[33] The soul, according to Tertullian, oscillates between the material and the spiritual, and is sure to fall at last on the side towards which it has mainly gravitated.[34] As a consequence, the bodies of the saints (not their souls, which are merely *completed* by the addition of the Spirit of God) become spiritual, though only after the resurrection of the flesh when, by a second step, we enter the kingdom after being changed, that is, made incorruptible and immortal.[35]

Tertullian's anthropology, however, cannot be considered as a typical Christian anthropology in spite of the body-soul-spirit scheme, because of his materialism inherited from the Stoics.[36] Though accepting the soul, Irenaeus can speak according to the flesh-spirit scheme inherited from Scripture:

> If, therefore, anyone admit the ready inclina-
> tion of the spirit to be, as it were, a stimulus to
> the infirmity of the flesh, it inevitably follows
> that what is strong will prevail over the weak, so
> that the weakness of the flesh will be absorbed
> by the strength of the spirit, and that the man in
> whom this takes place cannot in any case be
> carnal, but spiritual, because of the fellowship
> of the Spirit.[37]

However, the flesh of this man is not changed in its
substance because man is engrafted onto a fruit-bearing
olive tree (Christ), but his works are changed and become
spiritual.[38]

In his first *Homily on Genesis,* Origen explains the
drama of the fall of man as that of the soul divorcing the
spirit, instead of renouncing the flesh in order to unite
with the spirit.[39] Origen's analysis of man is the most
developed since it includes the body, the flesh, the soul,
the spirit of man and the Spirit of God.[40] The soul is
tripartite: flesh, 'soul' and spirit. When Christ died His
flesh was buried, His soul visited the dead in Hades, and
He entrusted His spirit to the Father. He recovers His
spirit from the Father only after He has taken back His
soul and raised His flesh. What is this human spirit? It is
not the soul, but it is a spiritual counterpart of every
organ of the body, of the senses and faculties of the soul
when they are quickened by the Spirit of God.[41] In this
regard the spirit of man is a gift of God for which man
ought to give thanks to God, although it develops in man
and not without his will.

Origen certainly depends for this doctrine on Philo
who explains the fall of man with the allegory of the birth
of Eve from the side of Adam.[42] When Adam, the earthly
man, fell asleep, when, because of pride and negligence,
his soul was not quickened any more by God—and severed itself from God, Eve was born, that is the irrational
part of man took the leadership. Sense-perception, and

the passions which derive from it, developed, and he became one flesh with the irrational part corrupted by lust. Because of this marriage to the irrational part, where the mind becomes a slave to the passions, man does not welcome the full strength of the wind of the divine Spirit. Only a spiritual breath is left to him, just enough to make possible the choice between good and evil or, rather, the choice of evil which supposes the presence of some good. Philo interprets in the same sense the episode of the sons of God marrying the daughters of men, and God's declaration, "My Spirit shall not abide in man for ever, for he is flesh" (Gen. 6:3). Through repentance—through our fight against and victory over the passions—with the power of reason and the help of the grace of God, we restore the order disturbed by sin. And we thus return to the ideals of the man created in the image of God, a man enlightened by the Logos of God and quickened by the divine Spirit without hindrance.

The resurrection of our body is also the work of the Spirit of God[43] according to the early Church Fathers. Here, the problem is more simple: just as God created man in the beginning out of the dust, He can create him anew after the body has returned to the dust. The Fathers generally compare the resurrection to creation, pointing out that the difficulty is the same, or that there is less difficulty in the resurrection.[44] As for the resurrected body, which is spiritual and glorious, not earthly and carnal, the explanation lies in its *transformation,* not only into a celestial and glorious body, but into a spiritual one. According to *Didascalia Apostolorum,* which represents the more popular view of the resurrection, the resurrected body is the same as that of the present time.[45] According to Origen[46] (who, however, affirms the resurrection of the dead body), the transformation is understood as the acquisition of spiritual senses[47] and a rearrangement of matter according to our new celestial environment.[48] For Augustine, there is no radical transformation, yet after the resurrection our bodies are weightless and subject to no needs—a theory which is almost inconceivable. Even Tertullian affirmed a transformation after the resurrection.[49] Athanasius is closer to Augustine,[50] and Gregory of Nyssa is closer to Origen.[51]

The scriptural basis for the creation of man is, obviously, Genesis 1–3, and this text is also used, as indicated above, for the resurrection. Of course, the most striking text for the resurrection of the body by the Spirit of God is Ezekiel 37, the chapter on the dry bones, which many Fathers,[52] for instance Irenaeus, interpret in this sense. In this passage the Creator is represented as vivifying our dead bodies, promising them resurrection and resuscitation from their sepulchres and tombs, and actually conferring resurrection upon them.[53] Other texts cited for this same purpose are Isaiah 26:19 or 6:13,[54] and some verses of the Psalms such as, "You send forth Your Spirit; they are created; and You renew the face of the earth" (Ps. 104:30),[55] or,

> Create in me a clean heart, O God, and put a new and right spirit within me. Cast me not away from your presence, and take not your Holy Spirit from me. Restore to me the joy of your salvation, and uphold me with a willing spirit . . . O Lord, open my lips, and my mouth shall show forth Your praise (Ps. 51:10–12).[56]

or, "Where shall I go from Your Spirit? Or where shall I flee from your presence?" (Ps. 39:7).

Of course, the most important reference is to Paul, especially I Cor. 15 and Rom. 8:11, "If the Spirit of him who raised Jesus from the dead dwells in you, he who raised Christ Jesus from the dead will give life to your mortal bodies also through his Spirit which dwells with you".[57] The resurrection of the body is therefore ascribed to the creative power of the Holy Spirit, and even the notion of the 'spiritual body' suggests the idea of a transformation which supposes a difference between our present earthly body and the body of the resurrection (I Cor. 15:51). For their representation of heavenly life, the early Fathers rely also on Matt. 19:12, about the sons of the resurrection who do not marry but live like the angels of God, and about the eunuch for the sake of the Kingdom. Melito was such a eunuch, that is, a man who lived in celibacy or continence; for this reason he was called a prophet and the angel of the Church in Sardis.[58] With him we may compare the virgin daughters of Philip, who were prophetesses[59] (Cf. Acts 21:9). These are prophets living an angelic or heavenly life in the Spirit.

The change from the carnal to the spiritual man is also the work of the Spirit.[60] The spiritual man is one renewed interiorly according to the pattern of the man created in the image of God in justice and holiness. The characteristic of the inner man is the possession of spiritual or inner senses. According to many early Fathers, especially Origen, the spiritual man has developed spiritual senses which are like a second nature, with which he understands the spiritual sense of scripture, sees and feels the things of God, and performs the will of God. This seems to be the characteristic effect of the divine spirit in man: a spiritualization of all his faculties, which supposes the presence and the influence of the Spirit of God. Of course, in order to grasp this spiritualization, we must raise our thoughts above the level of carnal things, since the same words and images are used for both carnal and spiritual realities in scripture, for instance, eyes, ears, nostrils, taste, touch, heart, bowels, blood, circumcision. We must think of 'spiritual eyes' etc.[61]

If man does not return to sin, spiritual life endures forever and subsists after death, even if he is for a while deprived of his body, or "asleep" in his soul. However, the beginning of spiritual life is not called properly a resurrection but a new birth, because it is a beginning conferred at baptism with the gifts of the Holy Spirit following the remission of sins and the purification of the soul. More exactly, it is a rising together with Him with whom we are both buried and raised again at baptism; but for us it is properly a regeneration in which we receive a spirit of adoption enabling us to say, "Abba, Father!" But this consideration leads us to sacramental theology, with which we shall deal after we discuss the role of the Spirit in Christology.

The Role of the Holy Spirit in Christology

Christology is not concerned simply with the incarnation of Christ, or His human life beginning with His birth on earth, but must be understood in the general context of the redemption. For the first generation of Christians, and perhaps for the disciples themselves, Jesus was the Word of God speaking to them in the flesh, the 'Anointed one' (*Christ*) who possessed the Spirit of God more fully than John the Baptist and the prophets. Christ was able through His spiritual power to heal the sick and raise the dead, to read hearts and preach with divine efficacy, finally, to raise Himself from the dead, to send the Spirit from the Father, and to impart Him to His disciples.

The 'Holy Spirit', or the 'Spirit of God,' is also the 'Spirit of Christ,' and that even before the incarnation, since Christ is the pre-existing and eternal Son of God, born now in the flesh. Therefore, the whole economy of the Spirit is closely connected with that of the Word. Their association appears from the creation of the world,[62] develops throughout the Old and New Testaments, and shall last until the end. We can read in the Fathers both that the Word of God and that the Spirit of God spoke through the prophets, with light coming to them from the Word and inspiration from the Spirit, insofar as such a distinction is possible. A complete demonstration would be too long, since, until Augustine questioned the traditional attribution of the theophanies to the Son and the Spirit respectively, preferring to ascribe them directly to the divine essence,[63] all the Fathers supported a preparatory mission of the Word and the Spirit in the Old Testament.

Justin summarizes the history of prophecy thus: it flourished among the prophets of the Old Testament, culminated in Christ (when it was withdrawn from the synagogue), and developed among the Christians:

> The scriptures say that these enumerated powers of the Holy Spirit (Isa. 11:1ff) have come upon Him, not because He stood in need of them, but because they were to rest in Him, i.e., would find their accomplishment in Him, so that there would be no more prophets in your nation according to the ancient custom; and this fact you plainly perceive ... Solomon possessed the spirit of wisdom, Daniel that of understanding and counsel, Moses that of might and piety, Elijah that of fear, and Isaiah that of knowledge; and so with the others ... It was necessary that such gifts should depart from you; and after coming to rest in Him, should again, as had been predicted, become gifts which He imparts by the grace of His Spirit's power to those who believe in Him, according as He deems each man worthy thereof (cf. Ps. 68:18; Joel 2:28f).[64]

The Spirit inspired the whole of scripture: Moses, David, the prophets, Solomon.[65] It is even said by Tertullian[66] that Noah, who probably had to rewrite the book of Enoch and other memories of the beginnings, which may have been destroyed in the flood, was inspired. So likewise was Esdras, who had to rewrite the books of Moses and other scriptures destroyed in the ruin of Jerusalem. Another famous example of inspiration is the *Septuagint,* according to the story of the 70 scribes inspired by the Spirit, who, working individually, produced the same verbal translation of scripture.[67] The Spirit inspired the prophets in such a way that they could see the deeper meaning and future implications of their visions and sayings, which refer to the coming of Christ in the flesh and the economy of the redemption.[68] We can say that the whole Law is spiritual[69] because of its Christological content and divine authorship. We shall see in a moment that it must also be interpreted spiritually, that is, with the inspiration of the Spirit in the Church.

All the Fathers repeat Luke and Matthew, and accept the virginal birth of Jesus, affirming that Jesus was born of the Blessed Virgin by the power of the Spirit.[70] Tertullian, however, interprets Luke 1:35, "The Holy Spirit shall come upon you . . . ," as the coming of the Word, since the Word is Spirit.[71] Tertullian also explains how the two substances in Christ, viz, the Spirit and the flesh, or the divine and the human nature respectively, work.:

> The property of each nature is so wholly preserved, that the Spirit on the one hand did all things in Jesus suitable to itself, such as miracles, mighty deeds, and wonders; and the flesh, on the other hand, exhibited the affections which belong to it. It was hungry under the devil's temptation, thirsty with the Samaritan woman, wept over Lazarus, was troubled even unto death, and at last actually died.

Tertullian counterbalances this sharp distinction, worthy of the Council of Chalcedon, with the principle of the *communicatio idiomatum:* "But by a transfer of functions, the Spirit carries out things usually done by the Flesh, and the Flesh is performing things possible only to the Spirit."[72]

A Christology free from the Stoic connotations which cause some ambiguity in Tertullian, can be found, for instance, in Irenaeus, who likes to speak of Christ as the Second Adam, i.e., the Son or Word of God who became man in order to bring us back to the Father, because He stood among us as the pattern of man among the deteriorated copies. This pattern was the image of God, in full possession of the Spirit of God, and ready to impart it to the disciples who were born as sons of the first Adam.

> This was the same (flesh) that the Lord came to quicken, so that as in Adam we all die, being of an animal nature, in Christ we may all live, as being spiritual, not laying aside God's hand-iwork but the lusts of the flesh, and receiving the Holy Spirit.[73]

It was traditional in Greek theology from the beginning to define Christ as the image of God, taken in two steps: 1) the Divine Word and, 2) the Incarnate Word as the New Adam, who is the pattern for man in both his creation and his redemption (being in both cases in possession of the Spirit).

Irenaeus added some distinctions, in opposition to the Gnostics, when dealing with the baptism of Christ: Christ is not a man receiving the Spirit of God in order to become a prophet, nor does the divine nature come upon Him at baptism;[74] He is the Word of God incarnate. The Spirit comes upon Him under the figure of the dove in order to learn how to dwell among men as in a temple, and not simply in visitations, as in the case of the prophets:

> For God promised that in the last times He would pour Him (the Spirit) upon His servants and handmaids, that they might prophesy; hence He also descended upon the Son of God, who had become the Son of man, and in fel-lowship with Him became accustomed to dwelling in the workmanship of God, working the will of the Father in them, and renewing

them from their old habits into the newness of Christ.[75]

According to the same Irenaeus, the spiritual powers of Christ, or the gifts of the Spirit, passed over the Christians,[76] as we see in Acts, in the Epistles of Paul, especially in 1 Cor. and, later on in the literature of the early Church. Particularly noteworthy among these diverse charisms are prophecy, wisdom, healing, discernment of spirits and exorcism. We shall meet them again in a following section. The help of the Spirit is felt particularly in prayer and contemplation.[77]

The gifts of the Spirit come to us in our earthly life, but not to all in the same way. However, the more general gift of the Spirit imparted to all the baptized, causes a thorough change in the meaning of Christian life since our hope of heavenly life governs the orientation of our will on earth.

According to Paul (Rom. 5:5 and 13:13), the Spirit pours charity into our hearts, and the gift of charity is the only one which survives in immortality, after faith and hope have been fulfilled.

The baptism in the Spirit is understood by Origen as a life spent in the union with God under the guidance of the Spirit, and as a higher understanding of the truth under His inspiration. Of course, the abolition of faith does not make knowledge or wisdom irrelevant in immortality (Rom. 13:12). Origen summarizes this teaching in *First Principles,*[78] presenting love and wisdom as the cause of beatitude in heaven. His notion of damnation corroborates this opinion, since he considers the divine judgment as an act of our moral conscience pricked by the awareness of sin,[79] and the condition of the damned as that of being "cut asunder,"[80] i.e., the soul divided from the spirit, or man from the gift of the life-giving Spirit of God, which sinners reject out of passion or pride.[81] In this sense, Origen can distinguish a death to God from death to sin and from natural death, and represent the condition of the damned as the "unending death", a phrase of Plato supported in scripture.[82] Moreover, our hope itself cannot deceive when interpreted according to the spirit and not according to the flesh, and when it points to spiritual, not to carnal goods. In this connection, Origen is opposed to the carnal or 'Jewish' interpretation of the promise.[83] The earthly prosperity promised to the people of God was a figure of the future possession of spiritual goods, since a literal or carnal interpretation would be impious. How can God incite us to look for lower, almost sinful goods as the fulfillment of our best hopes?

We can easily understand the relevance of a spiritual interpretation of the Old Testament since we know that the promises are spiritual, and that the chief object of prophecy is redemption through Christ, in which we are involved.[84] The letter is not enough, since the prophets themselves were able to know the spiritual meaning, and there is a disproportion between the literal and the spiritual meaning. In order to perceive the spiritual meaning, the reader must purify his soul and acquire spiritual senses.[85] In the *Dialogue with Heraclides,* before discussing the question whether the soul is the blood, Origen is insistent, almost insulting: "I beseech you, therefore, be transformed. Resolve to learn that in you there is the capacity to be transformed, and to put off the form of a swine." If the carnal approach is everything, how can we realise the importance and even the existence of the inner man with his spiritual senses?

Those among the early Fathers who do not develop a theory of the spiritual senses at least teach that for an understanding of the things of God, there is need of faith, given by the Spirit, or through the grace of God. For instance, Clement says:

Instruction leads to faith, and faith with baptism is trained by the Holy Spirit. Faith is the one universal salvation of humanity, and there is the same equality before the righteous and loving God . . . There are not, then, in the same Word, some illuminated (Gnostics); and some animal (or natural, Psychic) men; all who have abandoned the desires of the flesh, are equal and spiritual before the Lord.[86]

However, not everyone, or people of every condition, can interpret the scriptures correctly, as heretics contend, but only those in the Church, according to Irenaeus: "For where the Church is, there is the Spirit of God, and where the Spirit of God is, there is the Church, and every kind of grace."[87] Tertullian does not speak differently when he supports his theory of the 'prescription against heretics.'[88] All the Fathers agree that outside of the Church there is no Spirit; consequently, no right faith, no correct understanding of scripture, and even no true sacraments. As we shall see, especially with Cyprian and Augustine, this idea, which is right in principle, can become too narrow when too systematically understood. Whatever be the answer to this particular question, the necessity of faith, baptism and the Church in order to receive the Spirit of God and of Christ, to enter a spiritual life, and to understand scripture according to the spirit rather than the bare letter, leads us to consider the role of the Spirit in the sacraments and in worship.

The Holy Spirit in the Sacraments and In Worship

We can follow the work of the Holy Spirit in the making of a Christian through baptism and all the rites connected with it, in the eucharist and worship, in reconciliation and ordination. The sources are very rich, but here we shall use only the *Apostolic Tradition, Didascalia Apostolorum,* Tertullian's *De baptismo* from the ante-Nicene Church, and the catechetical works of Cyril of Jerusalem, Theodore of Mopsuestia and Ambrose who, though post-Nicene, represent the development of an older tradition.

In the *Didascalia* we read:

> Honor the bishops, who have loosed you from
> sins, who regenerated you by water, bred you
> with doctrine, confirmed you with admonition,
> and caused you to partake of the Holy Eucharist
> of God, making you partakers and joint heirs of
> God's promise.[89]

Baptism is conferred in the name of the Father, the
Son and the Holy Spirit,[90] but it is given after a special
training and is accompanied by meaningful rites.
Catechumens, who are not without the help of the Spirit
when they convert to faith and surmount their passions,[91] are prayed over with a laying on of hands by their
teachers before being dismissed,[92] and are exorcised
daily, also with a laying on of hands.[93] Just before baptism they are again exorcised as well as anointed by the
bishop.[94] After being baptised, they are prayed over by
the bishop with a laying on of hands in order to receive
the Spirit as becomes a fully initiated Christian:

> O Lord God, who counted these worthy of
> deserving the forgiveness of sins by the laver of
> regeneration, make them worthy to be filled
> with Your Holy Spirit and send upon them
> Your grace, that they may serve You according
> to Your will.[95]

Tertullian insists that the Spirit, who hovered over
the primeval waters, permeates the water of baptism,
conferring on it the power to purify and sanctify those
who are baptised.[96] Similarly, the baptismal ointment
"runs carnally, but profits spiritually" (*ibid.* 7), and the
imposition of hands after baptism is an invocation to the
Holy Spirit to enter those who are coming out of the
water, like the dove which came down from heaven and
rested upon Jesus (*ibid.* 8). The baptism of John could not
give the remission of sins and the Spirit, but, according to
John himself, Christ will come and give a baptism in spirit

and fire. This happened at Pentecost (*ibid.* 10:19), and according to the evangelist, Christ's baptism is given now in water and spirit (*ibid.* 4:5; cf. *John* 3:5). However, the baptism conferred by the disciples of Jesus could give the Spirit only after Pentecost, since Christ promised to send Him from the Father.

Tertullian refers to the types of baptism in the Old Testament, of which Christian baptism is the spiritual reality. For instance, in the flood the ark prefigures the Church, and the dove, the Spirit; the crossing of the Red Sea prefigures salvation from the bondage of the devil; the water purified by the tree prefigures the virtue of the cross; the rock gushing forth water figures baptism in Christ by water (*ibid.* 8;9).[97]

The Pauline theology of baptism, as a death and resurrection with Christ for a regeneration of the inner man and the gift of the spirit of adoption, underlies the early literature on baptism. More often, however, the latter insists on another aspect, also Pauline: the purification and restoration of the image of God in man according to Christ, the new man and the second Adam. Cyril of Jerusalem, in his *Procatechesis,* without insisting on the point, makes it clear:

> Baptism is a ransom for captives; a remission of offenses; a death of sin; a new birth in the soul; a garment of light; a holy and indissoluble seal; a chariot to heaven; the delight of Paradise; a welcome into the Kingdom; the gift of adoption.[98]

Cyril speaks abundantly of the action of the Spirit in Christian life as a consequence of baptism, for instance: "The indwelling Spirit fashions your mind into dwelling places for God. In the future, when you hear Scriptures concerning mysteries, you will understand things you know nothing of" (*ibid.* 1:6). He considers baptism as the seal of the Spirit (*ibid.* 1:17), and he gives two complete homilies on the Spirit in his catecheses (XVI, XVII), which deal with the theology of the Spirit and His work of sanctification. Gregory of Nyssa,[99] Theodore of Mopsuestia[100] and Chrysostom develop the figure of the burial and resurrection. Chrysostom says;

> The two creations, i.e. the birth of Eve, and the spiritual birth at baptism, cannot be understood. We must accept the mystery, and believe what is said. The divine covenant is fulfilled: death and burial, resurrection and life; and all these take place at once. When we immerse our heads in the water, as if in a grave, the old man is buried, and having sunk, is entirely hidden once for all; when we emerge, the new man rises again. Just as it is easy for us to be immersed and to emerge from the water, so it is easy for God to bury the old man and raise up the new. To the believer, a catechumen is a stranger, for he does not have the same Head [Christ, the Head of the Church, or of the Christian, His body], the same Father, the same city, or food, or clothing, or table, or dwelling.[101]

Ambrose says:

> Mark well the order of things in this faith: you died to the world, and rose again to God. And as though buried to the world in that element, being dead to sin, you rose again to eternal life. Believe therefore, that these waters are not void of [spiritual] power.[102]

Basil gives a definition of baptism which includes all the components mentioned above, and cites the Spirit as principle of the whole process:

> We are born to the Spirit by dying to the flesh; let us die that we may live. Baptism is the ransom of captives, the remission of debts, the death of sin, the rebirth of the soul, the shining garment,

the unbreakable seal, the chariot to heaven, the guarantee of the Kingdom, the grace of adoption, intimacy with God. We become His son, a soldier of Christ, a citizen of the heavens.[103]

In the case of baptism as well as that of the eucharist, there is the same emphasis on the presence and efficacy of a spiritual power conferred on the elements. This recalls Tertullian's idea that the Spirit of God permeates the water of baptism. The same reappears in catechetical writers, for instance, Cyril of Jerusalem:

Do not think of the font as filled with ordinary water, but think rather of the spiritual grace that is given with the water ... The ordinary water in the font acquires sanctifying power when it receives the invocation of the Holy Spirit of Christ and the Father.[104]

The same is said about the oil of the anointing after baptism, or chrism:

Having therefore become partakers of Christ, you are properly called Christ, ... or anointed. Now you have been made (new Christs) by receiving the anti-type of the Holy Spirit, ... by being given an unction, the anti-type with which Christ was anointed; and this is the Holy Spirit ... For Christ was not anointed by men with oil or material ointment, but the Father, who had appointed Him to be the Saviour of the whole world, anointed Him with the Holy Spirit ... But beware of supposing this to be plain ointment. For as the bread of the Eucharist, after the invocation of the Holy Spirit, is mere bread no longer, but the Body of Christ, so also this holy ointment is no more simple ointment, nor [so to say] common, after the invocation, but is Christ's gift of grace. By the advent of the Holy Spirit, it is made fit to impart His divine nature. This ointment is symbolically applied to your forehead and other senses; and while the body is anointed with the visible ointment, your soul is sanctified by the holy and life-giving Spirit.[105]

This is followed by a discussion of the spiritual senses of the inner man thus consecrated by the ointment (*ibid.* 4).

When we come to the eucharist in the catecheses and liturgical literature, we find the same approach. We have seen Cyril of Jerusalem comparing the change in the water and the oil to that in the bread and wine of the eucharist. Coming to the elements of the eucharist, in his explanation of the *Epiclesis,* he specifies:

Then, having sanctified ourselves by these spiritual hymns [the *Sanctus*], we beseech the merciful God to send forth His Holy Spirit upon the gifts before Him, that He may make the bread the body of Christ, and the wine the blood of Christ; for whatever the Spirit has touched is surely sanctified and changed.[106]

This emphasis on a spiritual change of the elements by the Spirit, or a spiritual endowment of the elements for the purpose of a communication of grace to the Christians who receive the consecrated food and drink, is common in the catecheses,[107] as we have said, and is already found in the *Apostolic Tradition:*

And we pray that You would send Your Holy Spirit upon the oblation of Your holy Church, and that You would grant to all [Your saints] who partake to be united [to You] that they may be filled with the Holy Spirit for the confirmation of their faith in truth.[108]

We do not have to discuss here whether this notion of the eucharist is primitive, or even primordial, or to refute the idea that it is close to magic: there is no proportion between a sacrament correctly understood and magic. The emphasis on the action of the Spirit in and through the elements implies that we live in the Church under the economy of the Spirit, who becomes the principle of our purification and sanctification, of our regeneration and consecration, of our spiritual nourishment, of the development of our spiritual senses, and who is the pledge of our inheritance.

This may be the point of entry for the notion of the eucharist itself, or, better, this doctrine commands the whole development of the eucharist from the beginning. In Judaism, the eucharist was essentially praise and sacrifice, a combination which our notion of thanksgiving, though good, can hardly represent in the fullness of its original implications.[109] The eucharist of Jesus is not only the offering of His flesh and blood for the remission of our sins, but also a spiritual sacrifice like the hymns and blessings of the Jews at the synagogue and at meals. How it was understood by His disciples after the coming of the holy Spirit is represented by the discourse after the Last Supper and the priestly prayer in John 13 to 17. In this context, one can grasp the sense of a spirit of adoption conferred on us, and crying, "Abba, Father!" or of a Paraclete speaking in our behalf, comforting and guiding us, or of a special ability to interpret scripture spiritually and to worship in the Spirit, that is to sing hymns with our hearts and not only with our lips, and even to invent new hymns.[110] Let us add that the Christians brought as to an altar their own offering, material gifts such as we see in *Apostolic Tradition*,[111] and what was necessary for the communion and for the support of the poor, widows and orphans, and of the clergy. Their gift must be pure, not the fruit of injustice, and may be offered only by baptized people living a blameless life,[112] because the Spirit would be offended if the offering were not pure, since the offerer would not be bringing a spiritual sacrifice, and the altar of God in the poor would be desecrated.

The Church itself is considered as the body of Christ, quickened by the Spirit. This idea is clear throughout the Fathers, and is given a beautiful expression in both Augustine and Chrysostom. According to the former, the Spirit builds the Church by pouring divine love into our hearts.[113] According to Chrysostom, the Spirit Himself is the soul of this great body of Christ, which is the Church.[114] With Cyprian, in third century Africa, we find a crisis in ecclesiology, where the controversy concerned the claim of a group of heretics to be a Church and to possess the Spirit. Ignatius of Antioch had already opposed this claim by heretics[115] in the second century. Because of his deep sense of the unity of the Church as the body of Christ and the temple of the Spirit, Cyprian denies to heretics the possession of the Spirit, and therefore the right to be a Church with valid sacraments.[117] His dispute with Stephen, the bishop of Rome,[118] and later on the theological problem of Donatism, are the consequences of this position. Cyprian emphatically denies the possibility of a heretic or schismatic being a minister of Christ or giving baptism. Augustine explained that God—not the minister—is the author of baptism, and that the baptism conferred by a heretic, though valid, is "dead" because the Spirit is given only in the Church.[119] When they reject the bond of love and the unity of the Church, which is His work, they offend Him.[120] Like Cyprian, whom he refuted, Augustine also may be too systematic, limiting the freedom of the Spirit and binding Him too narrowly to human divisions.[121] Moreover, the principle of the communication of the Spirit in the Church through a holy minister is basically correct, as we see in the prayers for ordinations and sacraments; and an adequate sacramental theology cannot be built on the negative aspect of the notion of unworthiness, which ought to be the exception.

In ordination, for instance in the *Apostolic Tradition,* the bishop, priest, and deacon are given respectively a princely spirit, a spirit of government and counselling, and a spirit of service.[122] These are the lawful ministers of baptism and of reconciliation after repentance. They communicate the possession of the Spirit and the right to receive communion through baptism and, if necessary later on, through the laying on of hands of absolution or reconciliation,

> As you baptize a heathen and then receive him, so also lay hands upon this man [a repentant sinner], while all pray for him, and then bring him and let him communicate with the Church. For the imposition of hands shall be to him in the place of baptism: for whether by the imposition of the hand, or by baptism, they receive the communication of the Holy Spirit." (*Didascalia*).[123]

In *Epistula* 57, Cyprian proposes to reconcile the lapsed because a persecution is coming, and they should be strengthened by the flesh and blood of Christ. How, he asks, could the Spirit of the Father speak in the confession of a Christian who has not recovered the Spirit of the Father through the gift of peace?[124]

The power of the Spirit also works in the remission of sins, but here some distinctions are necessary. The association of the gift of the Spirit and of the power to forgive sins in John 20:22–23 does not necessarily mean that the gift of the Spirit is the power to forgive sins, though we find support for this meaning in the text of Basil given at the beginning of this essay.[125] The remission of sins is the fruit of the blood of Christ, an association which is very strong in patristic literature, because it is rooted in the tradition of sacrifices in the Old Testament and in Christ's offering of His own blood for the remission of the sins of the multitude (Mat. 26:28 and parallels).[126]

Furthermore, God is the author of forgiveness, and the remission of sins is asked for in prayer by the bishop and the congregation.[127] The purification of the soul is both a prerequisite for and a result of the presence of the

Spirit, in the soul of a repentant sinner, according to Psalm 51.[128] We can say also that love is restored to our heart by the Spirit, according to Rom. 5:5, and the presence of love is the elimination of sin, according to Augustine.[129] The text of John 20:22–23 is addressed by Christ to the Apostles, but it could also mean that those in possession of the Spirit and who are not Apostles, have this power. Tertullian, for instance, takes the power of the keys away from the bishops and turns it over to the 'spirituals', who, for reasons of prudence, will not use it.[130] The truth underlying the exaggeration and therefore the error of Tertullian seems to be explained much better by Origen, and the intervention of the spiritual man in the healing of sinners is a matter of spiritual discernment and brotherly warning:

> Because having received the Holy Spirit and become spiritual, he obeys the impulse of the Spirit as a son of God and conducts himself according to reason in all things: he forgives what God forgives and retains the sins that cannot be healed. In this he resembles the prophets who do not speak their own thoughts, but those rather of the will of God; and so in this too he serves God, who alone has the power to forgive.[131]

In the same section, Origen, acknowledges this power in the successors of the Apostles:

> In the same way, the Apostles also and their successors, priests according to the great High Priest, having received the science of divine therapy, know from their instruction by the Spirit for what sins, when, and how they must offer sacrifice. They know also the sins for which they must not do so.

According to Origen, the official hierarchy ought to be spiritual and usually is, in spite of exceptions. This charismatic aspect of the healing of souls introduces us to the next section on charismatic life in the Church.

Charismatic Life in the Early Church

The whole question of charismatic life in the early Church is still very confused, not because the evidence is no good or too scarce, but because scholars come to it, even today, with their own presuppositions. For some of them, charismatics were the spiritual leaders of churches which had no other leadership than the Twelve, until the hierarchy of office (bishop, presbyter, deacon) became established toward the end of the first century or even in the second, under the influence of patterns of Greek society.[132] For others, the churches were structured from the beginning, and charismatic manifestations were looked upon with suspicion.[133] For still others, charismatic life was a rediscovery of the Montanists in the second half of the second century, and important texts on Christian prophecy are ascribed to the influence of Montanism.[134] In spite of the persistence of some scholars today, following the views of their school or church, we will assume that Pierre de Labriolle has given a good account of Montanism in his two books, La Crise Montaniste, and Les Sources de l'Histoire du Montanisme (Paris 1913). Therefore we do not need to bother with Montanism when we discuss the Didache, Hermas, or the Odes of Solomon; Perpetua is probably not a Montanist, and Irenaeus dealing with the martyrs of Lyons certainly not, in spite of their sympathy for the churches of Asia.

Labriolle rehabilitates Montanus and the prophetesses in his analysis of the extant Montanist oracles which he considers as orthodox prophetic statements,[135] thus disagreeing with the ancient opponents of Montanism.[136] Tertullian is the great literary representative of Montanism in Africa. Through him we know that the role of the Spirit was essentially to enforce Church discipline according to the counsels of the Gospels.[137] Because of their laxity, the *psychikoi* (the actual leaders of the Church) were bad shepherds, and leadership—even the power of the remission of sins—should be ascribed to the spirituals to whom it belongs essentially.[138] It is interesting to notice genuine manifestations of the Spirit in Montanism: in addition to the gift of tongues,[139] there were visions and prophecies,[140] and a strong Encratist tendency, the positive values of which lay in its emphasis on asceticism and continence.

What was the destiny of prophecy in the Church of the first centuries? The gift of tongues was known,[141] though the evidence for its existence is scarce. But the Spirit can also inspire a silent prayer,[142] and the devil, imitating the Spirit, can cause an energumen to speak in tongues.[143] A few prophets are mentioned, especially the four daughters of Philip, and Melito of Sardis.[144] Melito, and probably the daughters of Philip, at least when the latter prophesied, seem to combine prophecy and continence,[145] according to the ideals of the eunuch for the sake of the kingdom (Matt. 19:10–12). Hermas enjoys prophetic visions,[146] as does Polycarp who is called a prophet.[147,148] Perpetua has visions,[149] as do the martyrs of Lyons.[150]

Martyrs seem to become prophets, in some regards, when they confess their Christian faith before the judge and in suffering: they are inspired by the Spirit in their answers,[151] and they believe that they are given the power to overcome suffering,[152] as Perpetua said before her martyrdom: "Then there will be Another by my side Who will suffer for me, because it is for Him that I shall be suffering."[153] She observed, when she came back from the arena, that she had been in ecstasy during her suffering since she did not remember the cow which wounded her.[154] Martyrdom is considered a display of divine power, and a victory for the Christians.[155] Some of the pagans recognize the presence of God in the behaviour of Christians under trial, and the blood of martyrs becomes the seed of new Christians.[156]

Origen affirms the existence among the faithful of the charisms of exorcism, healing and revelations:

> Traces of that Holy Spirit who appeared in the form of a dove are still preserved among Christians. They charm demons away and perform many cures and perceive certain things about the future, according to the will of the Logos.[157]

According to Origen, however, charisms are less frequent in his time than in the beginning of Christianity,[158] but the power of prayer is not impaired: "I believe that the words of saints when praying are charged with great power, especially when they pray with the Spirit and with understanding."[159]

Another manifestation of the Spirit seems to be connected with the status of the widows in the pastoral epistles,[160] which became the charter of Christian widowhood for centuries. In the *Didascalia Apostolorum* we see these widows, now free from family duties, spending their time in prayer[161] and visiting the sick for whom they pray with a laying on of hands.

We can recognize several charismatic features in their style of life. They enjoy a power of intercession in their prayer for the sick, and perhaps a gift of healing. They may receive revelations and visions, at least if we can rely on a late document, the *Apostolic Church Order* (from the beginning of the fourth century in Egypt). Three widows are appointed, one to care for the sick and two to "persevere in prayer, because of all those undergoing temptations, and for revelations and instructions about what is needed".[162] Returning to the *Didascalia,* we find that widows exercise their power of intercession when they pray for the donors who support them in exchange for their prayer.[163] The reasons for these charisms and for their contemplative life as a whole, are the facts that they are poor (and the poor are heard by God)[164] and that they live in continence and purity of soul. They enjoy the dignity of the altar[165] when they consume the offerings of the faithful, and thus must not be desecrated by gifts that are the fruit of injustice.[166] As living altars they offer the spiritual sacrifice of praise and intercession. This form of charism should not be minimized on the grounds that widows were an institution; on the contrary, the elevation of poor widows to the status of the contemplative life should be considered an inspired act of a Church still breathing the spirit of Pentecost. So also was the determination to support them as providing a precious spiritual contribution to the life of the congregation. Poor old men also, as well as poor widows, possess the charisms of healing the sick and comforting the weak, as we see in Clement of Alexandria: "If a Christian has a presentiment that he is going to fall, he may say, 'Brother, lay your hand on me lest I sin,' and he will receive help both spiritually and physically."[167]

Should we consider as prophets or healers those whose prayer is powerful and advice spiritual? They may be simply the poor of the Church, who are the mainstay of the community, and who practise seriously their duty of brotherly admonition. Clement sends his rich man, who is poor in spiritual goods, to them:

> Collect for yourself an unarmed, unwarlike, bloodless, passionless, stainless host: pious old men, orphans dear to God, widows armed with meekness, men adorned with love. Obtain with your money such guards for body and soul. For their sake a sinking ship is made buoyant, when steered solely by the prayers of the saints; disease at its height is subdued, put to flight by the laying on of hands; and the attack of robbers [devils] is disarmed, foiled by pious prayers.[168]

Clement thus describes the ministries of the faithful:

All these warriors and guards are trusty. No one
is idle, no one is useless. One can obtain your
pardon from God, another comfort you when
sick, another weep and groan in sympathy for
you to the Lord of all, another teach some of the
things useful for salvation, another admonish
with confidence, another counsel with kindness.
And all can love truly, without guile, without
fear, without hypocrisy, without pretence.[169]

It is the nature of a charism to be given by God
spontaneously or as the result of prayer. Never is the
Spirit given simply by a laying on of hands, or by any
other rite; these are always combined with an invocation.
There is an *epiclesis* at Mass, and at baptism a laying on of
hands with a prayer. In ordinations there is an accompanying prayer, and the Spirit will come upon the
candidates if they are worthy. For this reason, an un-
worthy bishop, according to the *Didascalia*,[170] is a cause of
corruption for his whole Church. However, sound
thinking supposes that the clergy are worthy, and that we
do not have to refer regularly to the formula, *ecclesia
supplet,* as even the Donatists were obliged to do in certain
cases.[171] By their ordination priests are in possession of
the power to exorcise and to bless.[172]

However, the power to exorcize and to heal belongs
also to the laity, since healers and exorcists are neither
ordained nor appointed, as we read about healers in the
Apostolic Tradition: "If anyone among the laity appears to
have received a gift of healing by a revelation, hands shall
not be laid upon him, because the matter is manifest,"[173]
and about exorcists, in the *Apostolic Constitutions.*[174] The
existence of these gifts in the Church is abundantly attested and apparently by eyewitnesses and not merely by
reference to I Cor. 12.[175] Actually, the power of casting
out evil spirits is attested everywhere and in every writer
in the early Church,[176] for instance in Justin:

For numberless demoniacs throughout the

whole world, when many of our Christian men
had exorcized them in the name of Jesus Christ,
have been and are being healed. The possessing
devils have been rendered helpless and driven
out of the man, though they could not be cured
by all the other exorcists, or those who used
incantations and drugs.[177]

Here we see that in a Church which is charismatic by
essence, the difference between the man endowed with a
special charism of exorcism or of healing, for instance,
and the average good Christian, is one of proportion only
and not a matter of being or not being at all a charismatic.
For instance, Irenaeus states against the Gnostics that
"The Spirit is found in all of us, as the living water from
the Lord in those who believe correctly in Him, who love
Him, and know there is only one Father who is above all,
and through all, and in all."[178] Every Christian practises
exorcism privately, first upon himself and the things
which he uses, the most usual device of exorcism being
the sign of the Cross,[179] as we read in the *Apostolic Tradition:*

When tempted, always reverently seal your
forehead [with the sign of the cross]. For this
sign of the Passion is displayed and made
manifest against the devil if you make it in faith,
not in order that you may be seen by men, but by
our knowledge putting it forward as a shield.[180]

Already Justin noticed that the words of Jesus have an
amazing power to inspire awe and turn away from sin;[181]
but this can also be used in exorcism against the devil:

... by the name of Jesus with the recital of
stories about Him. For when these are pronounced they have often caused demons to be
driven out of men, especially when those who
utter them speak with real sincerity and genuine
belief.[182]

Tertullian portrays a Christian woman married to a pagan, who finds it difficult to perform without hindrance the practices of her religion in her private life.

> Shall you go unnoticed when you make the sign of the cross on your body; when you blow some impurity away; when even by night you rise to pray? Will you not be thought to be engaged in some work of magic?[183]

If now we try to give a description of a Christian prophet which would fit, for instance, the prophets of the *Didache*[184] about whom so much ink has been spent that no one dares to assume that anything sound can be said on their behalf,[185] what could we say? In my opinion, we must first distinguish the case of prophets or apostles coming from outside as visitors, who most often were probably holy men who truly lived and spoke in the Spirit but needed to be scrutinized as a precaution against false prophets or simple beggars, and the case of the prophets belonging to the community, who enjoyed the esteem of all and exercised their spiritual gifts, especially that of prayer, since they were contemplatives. The community supported them, like the widows referred to earlier, who lived by the ideals of prayer and continence. We should not be surprised by the title, 'high priest,' which is introduced as a justification for the benefit of the tithes enjoyed by the prophets, because this title does not mean 'priest' properly speaking. For there is no *cohen* in the New Testament, but rather intercessors, those who offer the sacrifice of thanksgiving for the nation, and intercede for their salvation and the remission of sins. In the early Church, the dignity of 'priest,' or 'high priest,' is attributed to those who offer spiritual sacrifice, according to I Peter 2: 5: "Like living stones be yourselves built into a spiritual house, to be a holy priesthood, to offer spiritual sacrifices acceptable to God through Jesus Christ."

The notion of spiritual sacrifice coming from converted Gentiles and acceptable to God derives from

Malachi 1:11, which is understood in this sense by the early Church. As 'priests' the prophets do not substitute for bishops, who are not yet designated technically as priests, even though they preside over the community in every regard, especially in worship. The prophets are allowed to "give thanks" as much as they like.[186] Should we understand that they recite or improvise—the difference is one of degree only—the *anaphora*? First, why should only one person give thanks, when we see the priests, even in the time of Augustine, invited to give a word of exhortation after the bishop? Moreover, why should not the prophets be allowed to make the prayer of thanksgiving since they are particularly gifted for prayer, and since the presidents are presiding in any case? Perhaps in the early Church, when the exigencies of unity had not yet increased the role of bishops, there was more freedom without danger to the exercise of authority.

Later Forms of Charismatic Life

We would not be complete if we did not say a word about three forms of charismatic life which flourished in the early Church and took on great importance: martyrdom, the ideals of the *didascale*, and monastic life.

Martyrdom continued to occur with varying frequency until Constantine, and is a recurrent phenomenon in the history of Christianity. However, we have said enough to prove that it is *par excellence* a fruit of the Spirit. Those who die under trial enter the glory of the kingdom,[187] and even the sins they have committed since baptism are wiped away by the superabundance of the Spirit.[188] Confessors—those who publicly professed their faith but were not executed—are considered as spiritual men,[189] allowed to sit with the priests[190] and to take some part in the reconciliation of sinners.[191]

Monasticism is a phenomenon of the fourth and subsequent centuries. The first monks who withdrew from their local church and city in order to live in a desert or in some kind of solitude, were the successors not so much of the martyrs as of the prophets and the servants of God who lived in prayer and continence during the first centuries. As evidence, we could compare *Shepherd of Hermas* and *The Life of Antony.* As it would be too long and unnecessary to develop this point, let us simply mention the discernment of spirits as an important practice or gift in this type of life, common to the two documents.[192] (According to *Hermas,* however, discernment of spirits is a necessity for every Christian who is concerned with the regulation of his own thoughts.)[193] Monks are visited by good and evil spirits, and should know how to live by the spirits coming from God, be they angels or simply the energies imparted to us by the Holy Spirit.[194] When Anthony came forth from his retreat, he appeared as a man "initiated in the mysteries and filled with the Spirit of God, being guided by reason and abiding in a natural state."[195] He is a man living according to the image of God, and developing a harmonious set of virtues since, "When the soul has its spiritual faculty in a natural state, virtue is formed."[196] Throughout the *Sayings of the Fathers,* the most interesting thing to observe is not the eccentricities, or even the great spiritual feats, but the beautiful sense of humanity, a genuine form of religious humanism, which these Fathers develop and teach to those who want perfection.[197]

The *didascale* was a type of charismatic gifted with wisdom and knowledge (I Cor. 12:8, cf. Isa. 11:2), two gifts which are frequently mentioned in the early Church,[198] especially by the two great *didascales,* Clement of Alexandria and Origen. Clement formulates his ideal of the 'true gnostic',[199] who is a man living in the Spirit and so spiritual in his judgments and motivation that he thinks and behaves according to the wisdom of God: "He perseveres without sin, acquires self-control, and lives in

the Spirit with those who are like him in the choirs of the
saints, even though he be still detained on earth."[200] He is
not, however, indifferent to the welfare of his fellow men
since, like divine wisdom, "he teaches his son," that is, his
disciples.[201]

Origen insists on the necessity of the gift of wisdom
in order to discover the spiritual meaning of scripture[202]
and to understand the object of faith, especially Christ, in
a more and more spiritual way.[203] He ascribes this wisdom to many uncultured Christians who are able easily to
reach a spiritual understanding of scripture:

> In the past very few, almost the prophets alone,
> could with the grace of the Holy Spirit, detect a
> spiritual sense in the law and the prophets; but
> now there are innumerable multitudes of be-
> lievers who, although unable to explain logically
> the process of their spiritual perception, have
> yet almost to a man the firm conviction that
> circumcision ought not to be understood lit-
> erally, nor the Sabbath rest, nor the pouring out
> of animal's blood, nor the fact that oracles were
> given by God to Moses on these points; and
> there is no doubt that this discernment is
> suggested to them all by the power of the Holy
> Spirit.[204]

However, there is a difference between the ability of
faith to reach the spiritual meaning in the average
Christian, and the gift of wisdom which is the first
charism, coming before knowledge which is the second,
and faith, which is the third. The simple people who
struggle for piety must be saved, but:

> You would not find ordinary people partaking
> of divine wisdom, but those whose ability is
> superior and stands out among the adherents of
> Christianity. . . . We do not hold that a man
> untrained in human wisdom can receive the

more divine, but we hold that all human wisdom
is foolishness in comparison with the divine.[205]

Origen does not, however, identify divine wisdom
with Greek philosophy or human wisdom. The saints in
heaven will find their delight in the knowledge of the
truth about man and the world, in the divine patterns,
not in the contemplation of the earthly copies.[206] On
earth divine wisdom is to be learned in scripture, for
instance in the spiritual interpretation of the Song of
Songs: the soul which does not know herself as the bride
of God, but reasons according to the problematics of the
schools of philosophy, is sent back "to the footsteps of the
flocks, among the shepherds' tents," where she belongs.[207]

Conclusion

Our inquiry has led us to discover many aspects of
the Spirit and His operations according to the early
Church. We should note the depth of this doctrine, its
theological and anthropological connotations, and its
extension to the details of the moral and liturgical life.
The notion of grace can compare with it, and has much
the same meaning.

In Augustine, who comes to ascribe the divine
operations to the essence rather than to the persons in
the Godhead, the Spirit pouring forth charity into our
hearts comes to be identified as Love itself, or the source
of love in which we participate and which enables us to
perform every kind of good. And Love, as a divine
energy, is a power given by God as a grace.

Unlike Augustine, Greek theology does not build
upon the definitions of Nicea and Constantinople, but
lives on a tradition dating from the first centuries and the
New and Old Testaments. Nor does it systematically
reinterpret the data or the operations of the Spirit as does

Augustine. Even the Arians, who attack the divinity of the Spirit in the second part of the controversy, do not question the Spirit's operations.

The details of these operations suggest that a pneumatology lies at the base of every theological treatise, from inspiration to ethics, anthropology, the Trinity, prayer, hermeneutics, Christology, ecclesiology, the sacraments, spirituality. The Spirit is rich in all regards because He appears as an energy involved in every activity of the Christian life. He is more particularly manifested in charisms which, due to their extraordinary repercussions either in the form of miracles or wisdom, mark the presence of His power.

It is to be noted that what we call the evangelical counsels, in contrast with the commandments and ordinary spiritual life, are the matter of a charism supported by heroism of the will. This is the case of the life of celibacy or continence, which Paul recommends but refuses to impose systematically, and in fact dissuades those who are either married or unable to follow such a life.

We should also note the biblical character of the entire theology and practice of spiritual life of the Greek Fathers. It is rooted in every detail of the Old and New Testaments, and makes use of corrected aspects of pagan Greek pneumatology, both the materialistic pneumatology of the Stoics and that of Plato and Aristotle.

To those interested in the spiritual life and the Pentecostal renewal today, I would say that the pneumatology of the early Church can provide a theological basis and an experiential guideline which can only improve their openness to the action of the Spirit.

IV. ━━━━▪

Several things in Islam might seem to offer parallels to the charismatic aspects of Christianity: the revelation of the Koran, belief in prophecy (especially as exemplified in Mohammed), the dervishes, the sufi mystics, etc. One point, however, on which we might not expect a parallel is the doctrine of the Holy Spirit. Islam's emphatic monotheism, its conscious and even passionate rejection of the Christian theology of the Trinity, would seem to make an inhospitable soil for the flourishing of any comparable notion.

In fact, however, not only does the very term 'Holy Spirit' occur in the Koran, but the notion that develops around it, at least in certain circles, manifests some thought-provoking parallels to the third person of the Christian Trinity. Is this another case of the hypostatization of a divine attribute, such as occurred in the Wisdom books of the Old Testament in regard to the Spirit (and the Word) of Yahweh? The latter development prepared the way for the New Testament revelation of the Trinity; may the Islamic parallel have a similar value? In any case, the fact that it occurred above all in mystic and contemplative circles makes it all the more significant.

—The Editor

HOLY SPIRIT IN ISLAM

JAMES KRITZECK

There are two Koranic terms to designate the notion of 'spirit' in Islam, *nafs* and *rūh*. At first acquaintance they may appear to be easily and sharply contrasted, as they often are in their Semitic cognates, almost like the Taoist (and proto-Taoist) *yin* and *yang* principles. *Nafs* may be taken to mean 'soul,' 'self,' the subjective, 'fleshly' spirit; while *rūh* is 'wind,' 'breath,' the objective, 'heavenly' spirit.

But few distinctions are that simple within Semitic languages, in which terms frequently denote strangely variant and even directly opposite notions. In Arabic we find not only a multiplicity of meanings for each of these words before and especially after the *Koran,* and from time to time interchangeable usage of them, but also a distinct set of different usages and seemingly a development of *rūh,* particularly, within the *Koran* itself.[1]

This is not meant to be a philological study and will not be such, but the unique nature of revelation to which Islam lays claim, and the widespread lack of understanding of it outside the Islamic community, suggest that some basic matters be clarified immediately.

There is no theory of scriptural inspiration in Islam corresponding to those in Judaism and Christianity, its acknowledged predecessors and highly favored rivals within the Abrahamic family. It is the orthodox position of Islam on this subject, seldom marred by heresy or even sophistry, that each of the 114 chapters, 6,239 verses, 77,934 words, and 323,621 letters of the *Koran* are (with

101

the possible exception of some allegedly abrogated verses, about which there is disagreement) verbatim the
dictation of God Almighty, under the name of *Allāh*,
through the Archangel Gabriel, to the 'messenger' (*rasūl*)
and 'prophet' (*nabi*) Mohammed (*Muḥammad*). Thus
Mohammed is regarded by Moslems (more accurately,
Muslims) as in no sense the author of the *Koran*, but rather
its 'reciter.' Indeed, *Koran* (*al-Qur'ān*) means 'recitation.'
Compared to the 'miracle' (*āyah*) of the *Koran* (each verse
is termed an *āyah*), the only miracle Mohammed admit-
ted to have been accomplished in some sense through his
agency, he himself is almost uncelebrated.[2]

For our immediate purposes, we may disregard the
Koranic usage of *nafs,* with its plurals *anfus* and *nufūs,*
which is either reflexive (one's 'self'—even God's) or
means the 'human soul,' with the same basal idea as the
Hebrew *nefesh,* the 'physical appetite' or 'desire.'[3] It is the
word *rūḥ* which we must examine most carefully. The
noun is feminine, by way of exception, and never used in
the plural or even 'derived' in the usual sense in Koranic
Arabic.[4] Its onomatopoeia is obvious. Indeed, from its
claims, it is the original onomatopoeia. *Rūḥ* is used
precisely twenty times in the *Koran,* in four sense-groups
with four anomalous texts.[5] It is customary among
Islamologists to divide the Koranic chapters of the Meccan period into three chronological groups, following the
order established by Theodor Nöldeke (and successors),
somewhat improved upon by Régis Blachère.[6] The
sense-groups for *rūḥ* conform very closely to that tripartite division of the Meccan chapters, followed of course
by the Medinan chapters, a fact which was not offered as
a major proof of the validity of that dichotomy but which
certainly reinforces it.

Because all of Islamic thought on the spirit depends
for its correct interpretation upon the recognition of this
development in meaning, and because it is no lengthy
matter, we may simply outline it from the twenty texts
themselves.[7]

In the chapters of the first Meccan period, the *Koran* associates the spirit with the angels:

1. "On the day when the spirit and the angels shall stand in ranks, they will not speak." K 78:38

2. "In it (the "Night of Power") the angels and the spirit let themselves down." K 97:4

3. "Someone has asked about a punishment... from Allah, master of the stairs, on which the angels and the spirit mount up to him." K 70:4

In the second stage of development, predominantly chapters of the second Meccan period, the spirit is what God breathed into Adam and the Virgin Mary, to give them life in different but similar ways, and Jesus is "a spirit from Him:"

5. "Thy Lord said to the angels: See, I am going to create a human being from potter's clay... So when I have formed him (Adam) and breathed some of my spirit into him, fall in obeisance to him." K 15:29

7. "Thy Lord said to the angels: See, I am going to create mankind from clay: so when I have formed him and breathed into him of my spirit, fall down to him in obeisance." K 38:72

8. "And her (Mary) who guarded her private parts... so we breathed into her some of our spirit and made her and her son a sign." K 21:91

9. "He created man... from clay... Then he formed him and breathed into him some of his spirit." K 32:8

19. "And Mary... who guarded her private parts, so we breathed into them some of our spirit." K 66:12

> 6. "We sent to her (Mary) our spirit, who took for her the form of a human being, shapely... He said: I am the messenger of thy Lord."[8] J 19:17
>
> 17. "Jesus... is only the messenger of Allah, and his word... and a spirit from him."[9] K 4:169

The third stage of development, during the third Meccan period, is marked by a very decisive association of the spirit with the *amr* ('affair,' 'command,' 'will to action')[10] of God, spent on men and angels, but increasingly an attributive 'part' of God in some way compatible with the uncompromising monotheism of the revelation being 'recited':

10. "They ask thee about the spirit, say: The spirit belongs to my Lord's affair, but ye have not knowledge bestowed upon you except a little." K 17:87

11. "He (Allah) sendeth down the angels with the spirit belonging to his affair upon whomsoever he willeth of his servants that they may give the warning." K 16:2

13. "Lofty in degrees, possessor of the throne, casting the spirit belonging to his affair upon whomsoever he willeth of his servants, that he may give warning." K 40:15

14. "It belonged not to any human being that Allah should speak to him except by suggestion or from behind a veil, or by sending a messenger to suggest by his permission what he pleaseth . . . Thus we have suggested to thee a spirit belonging to our affair." K 42:52

Finally, predominantly in the Medinan chapters beteen 622 and 632, the spirit becomes 'the Spirit of Holiness '(*rūḥ al-qudus*). There are only four undoubted references with this meaning, together with a plausible fifth, but it may be recalled that they represent a quarter of the sum total of usages of *rūḥ* in the Koran:

12. "Say: The spirit of holiness has sent it (the Koran) down from thy Lord . . . that it may strengthen those who have believed." K 16:104

> 4. "It is the revelation of the Lord . . . with which hath come down the faithful spirit upon thy heart, that thou may be of those who warn in clear Arabic speech." K 26:193

15. "We gave Jesus . . . the evidences and supported him by the spirit of holiness." K 2:81

16. "We gave Jesus . . . the evidences and supported him by the spirit of holiness." K 2:254

20. "O Jesus . . . remember my goodness to thee . . . when I supported thee by the spirit of holiness in speaking to the people in the cradle[11] and as a grown man." K 5:109

Seven of the references to the spirit are to Adam, the Virgin Mary, and Jesus as 'a spirit of God.' Four references are to 'the spirit of holiness,' of which three identify 'the spirit of holiness' as the strengthening authentification or 'proof' of the Virgin Birth and Mission of Jesus.

Thus the development of the Koranic revelation of *rūḥ* would seem to have reached its logical conclusion, and in Christian terms to have been perfectly completed. There being no philological reason for distinguishing "the spirit of holiness" from 'the Holy Spirit' in the last sense-group, and indeed in the clearly Christian context of all but one of them, the conclusion is all but inevitable: the Holy Spirit was clearly proposed to Moslems in the *Koran,* and speaks in His own name.

Unsurprisingly, however, the different and even somewhat confusing Koranic references were not the end of the matter, but rather the beginning. Again because of the unique nature of revelation to which Islam lays claim, according to which for example, the texts of K 78:38 and K 5:109 bear the same divine authority and are somehow supposed to mean the same *rūḥ,* it required thirteen centuries to put the sense-groups for *rūḥ* together properly.[12] In the meantime, the Holy Spirit was alive in Islam. Philologists, exegetes, tradition (*ḥadīth*)—collectors and evaluators, philosophers, legists, theologians (*mutakallimūn*) and plain believers had much to say about an unclear subject.[13] Reinforced to some extent by the others, it was really the plain believers who, as it were connaturally, clarified the notion and witnessed to the living reality of the Holy Spirit in the context of *at-Taṣawwuf* or Sufism. Broadly speaking, Sufism is the contemplative branch or side of Islam which has a very long and elusive history, and about whose orthodoxy there continues to be a division of opinion among Moslems.[14]

For the Sufis, the *Koran*—early to be declared by the religious legists and theologians on a par with God as 'uncreated'—held a wealth of esoteric meanings. Peripherally, they forged their own theology from a stubborn and inadequate (at times, to some) revelation. This, in turn, became the basis for an immensely supple spiritual life.[15] The 'Spirit of Holiness' or the 'Holy Spirit' began to be identified by many of them, unabashedly, with God Himself, as it were God under an assumed name. Indeed, the 'names' of God, which are more than mere 'attributes' (because adjectives are considered nouns in Arabic) favored the type of popular speculative theology and devotional life especially preached by the Sufis with enormous success, to the utter horror of the *mutakallimūn*. Even today the ubiquitous *misbahah*, Moslem prayer-beads which in one form at least are the proto-form of the Christian rosary, are meant to remind Moslems, one by one, of God's names. For the Sufis, then—or at least for a significant number of them—there could be God 'the Father,' God 'the Word,' and God 'the Holy Spirit' without the slightest deviation from Islam's absolute monotheism—any more than the Holy Trinity deviates from the absolute monotheism of the Christian Church—with Islam blessedly spared the Christological heresies.

It was the Sufis who made a 'church' out of a 'community' (*ummah*), 'sacraments' and 'sacramentals' out of 'pillars' (*arkān*) and pebbles, and disengaged and gave primacy to the attributes of grace-giving and love on the part of *Allāh,* otherwise an impersonal and transcendant God, static and silent to a point which would have shocked John Calvin and would frighten a modern atheist. The Sufis were also, somewhat paradoxically for ascetics, the first and only real 'professional' missionaries in Islam, as their spiritual descendants still are.[16] They experienced the Holy Spirit, and felt it their obligation to share that experience with others, and to recruit and train others for it.

The subject of the Holy Spirit as such, whether as *rūḥ* or, increasingly, as *nafs,* was only rarely made the principal theme of Sufi sermons and treatises, however. We know that the earlier Sufis considered that *rūḥ* in man was a material, "fine, created substance (*'ain*) or body (*jism*), placed in the sensible body like sap in green wood."[17] Together with *nafs,* the seat of the blameworthy characteristics, it constituted man himself. What is particularly interesting about this naive-appearing view, which had the authority of both Al-Qushayri and Al-Hujwīri, two eminent Sufi theorists, is that it makes man *all* material and *all* spiritual at one and the same time.[18] This certainly reflects the intellectual discomfort and awkwardness in early Islam generally, and somewhat later in early Sufism particularly, at the alien and conflicting notions which, it was felt, had to be accommodated and harmonized into a coherent theory. It may also reflect a part of the Hindu influence on Sufism which must have led to bewilderment by its positive denial of the principle of non-contradiction and even of "self."[19]

Such an accommodation and harmony was provided most successfully by Abū-Hāmid Al-Ghazāli (d. 1111), a terrified convert to Sufism from the traditional sciences, philosophy, and *kalām* (dialectical theology) and one of the towering figures in all of Islamic intellectual history.[20] To simplify something which is very nuanced in Al-Ghazāli's Arabic treatment, the *rūḥ* (now definitely, when convenient, 'soul') of man is held to be immaterial, purely spiritual, of the same nature as the Holy Spirit, *Allāh*'s own *rūḥ,* with which it can enter into direct communication. If devoted, persevering, receptive, and fortunately graced, it may even attain a state of union.[21]

It might be thought that this was as far as the notion could reasonably be expected to go. Actually, it went much farther.

Relative coevals from opposite ends of the Islamic

world, the Persian poet Farīd ad-Dīn 'Attār (d. ca. 1225), and the Spanish poet Muḥyid-Dīn Ibn al-'Arabi (d. 1240), arch-Sufis both, said about the same thing at about the same time.[22] 'Attār said of *Allāh*, God, that He was *rūḥ kullī*, "the Universal Spirit."[23] Ibn al-'Arabi, possibly the most accomplished and erudite Sufi of them all, propounded the same theory of *rūḥ:*

> Ibn al-'Arabi divides things into three classes: Allāh, Who is Absolute Being and Creator, the world; and an undefinable *tertium quid* of contingent existence that is joined to the Eternal Reality and is the source of the substance and the specific nature of the world. It is the universal and common reality of all realities. Man likewise is an intermediate creation, a *barzakh* between Allāh and the world and a vicegerent connecting the eternal names and the original forms. His animal spirit (*rūḥ*) is from the blowing of the divine breath and his reasoning soul (*nafs nātika*) is from the Universal Soul (*al-nafs al-kullīya*), while his body is from the earthly elements. Man's position as vicegerent and his resemblance to the Divine Presence come from this Universal Soul, which has various other names, Holy Spirit (*rūḥ al-kudus*), the first intelligence, vicegerent (*khalīfa*), the perfect man, and the *rūḥ* of the world of command (*'ālam al-amr*).[24]

Theoretically then, *rūḥ* has become *nafs*, and the 'Holy Spirit' the 'power' of the soul. It only remains for *nafs* to become *rūḥ*, and the 'power' of the soul to become the 'Holy Spirit.' Providentially for Islam, and conveniently for this study, that comes immediately.

In the works of 'Umar Ibn al-Fāriḍ (d. 1234), a contemporary of both 'Attār and Ibn al-'Arabi, incarnation (*ḥulūl*) and identification (*ittiḥād*) with *Allāh* are impossible. But there is real 'passing away' (*fanā'*), and union (*waṣl*) of the *nafs* and *rūḥ* of the person with the *nafs* and *rūḥ* of *Allāh* becomes possible, because the Holy Spirit and the person's soul become the same *nafs* and *rūḥ*.[25] Al-Jilāni carries this "position of existential monism on to straight animistic pantheism," and the 'Holy Spirit' is the name for a special aspect of *Allāh* in relation to which, or whom, all created spirits stand, and by the power of God the angelic and holy Spirit becomes the 'reality' and 'real meaning' (*ḥaqīqa*) of Mohammed. Mohammed thereby becomes the 'perfect man,' and— even Al-Jilāni hesitates to conclude the thought—all of this (now completed) circular speculation forces upon him—*Allāh* Himself.[26]

That, in brief, is one thing which Sufism did to and for Islam by its *tafsīr* and usage of the notion of 'Holy Spirit': it came one step short of divinizing Mohammed, who not only would not have entertained for a second such a suggestion, but reluctantly approved killing for much less. An uncompromising monotheism pervades the Koran. Take Sura 112, for example:

Say: "He is God, One,
God, the Everlasting Refuge.
He did not beget and was not begotten,
and there is none equal to Him."[27]

So much for Sufi theory. There are easily hundreds of thousands of references which could be employed to show the single short and long steps which individual Sufis took in this direction—and others. But to multiply such references to prolixity would be foolish in the structure of this short chapter, and would in fact tend to give a false picture of the Sufis and of the role of the Holy Spirit in their own lives, not to speak of the lives of ordinary Moslems.[28]

The Sufis were not, for the most part, theorists. Certainly they were not book-worms; their literature consists largely of hagiography and training manuals.[29] They were men and (many) women who embraced a contemplative life of journeying for the purpose of reaching a destination and goal. Whether in an eremetical or, more usually, in a cenobitical form of life in 'religious orders' or *tarīqāt,* or as mendicants, their inexpressible experiences of *Allāh,* through or as the Holy Spirit (or indeed, His as *themselves*) were what was all-important.

At their finest, they were mystics like Rābi'a al-'Adawiyya (d. 801), the most beloved woman Sufi in Islam, and Husayn ibn Mansūr Al-Hallāj, who was so full of the Holy Spirit that he could no longer distinguish himself from God. Unfortunately he said so, and was therefore crucified, beheaded, and otherwise dismembered in Baghdad in 922. By a kind of *ijmā'* (common consent of scholars), his life more than that of any other Sufi illustrates the intensity of the spiritual experience in Islam.

The lives of most of the Sufis are preserved, not in highly structured and wordy treatises but rather in hagiography, in stories, anecdotes, and aphorisms which are not so much to be found in libraries as on the lips of Sufis.[30] The Sufi life centers around *dhikr,* 'recollection,' a spiritual exercise designed to render God's presence throughout one's being, and in which usually there is a rhythmical repetitive invocation of God's names, that is His attributes, or merely *Allāh,* or *Hūwa* ('He'), or the simple expiration of breath.[31] Of course there developed many forms of *dhikr.*[32]

Sufism is vital at this very moment, not only within the Islamic world which is an enormous portion of the inhabited earth, but even outside the Islamic world, in Europe and particularly America, for example, where it has come to enjoy a certain vogue.[33] It is of course not as popular as it has been at other times, but it is perhaps all the healthier for that. Sad to say, Sufism won so many adherents by the 16th, 17th, and 18th centuries that it was in the hands—more than in the minds and hearts—of amateurs and even disinterested persons, and of persons more interested in hashish or membership in the local "club" than in spiritual life. The very word 'Sufi,' never exactly a respectable term, thereafter became almost synonymous with 'drifter,' 'hippie,' 'hustler,' or 'nut' (*majnūn*, 'possessed by a *jinn*').[34]

That is not to say the Sufi theories of *nafs* and *rūḥ* suffered any decline or diminution. On the contrary, in some Sufi circles they were expanded into a kind of *Divina Commedia*.[35] It is questionable, of course, whether or not that was a good thing.

The important fact is that much authentic Sufism has survived, here and there. It is also playing its age-old missionary role on the frontiers of Islam, notably in Africa.[36] It is producing some saints; one might cite the recent remarkable life and work of Shaykh Aḥmad Al-'Alawi (d. 1934) of Algeria.[37]

In the honest and serious search for and with the 'Holy Spirit' lies one of Islam's most appealing and endearing aspects. It may prove to be the most significant one of all to be considered if the Sons of Abraham are ever to be one in faith, in hope, and in love, praising forever the glory of the Father, the victory of the Son, and the comfort, the gifts, and—as Blessed John Ruysbroek (d. 1381) phrased it—the "delicious taste" of the Holy Spirit.

V. ▪▪▪

History offers many instructive precedents for the contemporary charismatic movement. Although many of them are treated lengthily and wittily by Ronald Knox in his Enthusiasm *(Oxford: University Press, 1950), his derisive disaffection for them is so total (despite avowals to the contrary) as to exclude any possibility of even a partially positive appreciation. The following survey attempts to be more open and balanced.*

Not all the movements touched on here would be charismatic according to the same definition. But since it is a question, not of defining an essence but of proposing analogies for consideration, it is better to be as open and flexible as possible in extending the term to movements which, from various angles or at different levels, offer an instructive resemblance to the contemporary renewal.

—The Editor

SOME CHARISMATIC MOVEMENTS IN THE HISTORY OF THE CHURCH

LOUIS BOUYER

Is the Pentecostal movement something as new in the Catholic Church as it seems to many people? And, if not, what kind of reactions have analogous movements in the past provoked on the part of the theologians and Church authorities? These are the two main questions I shall try to answer. I shall not make any attempt to be exhaustive; rather, I shall take a few, but very remarkable samples of such movements through the centuries. It will be enough, I think, to show that such movements are a quasi-permanent, or ever-recurrent, feature of the life of the Catholic Church. This will also enable us to see that they have ever been raising more or less the same problems.

Faced with these problems, the best theologians—when they were also spiritual men—have always had two main reactions. The first one has been to advise the people engaged or attracted, of the necessity of what is called discernment of spirits, while trying to set sound and practical rules toward that end. The second has been to insist that however positive what we may call the Pentecostal phenomena may seem and be, they are not to be considered and pursued as an end in themselves. However, as we shall see, they have always diverged on the question whether this meant that such phenomena had to be gone beyond, more or less quickly, and dis-

113

appear in the course of a right spiritual development; or
that they simply had to be referred and submitted always
to higher ends.

The Church authorities seem to have been ever
anxious to avoid, and if need be to condemn, eccentric or
sectarian forms of such movements, while remaining
persuaded of the necessity of never 'quenching' the
Spirit, when and where its manifestation can be au-
thenticated. Far from what has been the *a priori* suspicion
of some Protestant historians, it can be said on the whole
that the bishops in the past have been disposed to integ-
rate these movements into the life of the Church so as
fully to exploit for the whole Christian body the riches of
their experience, rather than to discourage them. Of
course, such a positive reaction has been at times
weakened, especially after some violent outbursts of a
sectarian spirit. However, it remains the basic reaction of
authority throughout history. The comparatively modern view that charism and regular organization in the
Church would normally be in a state of nervous tension,
if not of war, is not based on fact but on prejudice. It is a
view that was launched in the eighteenth century by the
brilliant but very superficial and overly systematic history
of these movements, written by the pietistic teacher
Gottfried Arnold.[2] Many others have developed this
theme after him, but they have never been able to support it otherwise than by a selective and distorted presentation of the facts.

Here we shall first summarize the essentials of what
we find on the subject in the New Testament itself. Then
we shall study the charismatic phenomena connected
with martyrdom in the early Church, together with what
is called Montanism. After the period of persecutions we
shall come to the so-called Macarian school in primitive
(or nearly primitive) Monachism, in connection with the
development of Messalianism. Then in Byzantine
monasticism we shall see the development of a charismatic tradition, first with Symeon the New Theologian, in

some tension with a more institutional conception connected mainly with the great monastery of Stoudios in Constantinople. After that we shall follow the development of the same line in the so-called *hesychast* tradition, connected with the monasteries, first of Mount Sinai, later of Mount Athos. We shall say something of the controversy this movement aroused in the fourteenth century, when it was defended by St. Gregory Palamas, Archbishop of Thessalonica, and of a later conflict between St. Nilus Sorsky and St. Joseph of Volokolomsk, provoked by the propagation of the movement in Russia at the beginning of the modern era. Then passing to the West, we shall have to say something first of the opposition between two great English spiritual writers, also of the fourteenth century: Richard Rolle and the unknown author of the book called *The Cloud of Unknowing.* This will prepare us to study some marked features of the mystical doctrine of Saint John of the Cross, in opposition to certain forms of popular mysticism in Spain, such as the *alumbrados* movement, and perhaps also to some aspects of the teaching of his own friend and *dirigée,* Saint Teresa of Jesus.

After a few words on Quietism and some surprising aspects of late Jansenism, we shall try to draw some general conclusions, mostly practical, from this study.

Scripture

We do not need to study in detail here the well known texts of the Acts of the Apostles which connect the first outpouring of the Holy Spirit in the Church, after the resurrection and ascension of our Lord, with extraordinary manifestations, especially 'speaking in tongues' on the day of Pentecost. Similar manifestations seem to have taken place on later occasions in the primitive Church, as when the apostles were sent back from the sanhedrin, or when the family of Cornelius converted. In addition to speaking in tongues, we notice prophetic gifts, either in the specific sense of prevision of the future, or, more generally, of inspired hymns or exhortations; also gifts of a healing power. We must not forget the collective visions, such as that of the divine fire coming down from heaven, reminiscent of the manifestation on Sinai, nor, more widely, what may be called a mysticism of the Shekinah (the visible presence of God with His people in the cloud and fire) or the Merkabah (the immediate vision of His throne, borne by the angelic powers) which seem to have developed already in Judaism.

According to Paul's own witness in I Cor. 12 and 13, we see that similar manifestations were commonly found even in a Church consisting mainly of Greek converts, such as that of Corinth. And it is clear from what is said that Paul himself had a personal and very intense experience of such gifts.

What makes these two chapters especially interesting to us is that they give not only a description of phenomena connected with the coming of the Spirit, but also some criteria of their authenticity, together with an appreciation of their significance, of their right use, and of the perspective in which they are to be seen in connection with the whole development of the life of the Spirit in us, both individual and collective.

On the first point, according to Saint Paul, there is no inspiration which comes from the Spirit of God and does not confess Christ as the Lord. This certainly means more than a purely verbal confession of faith; it implies obedience to the teaching of Christ and fidelity in following Him. Even if they are authentic in their root and origin, the gifts of the Spirit are distorted if they become an occasion of vain glory, or if they make us forget that we ought to put our own gift to the service of others and acknowledge the need we have of theirs.

In this connection, it is extremely important to

notice that in modern times, largely as a result of the influence of Gottfried Arnold, we have come to use 'charism' in a sense which is not at all that of the apostle, and which more or less implies an opposition that he was most anxious to reject. That is, by 'charism' we mean, or tend to mean, only a very individual and more or less extraordinary gift. By the same token, we tend to oppose 'charism' and 'office' (*Amt,* as the Germans would say): any function regularly exercized by appointed officials in and for the community. In the view of Paul, this is completely wrong. He applies the word indifferently to the extraordinary gifts (such as speaking in tongues), to the regular functions of officials (such as the apostolate, teaching or government), and even to the most humble capacities of "helping" in any way.[4]

On the other hand he insists that *all* these gifts (not only the official functions) are to be considered by their possessors not, in fact, as their own, to be enjoyed freely and without regard to others, but as 'ministries' (διακονίαι) given to them not for themselves primarily but for the good and service of all.

This will lead him directly to the great conclusion that of all the gifts, the most important, and the only one which is to last for ever, and therefore to which all the others have to be submitted, is the gift of charity:[5] unselfish love, like that which God has manifested to us in Christ.[6]

I need not say that throughout the whole of Christian history, this text of I Corinthians was to be used again and again as the great charter of the Pentecostal gifts, as regards both their use and interpretation.

To this must be added another characteristic of Saint Paul's teaching: the close connection he sees between the life of the Spirit in us and what he calls our life "in Christ," to quote a phrase which comes up again and again through all his letters. Note also the verbs beginning with συν, so characteristic of his style, to express a community of activity and life between us and Christ himself. This point has been developed abundantly, especially by authors such as Albert Schweitzer,[7] Msgr. Lucien Cerfaux[8] and Bishop Moule,[9] and I shall not say more on the subject. However, it must be noticed that the connection between the risen Christ and the Spirit is so strong in the teaching of Saint Paul that some have come to the conclusion that, for him, they were one and the same. This opinion takes its stand especially on the famous sentence of II Corinthians 3:17–18: "The Lord is the Spirit." However, as the context shows, he means that, "just as Moses and the gift of the Law were one to the Jews, so for us Christians, Christ and the gift of the Spirit are one also." As the following verses express it, in the risen Christ, the whole human being has become as it were permeated by the presence of the divine Spirit. In the same way, in the measure in which we become one with Christ by faith, the Spirit takes possession of us. It can be said equally well, either that we live in Christ through the Spirit, or that Christ lives in us through the same Spirit.

The Martyrs and Early Monasticism

This is what will be exemplified remarkably throughout most of the literature of the ancient Church connected with martyrdom. Here we must consider first the Apocalypse of Saint John, and later the documents connected with Ignatius of Antioch and Polycarp of Smyrna (their correspondence and the story of the martyrdom of Polycarp), and more generally the *Acta martyrum* whose authenticity is acknowledged by all historians, together with some letters or treatises connected with martyrdom (mainly of Tertullian, Saint Cyprian and Origen).

Already in the Apocalypse, the main theme is that those who suffer death out of fidelity to Christ are united with him in the process of his passion and resurrection, so much so that their death becomes, like His, the beginning of their glorification. It is thus that they are his martyrs, i.e. 'witnesses,' par excellence. However the same book identifies the 'testimony' or 'martyrdom' of Jesus with the Spirit of prophecy (19:10), while the Spirit and the Bride of Christ, the latter being the Church considered in her present trial, are seen as one in crying "Come, Lord Jesus, come soon!" (22:17 and 20).

It is by an extension of this line of thought that most of the later texts agreed in their description of the martyrs as undergoing a special experience of the Spirit, which will be made manifest through their gifts of vision and prophecy. But above all the presence of the Spirit will be demonstrated by an identification with Christ during their passion, so that He will appear to suffer in them and instead of them. This is more than implicit in the teaching of Ignatius of Antioch (ca. 35-ca. 102). It is fully explicit already in *The Martyrdom of Polycarp,*[10] together with some visible manifestations directly reminiscent of Pentecost. But its best expression is to be found in the *Passio Felicitatis et Perpetuae,* where a martyr does not hesitate to say to one of the soldiers guarding her in jail, "Another will suffer for me."[11] This *Passio* especially is so strikingly marked by all kinds of Pentecostal manifestations that some critics have suspected it of being tainted with Montanist influence.

The first case we know in history of a Pentecostal movement turning to heresy is that of Montanus[12] and his followers.* It seems that the sectarian and heretical tendency developed among them progressively, to such an extent that they came to see their extraordinary gifts as the only authentic gifts of the Spirit, while expecting a second coming of our Lord very soon. They considered as imperfect all those Christians who did not experience the same gifts and submit to radical asceticism; and they rejected the regular hierarchy as not sufficiently spiritual. Their greatest adept was to be the genial but extremist African theologian, Tertullian, in whose writings we can

*For a somewhat different appraisal of Montanism, see chapter III, p. 61f. (Editor)

see the progressive development of a one-sided absorption into such a conception of the life of the Spirit.

The inevitable condemnation of Montanism did not, however, mean a disappearance in the Church of what we can call 'charismatic' or 'Pentecostal' tendencies.

Just when the evolution of the ancient world in its relationship with Christianity was making the perspective of martyrdom fade away more or less into improbability, monasticism appeared as a new way of following Christ in a poverty freely embraced and a general renunciation of the world. As has been shown already by Karl Holl,[13] there is no doubt that early monasticism, like the spirituality founded on the perspective of martyrdom which it succeeded, was in its origins a definitely charismatic movement. Not only was the monastic vocation to take the demands of the Gospel literally interpreted from the beginning as a direct call of the Spirit, but the whole of monastic asceticism was understood as a victorious struggle of the Spirit with the powers of the world, taking place in the believer. This appears already in the oldest document on monasticism, the *Life of St. Antony*,[14] written by St. Athanasius (ca. 296–373). The true monk therefore will be acknowledged as a man in whom the presence of the Spirit and its dominion have become manifest through the gifts of "word and power." (Throughout the literature of the *Apophtegmata Patrum*,[15] this expression refers to words of prophecy and miraculous powers, especially of healing, both spiritual and physical.) In the measure that this is realized, the complete monk returns to the world as a "spiritual father," able, through the testimony of his whole life, to awaken the life of the Spirit in others.

We must remember in this connection that the monastic movement, in its beginnings, was essentially a lay movement which had sprung up spontaneously. Hence there is all the more significance in the fact that the Church authorities, beginning with Athanasius, the famous theologian and bishop of Alexandria, far from opposing the movement or looking at it suspiciously, tended very early to make full use of the opportunities it offered for recruiting a better clergy, and first of all a better episcopacy. The letter of Athanasius to the monk Dracontius on this subject is most characteristic.[16] In addition Saint Basil (ca. 330–379), the great leader of the Cappadocian Church in the following generation, worked strenuously to make monasticism the principle and focus of a renewal of the whole Church life.

Conversely, some of the first monks, such as Anthony himself (ca. 250–356), were among the strongest auxiliaries of the bishops in their fight with heretics such as Arius, or paganizing emperors such as Julian the Apostate.

Some, however, in the course of the fifth century, were already found falling into a specific heresy, called *Messalianism* in Syriac, *Euchism* in Greek, both words meaning the heresy of the *praying people.* They maintained that prayer is the only work required of a monk or spiritual man, while identifying the only true prayer with that which is accompanied by sensible gifts of the Spirit. When these have been received, they held, there is no need of any other practice, not even of the Eucharist, nor of any effort to resist one's desires or passions. For the spiritual man, nothing could be a sin any more!

The Messalians were condemned at the Synod of Side (388 or 390), and repeatedly thereafter. But so far is this from implying an attempt to "quench the Spirit," that traces of Messalianism have been found by some modern scholars in the famous homilies ascribed to Macarius, which remain one of the greatest classics of monastic spirituality, particularly in the East. Even in the work of Diadochos, Bishop of Photike (ca. 451) whom Christian antiquity regarded as one of the best defenders of orthodoxy *against* Messalianism, modern research has in fact detected traces of the heresy.

How can we explain this? First of all, although Pseudo-Macarius[17] insists that prayer cannot be separated from useful work, nor be fruitful apart from a pure and generous Christian life, there is no doubt that for him prayer in its most personal form is the fundamental activity of the Christian. He also insists that a prayer worthy of the name will normally produce a sensible experience of the Spirit, filling the soul of the true Christian with light and joy.[18]

Against that view of a presence of the Spirit manifested in us by a sensible experience of light, other contemporary spiritual writers, e.g. Evagrius Ponticus (346–349), insist that true 'knowledge' of God must be above any kind of feeling, or even any idea. All that is created must be transcended and utterly disappear for him who prays. Others, such as the Pseudo-Dionysius,[19] will attempt a reconciliation between the two views, saying that we cannot meet the true God experientially except in an utter darkness in which all created lights have vanished. Yet this very darkness is identical with that "unapproachable light" in which God is said to dwell (I Tim. 6:16).[20]

Diadochos of Photike attempted a similar synthesis, while insisting on the struggle in us between the Spirit of God and the evil spirit, which is to end in an experience of light and joy when the Holy Spirit has become entire master of our most inner being.[21] In order to reach and persevere in such a state, the same author insisted on the necessity of keeping our minds and hearts fixed on "the Lord Jesus." He supports this position by citing I Corinthians 12:3: "No one can say, 'Jesus is Lord,' except by the Holy Spirit." Note that this was a first step in the direction of what would be known later as the 'hesychast' spirituality.

However, the greatest forerunner of this later Byzantine school was Saint Symeon the New Theologian (949–1022), a monk of Constantinople. For him, the experiences of the primitive Church connected with Pentecost are not to be considered a thing of the past (as was taught at Stoudios, his monastery, by many monks, who made the whole Christian life consist of liturgical prayer, a strict discipline of life and an active charity).[22] The normal development of the inner life, according to his own experience and teaching, should be into a sudden and conscious outpouring of the Spirit in us, making us aware of our actual union with Christ and of our adoption by the Father through a joyful surrender of our whole being to divine love. But along with a dominant of light, there is in this experience a deep 'compunction', that is to say a breaking of our heart in loving contrition for our sins, at the very time when we experience at last that we are washed from them in the death and resurrection of Christ.[23]

According to Symeon, only those bishops and priests who have gone through an experience of this kind are to be true spiritual leaders. If such is not the case, it is better to take for your master a simple layman who knows these things by his own experience. If we do not observe any tendency in Symeon himself to draw anarchical conclusions from these ideas, such is not the case with all of his disciples (beginning with his first editor, Nicetas Stettatos). Of course, such reactions did not tend to mellow the opposition already manifested by monks of a more moralistic tradition, such as those of Stoudios. Nevertheless, throughout the monastic tradition of the East (and a good part of that of the West), it will be maintained that the true monk, or spiritual man, is not he who merely conforms to an external rule, but only he who has attained a personal experience of the inner light. By the same token, even if he is a layman, such a one has more right to be a spiritual father than any priest or bishop who knows nothing of this experience.

Mediaeval East and West

The spiritual heritage of the Macarian homilies, Diadochos of Photike and Saint Symeon, developed into 'hesychasm' a spirituality aiming at a supernatural 'quiet' or repose in God. This came about when it was combined, under the influence of St. John Climacus (ca. 570–649), the great abbot of Mt. Sinai, with a simple practice of prayer concentrated on the constantly repeated invocation, "Lord Jesus, Son of God, have mercy on me, a sinner!" Later, at Sinai and above all Mt. Athos, it was turned into a method through the deliberate regulation of the breath, each exhalation being connected with the first part of the prayer, and each inhalation with the second. During the Byzantine middle ages, there grew up around this subject a whole literature, which has been well summarized and discussed by an Eastern monk, Leo Gillet in a little book *The Prayer of Jesus*.[24] The whole ascetical and mystical teaching connected with this practice tends to lead toward an experience of light, interpreted as a conscious domination by the Spirit of the man who prays, realizing literally the teaching of St. Paul: "We all, with unveiled face reflecting the glory of the Lord, are being changed into his likeness, from one degree of glory to another, for this comes from the Lord who is the Spirit" (I Cor. 3, 17–18).

In the fourteenth century, this whole school was violently attacked by other monks, under the influence both of Renaissance humanism and nominalistic philosophy. It was at the same time defended and systematized by a former monk of Athos, later Archbishop of Thessalonika, Saint Gregory Palamas (ca. 1296–1359) whose *Defence of the Holy Hesychasts*,[25] in its main theses, would be solemnly approved by an Orthodox Council of Constantinople.[26] Gregory's position has become common teaching among modern orthodox theologians and spiritual writers. Its significance has been made clear especially by the works of Vladimir Lossky and above all John Meyendorff. According to Gregory Palamas (who borrowed from Gregory Nazianzen), the highest experience of the Spirit here on earth is an experience of the "divine energies" which radiate from the divine essence and transfigure our whole human being as in Christ's own Transfiguration. In such an experience (which was already found in Diadochos of Photike) not only is our soul fully united to the risen Christ in the Spirit of love, but even our body is associated with this spiritual experience, so that an element of sensible vision is connected with the most interior experience, as was the case of the disciples on Mt. Tabor (and already of Moses during the Exodus).

Later, the hesychast tradition was made available to everyone through the *Philokalia*.[27] This anthology of spiritual texts, compiled at the end of the eighteenth century by Saint Nicodemus the Hagiorite (1748–1809), at the beginning of a great spiritual revival of Eastern Orthodoxy, was soon translated into Slavonic by the Rumanian Monk, Paissy Velitchkovksy, and later into Russian by Bishop Theophane.

However, the hesychast tradition had already been transplanted into Russia during the late fifteenth and early sixteenth centuries. There it was well decanted and adapted by the great spiritual leader, Saint Nilus Sorsky.[28] But there again it met the opposition of another great monastic reformer: Saint Joseph of Volokolamsk (ca. 1439–1515), on the grounds that it was likely to encourage illusions and leisurely contemplation and to deter people from a full insertion into the framework of traditional discipline and social action.

It may be of interest to compare the hesychast controversy of the East with a not too dissimilar one which arose in the West about the same time between two of the greatest English mystics: Richard Rolle (1295—1349), the hermit of Hampole, and the anonymous author of *The Cloud of Unknowing*. The Holy Spirit is not often mentioned by Rolle, who on this point is representative of much medieval Latin mysticism. Instead, Rolle describes the heights of spiritual experience as an experienced union with Christ. However, the way in which he describes it in his two great treatises, *Incendium Amoris*[29] and *Melos Amoris*,[30] can be qualified as distinctly

Pentecostal. It is a sudden gift of love taking hold of our whole being as a sensible fire rather than as a light. According to his most original expression, the whole life of the being who has undergone such an experience is now transformed into a continuous song of love: the *melos amoris,* which gives a tone to everything we know, feel or do.

This, however, does not find favor with the author of *The Cloud,*[31] even though he fully agrees with Rolle that the whole matter of a Christian spiritual life is an experience of love, and goes so far as to acknowledge also that it should permeate our entire being, including our bodily sensibility. For him, however, such an experience remains deeply mysterious: it is altogether a matter of faith. Consequently, it is in an 'unknowing' of everything sensible or intelligible that the experience of divine love is to be attained. In the exultant descriptions and expressions of Rolle, this author can only suspect some illusion of the senses, a very questionable kind of 'enthusiasm.'

As I have already mentioned, we find the same reaction but much more systematically articulated, in the sixteenth century, in the spiritual master who has become the doctor par excellence of modern Western mysticism, Saint John of the Cross (1542–1591). For him the deepest and the only certainly authentic experience of the life of union with God supposes an entrance into the night, first of the senses, and then of the 'spirit'—the highest capacities of our natural intelligence. It is, therefore, in utter darkness that we must meet God by faith and be united to him through the highest form of spiritual grace. We must transcend not only every kind of feeling, vision, and sensible consolation but also all the human representations we can have of the divine reality. Even the loving thought of Christ's humanity has to be left aside if and when we are to reach the consummated union with His divine life, although it is of course through Him that this comes about.

In this, Saint John was consciously opposing not only

the more or less sensual mysticism of the contemporary *alumbrados,* but even the views of that other great Carmelite contemplative and fellow worker in the spiritual renewal, Saint Teresa of Avila (1518–1582).

It should be noted that two centuries before Saint John of the Cross, we find a doctrine not dissimilar to his but less trenchantly formulated, in that most balanced and evangelical of the Rheno-Flemish spiritual leaders, Ruysbroek (1293–1391).[32] He is likewise in the line, if not exactly of Evagrius Ponticus, certainly of the Pseudo-Dionysius, only with a directly psychological application of principles which for the latter remained mainly metaphysical. In our conclusion we shall come back to the problems raised here.

But we cannot leave the Western middle ages without saying something of two spiritual and theological approaches to this life of the Spirit in us which have not yet had, in the West itself, all the influence they should. The strange and quite unexpected lack of interest in the theology of the Holy Spirit even on the part of a 'spiritual' man, such as Richard Rolle, is very characteristic of a whole trend of Western spirituality which, in line with some developments of Augustinian theological spirituality, was more concerned with a mysticism of a union of essences between God and man than with a mysticism of personal union. (To this was added of course the corrective of a growing interest in some form of more or less imaginative union with the humanity of Christ.) However, it would be a great mistake to suppose that all of the spiritual developments of the medieval West were to follow this channel.

In the thirteenth century we find quite a different view of things in William of Saint-Thierry (ca. 1085—ca. 1148)[33], considered the greatest mind and spirit of the Cistercian or Bernardine school. For him, the whole development of spiritual life is a growth in faith through the development of obedience. From blind obedience to the teaching of Christ given in the Church, we should progress to the knowing obedience of a faith that blossoms into experience through love, and finally into what he calls *unitas Spiritus*. This is a state in which, directly moved by the Spirit, we experience the blessed identity of perfect freedom with perfect obedience to God in Christ.

In a similar line we must note the doctrine of Saint Thomas Aquinas (1224/5–1274) on the gifts of the Spirit, later greatly developed in the early sixteenth century by his Spanish disciple, John of Saint Thomas. Saint Thomas distinguishes three different ways in which the human soul can act. First, it can develop purely human and natural virtues, a development always checked by sin. Second, it can be brought not only to overcome that negative tendency by divine grace, but to illumine and transfigure natural virtues such as justice into infused virtues under the radiation of the purely theological virtues of faith hope and charity—virtues which are created immediately in us by God's grace and to which they are directly related. But beyond this ordinary and elementary stage of Christian life the soul can be brought to the regime of 'the gifts of the Spirit,' in the highest sense of the phrase. According to Saint Thomas, this means that through a more immediate and manifest action of the grace of the Holy Spirit in the soul, God not only pervades all our human activities with a divine influence but imparts to us a way of acting, a genial and properly filial correspondence to His own views. This communicates to us in its fullness a life worthy of the children of God . . . Here, in the theology of the "gifts of the Spirit,"[35] we could find a very interesting and fruitful interpretation of the Pentecostal experience.

To conclude this historical survey, let us say just a few words about the great controversies of Quietism and Jansenism in the seventeenth and eighteenth centuries.

Quietism involved a revival of the mystical tradition of the Rheno-Flemish and Spanish masters with some ambivalent developments which in the eighteenth century resulted in a tendency to confuse all extraordinary gifts, and every notion of a sensible experience of the life of God in man (in whatever sense the adjective can be taken), with unrestrained 'enthusiasm' and more or less openly pantheistic tendencies. However the essential contention of people such as Fenelon (1651–1715) or Madame Guyon (1648–1717) herself, was that the fully Christian experience is one of God taking hold of us through the Spirit, and therefore, as Saint Paul has it, "creating in us both the will and the deed" (Philip. 2:13). This is undoubtedly a basically Christian view of life and one that corresponds to the experience of the Spirit in the early Church. During the seventeenth century the Jansenists, owing to their strongly ethical ideal, had generally opposed the Quietist movement as tending to relax the Christian moral endeavour. It is rather surprising therefore that in the eighteenth century, in connection with the deacon, Francis of Paris, they experienced a sudden revival among their own disciples of spontaneous ecstatic collective experiences, very similar to those of the early Church . . . So true it is that the ways of God are unsearchable!

Conclusions

From what precedes it seems that a few general conclusions may be drawn. The Pentecostal manifestations of the Spirit, for example, have never truly ceased within the Catholic (or Orthodox) Church. From the very beginning, as we can see in the case of the Corinthians, they have always been in some danger of falling into schism or heresy but have never for that reason been condemned as wrong in principle, either by the greatest spiritual theologians or by the Church authorities.

However, it has always been considered essential that a discernment of spirits be practiced. Only those gifts of the Spirit are authentic which, rather than tending to break the unity and peace of the Church, lead those who experience them to a greater fidelity to Christ's teaching, in a more humble and generous cooperation with their fellow Christians in all the activities of the Church, under the loyally accepted leadership of the apostolic ministry. However, even authentic gifts of the Spirit may become distorted if those who enjoy them do not actually recognize that the highest ones are not the most extraordinary, but faith, hope and charity, and that the others tend to their own destruction when not fully subservient to these, and entirely submitted to the control of charity above all.

It is further a permanent feature of the teaching of the best spiritual masters in both East and West, that there is a tension that can never entirely be eliminated between two tendencies, difficult to harmonize but always to be kept in balance. On the one hand, not only is the life of the Spirit meant to become for us Christians a real experience, but it should involve the whole of our being—not only the deepest recesses of the soul, the apex of the intellect and the purest center of our free-will, but also our whole imagination and affectivity, implying certainly the bodily sensibility itself.

On the other hand, the experience of the Spirit remains something apart, which must never be confused with any of its concomitants in the mind and heart of man. These can all be counterfeited or corrupted by the devil, as well as by a purely natural human propensity towards an illusory self-satisfaction. Therefore all, even the greatest, gifts of God are to be freely accepted but also freely renounced if and when God wills it, for that gift which is God Himself and God alone, communicating Himself to us through His Spirit in the night of the senses and of the spirit itself, in an utter detachment from self, corresponding to the perfect unselfishness of God's love.

Now does that mean, as Saint John of the Cross tends to say, that we must go beyond all of the more sensible gifts of the Spirit in order to come as near as we can in this life to the deepest union with God in the Spirit?

Or is it enough, as was rather the tendency of Saint Teresa, to accept these gifts humbly and thankfully, always ready to accept the loss of them, in faith, if such is God's will even though He may not actually require this. . . ? It does not seem that we can choose between these two ways. Each of them has been followed by some very great saints, according to God's own inspiration and vocation. What we must never forget is that no one may impose his way as the only right one, no one should condemn the gift or the way of the others, nor believe that God will have to keep him always in that which, for the time being, seems appointed for him. Here more than anywhere we must respect the Catholic view of one of the greatest spiritual teachers of the West, although himself a disciple of the East, and acknowledged as the model of pastors by both East and West: St. Gregory the Great, who gave St. Augustine of Canterbury the following advice on such matters: "Let there be unity in things that are necessary, freedom in things that are doubtful, and charity in all things."

VI. ▬ ▬▬▬

Although the historical disciplines and the comparative study of religions provide invaluable perspectives for an understanding of the activity of the Holy Spirit, to rely on them solely would be to confine one's attention to the most external and therefore least typical manifestations. To be oriented towards the proper nature and principal features of life in the Spirit, it is necessary to learn from those in whom it attained its fullest and firmest development. The following essay is only a brief indication of what can be expected from such an exploration.

—The Editor

THE HOLY SPIRIT, CHRISTIAN LOVE, AND MYSTICISM

EDWARD D. O'CONNOR, C.S.C.

The life to which Jesus summons His disciples is not characterized primarily by a superior enlightenment or moral rectitude, but by love. The Holy Spirit, by whom "God's love is poured forth in our hearts" (Rom. 5:5), introduces man into a life in which love is not merely a motive and a goal, but an actually experienced and all-pervading reality. This radically new life is characterized by the living presence of God and union with Him. Apart from the gift of the Spirit, man relates to God as the Creator from whom he has originated, and as the Last End towards which all his striving ought to tend; but by the Spirit he is brought into an actual union with an immediately present God.

The Incarnation, which is the root and source of this new life, is also an index of its character. By the very fact of taking on our flesh, the Son of God makes Himself present to us and puts Himself in union with us. He does not hesitate to be called our brother (Hebr. 2:11ff), friend (John 15:15) and even bridegroom (Mt. 9:15; John 3:29; Eph. 5:21–32; Apoc. 19:7–9; 21:2, 9 . . .).

The Eucharist is a striking sign and instrument of this immediate living presence and union. From it we

133

learn effectively the Lord's intention to abide with us and be united to us, and that it is in no other way but through His Body that we can be united with the divinity, sharing in the divine life, and living by the Son as the Son lives by the Father.

The law of the Kingdom of God is a law of love. It does not prescribe just one particular act, but embraces all the commandments and the totality of human life. It governs man's relations with God and with his fellows, making him love God as God loves Himself, and his fellow man as a friend, an intimate, another self, even as one beloved. Under Jesus' new commandment we love God in our neighbor and our neighbor in God: not by reducing God to neighbor, as in secular humanism, nor by simply accepting our neighbor for God's sake without loving him really in himself, as in a caricature of Christianity. When we love our neighbor in God, the very person of our neighbor is loved most truly.

Furthermore the commandment of love unifies the activities of all the faculties and energies of the soul, making man imitate even in this the very life of God. It is the commandment proper to the 'unitive life'. On the other hand, it is a commandment given precisely for "little ones," who cannot be content with mere counsels or with an ideal that demands a complex ratiocination; they need a definite commandment that is capable of being applied here and now.

It is by the Holy Spirit that this is brought about, that Jesus becomes in deepest truth the bridegroom, that the meaning of the Eucharist is fully realized, and that the universal commandment of love is made particular, concrete and efficacious. The Spirit does this by taking hold of our humanity in a way that is at once a total embrace and a radical renovation, called a "new birth" (John 3:1–8), a "regeneration" (Titus 3:5), and even a "new creation" (II Cor. 5:17; Gal. 6:15). Although achieved in principle from the very first reception of the

Spirit, this renovation is brought to fulfillment only progressively over a lifetime. Hence it is not the newly baptized, even though the liturgy calls them "new born babes," that can give us an adequate notion of all that is entailed in being born again of the Holy Spirit. While it is not unusual for adult converts to have a certain genuine experience of this spiritual regeneration, it is only at the price of a thorough-going purification and confirmation that its full range becomes evident. Hence, for truly representative examples of the effects of the Holy Spirit we must look to the saints—those who have yielded wholeheartedly and uncompromisingly to His leavening action. The saints on whose experience the following pages will draw are not only those canonized, who are thereby our most reliable guides, but also those living today, who have at least the advantage of reminding us that the grace of the Spirit is forever working in new and unexpected ways, and that holiness is not so much a matter of impressive achievements as of being faithful to Jesus wherever we are.[1]

More precisely, it is from the experience of the mystics that we learn the true sense, the proper and specific character, of the work of the Holy Spirit. By 'mystics,' I do not mean recipients of extraordinary phenomena, such as supernatural visions, locutions, stigmata, etc., and still less someone who experiments with exotic cults. The mystic is properly one who has personal experience of the divine realities presented to us by faith. Taken in this sense, mysticism is not an extraordinary and marginal spin-off of the Christian life, but its connatural development. The aim of the present paper will be to draw upon the experience of the mystics in order to show concretely how the Holy Spirit makes the Christian life one of divine love.

Although all authentic religious experience pertains to mysticism in the sense just indicated, the term 'mystic' is generally reserved for those whose experiential contact with God is relatively firm and abiding.[2] According to this usage, the mystical life begins with the graces of quiet (or 'quietude') and culminates in the state of transforming union. Rather than trying to determine the precise distinction between these two phases of the mystical life, it will be more advantageous for our purpose to insist rather on the continuity by which one leads the other.

St. Teresa of Avila has given the classic description of the graces of quiet.[3] Beginning with the will, and progressively taking hold of the other powers of the soul, they quiet the habitual restlessness of the faculties by uniting them with God in a blissful repose.

Remarkable analogues to the prayer of quiet are to be found in many non-Christian religions and spiritualities, e.g., the stoic *apatheia,* the neo-Platonic ecstasy, and the Buddhist nirvana. From a theoretical point of view, it is comprehensible that any authentic religion, in proportion as it becomes more interior, should culminate in a kind of inner silence and immobility. If the essence of religion is worship of God, it is evident that external cult is vain except insofar as it expresses interior worship. The latter, in proportion as it becomes aware of the transcendence of its object,[4] naturally tends to turn into adoration and an awe which consist in a stillness of intellect and will together, while being at the same time their supreme act.

Nevertheless, there are decisive differences between the Christian grace and its non-Christian analogs, which can be briefly indicated even though it is not possible here to undertake the thorough-going comparison which this subject merits. In the first place, the Christian prayer of quiet results not from an intellectual contemplation or moral discipline (although it does in some measure presuppose them), but from an affection—a loving adherence to the divine spouse. Secondly, it is implanted at a deeper level than that attainable by any natural ascesis. Finally, whereas the inner quiet reached by other 'ways' seems to come as their culmination, in Christian mysticism it is only the starting point of a development that proceeds to a transforming union with the God who is love.

The grace of quiet, which pertains to that "peace which passes all understanding" (Phil. 4:7), is a sure sign of the presence of God and of union with Him. It does not consist in a mastery of one's own faculties and their inner activity. Even in its beginnings it has the character of a being-taken-possession-of rather than that of active domination. The will is embraced by God at a level deeper than the acts of which it is author, and at a point, so to speak, that is anterior to its own activity, even in its most radical acts, because it is precisely the latter that are quieted (which does not mean suppressed). This is a sign that it must come from a source prior to, deeper than, and even more interior to man than nature itself. Such can only be the very Author of nature. This peace embraces ultimately all of the faculties, something that deliberate human endeavor (being initiated and structured by the concurrence of intellect and will) can never do. Its radical immobility and deep inner silence, coming when the soul is in a state of supreme actuation, manifest the existence of a domain deeper than that in which our natural activities are carried on—even the most profound activities of the moral, aesthetic or metaphysical domains.

On the other hand, however, the grace of quiet is not opposed to the earnestness and responsibility demanded by the moral life, nor to the understanding sought after by philosophical reflection. Great mystics can be acute philosophers, as St. Thomas Aquinas, or effective men of action, as St. Bernard or St. Catherine of Siena. Their prayer gives a new depth and interiority to their activity, not so much on the side by which it has to do with the human community and the environing world, but insofar as it regards man's last end. It can be said that by the graces of quiet the mystical life, for all its intrinsic supernaturality, is rooted in human nature.

The grace of quiet is not, however, merely a repose

of the faculties; it is also and primarily their positive
actuation in a loving union with God. It is the fruit, not so
much of a turning away from the world, or of a turning
within (although on this point the language of many of
the mystics, seeking to free rude natures from captivity to
the external senses, can easily give rise to misunderstand-
ing), as of a turning to God. But the active turning and
striving, of which man himself is naturally capable and
which is required of him, is completed by a divine action
with respect to which man is fully passive, though
conscious and consenting.

Thus, he must observe a human silence; but there is
a kiss of the Holy Spirit (at times even sensed physically[5])
which seals man's lips and heart with a loving silence that
he himself cannot produce. Likewise, man has to avoid
unnecessary bodily movement, and adopt, as far as
possible, a restful posture. But the Holy Spirit, who first
inspires him to do this, may by His embrace confer on this
physical posture a value of union that transcends the
initial inspiration. In any case, the most important
preparation on the part of man is not a heroic asceticism,
but the littleness of a child and the loving fidelity of a
spouse.

It has already been noted that grace takes possession
of a person by progressive stages. Beginning with the
will, the starting point of all properly human activity, its
stilling influence extends first to the intellect. Still later, it
encompasses the memory and imagination, the dark
roots from which many of our less conscious motives
arise, and finally even the (external) senses themselves.

But it is not only at the level of faculties that the grace
of quiet takes possession of man, but even at the level of
substance. Mystics speak frequently of a 'substantial'
contact with God. Even more frequently, perhaps, they
speak of a divine embrace, which would seem to be
essentially the same thing but with more human over-
tones.[6] Theologians are somewhat ill at ease to explain
what this contact might be; but in face of the unison and

insistence of those who have experienced it, to adopt an explanation which diminished the strength of these affirmations[7] would seem unwise.

On the other hand, however, in the classic literature of mysticism it is usually the soul that is called the spouse of the Holy Spirit. Modern sensitivity to the wholeness of the human person, and the emphatic modern reaffirmation of man's essential bodiliness, make us somewhat uncomfortable with this singling out of the soul in distinction from the body. Despite the crudeness and gross exaggeration with which it is frequently expressed, this impulse of modern culture would seem to be in accord with the most authentic Christian anthropology; and there seem to be serious grounds for holding that even man's bodily substance is not alien to the divine embrace.

St. Paul himself teaches that in the resurrection, we will have "spiritual bodies" (I Cor. 15:44), by which is surely meant, not that they will be somehow immaterial (for then we could not speak of the resurrection of these present bodies), but that they will be completely pervaded by the influence of the Spirit.[8] That even in this life the action of the Holy Spirit at times goes so far as to have bodily effects is, moreover, commonly recognized. Reports are not rare of people who were visibly transfigured, sometimes so manifestly that it was evident to all, usually in a more delicate way that was sensible only to those who were rightly attuned. Even if we grant that such effects are not meant to be the ordinary results of grace in this life, still it seems better to take them, not merely as exceptional marvels showing what incredible things the power of God is able to do, but as signs that His Spirit espouses us in the fullness of our being, even in the bodiliness and materiality which seem the farthest removed from the domain of spirit.[9]

The profound unification of the activities of mind and body which constitutes the grace of quiet seems to be accounted for by the fact that the Holy Spirit takes hold of man in his substantial unity. It corresponds also with the experience of those who have thereby acquired an immediate awareness of the unity of their own being which they have never previously had. This awareness comes, however, not as the term of introspection, but in and by awareness of union with God. He is no longer merely the object of thought or the goal of desire; He is a present person who has united Himself directly and immediately to the substance, even the bodily substance, of the mystic.

The testimony of some would seem to indicate that in the very material roots of man's being there are fundamental dispositions enabling him to be docile and amenable to the action of the Spirit. Essentially passive in character, these dispositions are not actualized except by the graces of the mystical life, and cannot even be desired or conceived before they have thus been manifested.

This substantial contact with God is often said to be felt or sensed. Such language accords well with the notion of interior or spiritual senses which, starting in the patristic era, became one of the commonplaces of mediaeval spirituality.[10] The academic spiritual theology of modern times however, has been ill at ease, even embarrassed, with this notion, dismissing it, perhaps too hastily, as metaphor. But is it necessary to exclude *a priori* the possibility that the sense of touch may be involved in the so-called 'feeling' of God's presence? The vividness, realism and simplicity of the expressions used, not only by the classical and literary mystics,[11] but also by very ordinary contemporaries, obliges us to face this question. For example, the hymn *He touched me,* which is so beloved among Pentecostals, surely does not owe its popularity to the quality of its music, but to the fact that it expresses so well something that has been experienced.

That God is not a physical reality, capable of being an object of the senses, goes without saying. But the question which must be posed is whether, in the contact with God which the Holy Spirit brings about, the senses themselves may not be really affected, in particular the sense of touch, the least spiritual but the most realistic of them all. Is the *tactus* ('touch') connoted by the very term 'contact,' which is so naturally employed here, nothing more than a metaphor for a vivid spiritual apprehension, or may it not reflect a real bodily participation in man's awareness of the real, intimate and pervasive presence of God?

The starting point for consideration of this question should not be the external sense of touch, by which a person feels things outside of himself, but the inner or 'organic' sense, by which he is aware of the state of the inner organs of the body. On the other hand, the touch that pertains to mystical experience does not seem to be wholly identified with this organic sense. It is not purely internal; it transcends the distinction between internal and external. Furthermore, it has a mode of actual awareness, of living presence, and even of liberty, that are not found in the organic sense. The latter has a certain dullness about it; it must almost be regarded as more virtual than actual. On the contrary, the substantial touch of love which comes with mystical graces implies an awakening of the soul and the entire being with a new sensitivity.

In particular, there sometimes arises a new consciousness of the act of breathing, and of one's contact with the enveloping air. There comes a new experience of this element which God uses as a sign and instrument of His loving presence. Air takes on a new meaning and may acquire a consistency, a kind of substantiality. This is all the more remarkable because, in the graces of quiet, a person normally tends to lose consciousness of the things around him. His table and chair, or his pew and the chapel in which he is praying, lose their solidity for him and become vain. The air, on the contrary, receives a substantial character it had not had before. The person is conscious of touching it and bathing in it.[12] In order to be made aware of this living and substantial quality of the air, he has to be detached even from the light, and from all that belongs to the domain of light. By a revelation that comes without being sought, and which involves no poetic insight, love discloses to him a hidden, but real and objective, not imaginary, 'virtue' of the air, by which it puts him in immediate contact with the God who is Love itself.

Finally, it must be asked to what extent the Holy Spirit's embrace affects even man's external activity. The mystics commonly speak of states of close union with God in which the human person is moved by the Spirit, and acts as His instrument. Such assertions are commonly understood in the sense that man has been made so docile to divine inspirations that he responds faithfully to their least prompting. In such an explanation, the grace of the Holy Spirit bears directly only on man's intentional faculties, chiefly the intellect and will. The actions which follow are simply the actions of man, even though solicited and guided by the Spirit.

There are, however, testimonies which suggest that the grace of union may extend also to the faculties of execution. In such a case God would be moving man directly, and the latter would be fundamentally passive.

As 'Unmoved Mover,' of course, God moves not only man but every creature, and in everything it does, even though the creature remains truly, at its own level, the author of its own actions by the powers and tendencies of its nature, and, in the case of man, by the intentions he forms. This universal divine movement, which adapts itself to the nature of each being, belongs to the natural order and is, so to speak, hidden in it. The human soul is not naturally conscious of the divine movement; only by a metaphysical argument can one be led to recognize the necessity of supposing it.

There is also a supernatural way in which the Holy Spirit moves rational creatures by inspirations of which the latter are properly conscious even though they may not explicitly recognize their true character. But the grace of union, if what is proposed here be correct, entails still a third way of God's moving the human person. Unlike the transcendent, universal and hidden First Movement which underlies the natural order, it involves an influence of which the recipient is fully conscious and to which he freely consents. On the other hand, however, it is not simply an inspiration directed to his mind and will, inviting him to act. It is properly a movement in which God moves him.[13] There are not two moments or phases, first a receptivity or passivity, and then the execution of an action.

The words that are spoken, and the actions that are performed, under this grace spring immediately from the love by which man is united to God, and in which man is predominantly passive. Likewise the consciousness and consent by which man accepts the divine action are themselves the fruit of love and wholly impregnated by it. Love here is at once passive and active: it is peace and rest on the one hand, word and action on the other.

The words and actions that proceed from this grace deepen the love even of the person who speaks or acts. It is not, of course, unusual for words and actions to reinforce the emotion that generated them; but that is not what takes place in this wholly divine experience. The person does not think of the word before uttering it, but in the very act of speaking he as it were discovers it, and becomes aware of it as the immediate expression of his love.

This shows (as the mystic himself is fully aware) that love has a fullness about it, whereby it does not require the intervention of objective and conceptualized thought in order to express itself. In fact, as St. John of the Cross makes clear,[14] conceptual thought and figurative representations are not only unnecessary for, they are incompatible with the deepest union of love. The mind that is bathed in love has a direct and realistic mode of operation that is quite the opposite of the reflection and intentionality characteristic of ordinary psychological consciousness. However, while divine love does not need concepts in order to express itself, it does need to be expressed, and it uses words and actions. But it employs these signs directly, in a kind of expression altogether proper to divine love and the grace of transforming union. In a person fully yielded to the Holy Spirit, divine love not only pervades his attitudes and motivates his activity, but directly expresses itself through the latter, which becomes thereby a privileged instrument for the communication of this love to others.

Thus, when seen in the perspective of mystical experience, the Christian life is a life of love in a way quite incommensurable with the natural experience of love as passion, friendship or philanthropy. God is the proper and defining object of this love in such a way that, without detracting from the realism with which it embraces men, love acquires a depth and intensity it could not have in merely human terms. The communication of the Holy Spirit has the effect, on the one hand, of making the Divine Beloved actually and personally present, instead of being remote and 'unreal.' On the other hand, it absorbs man wholly in divine love, not only engaging his higher faculties of mind and his will, but reaching to the deepest and most material roots of his being. It stills the restlessness of the soul in a supernatural peace which is its supreme actuation, and it awakens latent dispositions which enable man to be both wholly passive in the reception of divine love, and active under the direct movement of the Holy Spirit.

VII. THE LITERATURE OF THE CATHOLIC CHARISMATIC RENEWAL 1967-1974

EDWARD D. O'CONNOR, C.S.C.

The literature concerning the charismatic renewal in the Roman Catholic Church began with newspaper accounts of events at Notre Dame in the Spring of 1967.[1] In the course of the next three or four years, the early trickle of journalistic reports swelled slowly into a stream. Nevertheless, at the beginning of 1970 when *Time, Newsweek* and other news journals featured reviews of the sixties and prognoses for the seventies, not one, so far as I have been able to determine, made the least allusion to the Pentecostal movement, even in reports devoted specifically to religion. But it was not long before they discovered it, and from 1971 through 1973 a small flood of journalistic reports and television programs appeared. Even the *Wall Street Journal* ran a front page article on the subject, March 12, 1974. Since then, the interest of the journalists has waned somewhat. Likewise, their tone has changed. Instead of being presented as sensational news, the renewal is alluded to routinely in a way that takes it for granted as an accepted fact of Catholic life.

In about 1969, someone got the idea of doing a classroom theme on the charismatic renewal. Since then, term papers, theses and dissertations, at the high school, college and university level, in sociology, psychology, religion and literature, have poured out. Most of these essays naturally were not published; and many of the more important ones seem to be still in process. Professional psychologists and sociologists have just begun to give serious attention to the charismatic phenomenon among Catholics, although they have been dealing with older branches of the Pentecostal movement for several decades. Apart from unpublished theses and short articles, the only major sociological study is that which Joseph Fichter has just published, and there is still no important psychological study. Neither is there as yet a comprehensive history.

The great bulk of the literature, if we set aside the journalistic reports, pertains to what may be called loosely the theological domain. It began with articles and pamphlets giving simple expositions of the renewal, or defending it. In 1969 came the first book on the subject, *Catholic Pentecostals,* by the Ranaghans. It was followed by three more books in 1971, and by one or two more each year thereafter. A newsletter for communities of central Michigan was expanded into a national newsletter in 1970, and became one of the principal organs of the movement, with the name (since 1971), *New Covenant.* Meanwhile, pamphlets continue to appear in increasing numbers.

The earliest writings were all in English. Since about 1972, however, a considerable body of literature has appeared in Spanish, French, Portuguese (from Brazil) and German, and there are beginnings in Dutch and many other languages.

Several trends can be recognized in this literature, interacting with one another in paradoxical ways that do not make it possible to forecast the course of the future, but do perhaps allow us to discern some of the issues on which the future will depend.

In the first place, the initial literature was focussed on the newness and distinction of the charismatic renewal, with stress on the peculiar experience and characteristics that set it apart from the life of the Church at large.

This was made inevitable by the need of expounding, propagating and defending a new movement. But in a reaction that set in very early, many leaders began to insist that such a mentality ought eventually—and the sooner the better—to be replaced by one which would see the renewal not as a distinct movement within the Church, but as nothing less than the Church itself being renewed. In both the practical and theoretical order, there has been a strong impulse to stress solidarity with the Church as a whole. This tendency, however, is ambivalent. It can have the sense either of moving toward a more wholehearted belonging to the Church, with filial acceptance of its authority, or of implicitly seeking to impose upon it, in the name of reform, an ideology not germane to it. There are seeds of both the filial and the imperial attitude in the actual literature.

In the second place, the early writings were concerned with the charismatic renewal as a whole: expounding, propagating, interpreting or defending it. Progressively, however, the literature has begun to devote itself to particular elements and aspects of the renewal, e.g., individual charisms such as healing and prophecy, prayer meetings, communities, etc. This trend, which is natural in any new movement, will undoubtedly continue; and since most of the particular elements of the charismatic life are common to Christian or at any rate Catholic life as a whole (prayer, the sacraments, participation in the Church, particular devotions, as well as the doctrines of grace, redemption, eschatology, etc.), this should reinforce the above-mentioned tendency to viewing the renewal in the perspective of the whole Church, rather than separately. Such writings will naturally tend to draw upon the doctrinal and spiritual riches already available in Catholic tradition, and at the same time will manifest more effectively than general treatises, the original contributions of the renewal to Christian spirituality.

Thirdly, the early literature tended to stress the

Catholic orthodoxy of the renewal in response to the reactions of a public that found it strange, bizarre and "Protestant." (By an ironic contrast, the charismatic renewal in the Protestant churches is often attacked as a reversion to Catholicism!) But in the measure that the public has grown accustomed to the notion of 'Pentecostal Catholicism,' there has been less need of such apologetics. In fact, the change has come about almost prematurely. No one has yet drawn up a thorough-going, well-informed, and trenchant critique of the renewal which might have evoked an equally serious reply; there have been mostly only enflamed denunciations and snide denigrations.

However, many charismatics have been restless under the constraint of having their orthodoxy measured by the criterion of a Church which appears to them in need of reform or renewal itself. Some of them have already abandoned it; as the pressure of demonstrating their own orthodoxy relaxes, and the visible success of the movement generates more assurance, it is not unlikely that many others will take a more independent and aggressive stand. The bellwether of such a development could well be Ralph Martin's proclamation at the 1974 International Conference, "We are moving from an apologetic phase into a prophetic phase."[2]

The crucial question here would seem to be whether the renewal movement is going to relate to the Church primarily as a human enterprise, subject consequently to the law of decay, and forever in need of being reformed; or primarily as a mystery of faith, the work of Jesus Christ and the form of His living presence among His brethren. It would be difficult to overestimate the decisive importance of this challenge to those concerned for the Church. They need not only to give an effective demonstration of the fact, but also to show concretely in what sense, the spiritual resources of the body, bride, building and instrument of the Incarnate Son of God are real, rich and actually available.

Simultaneous with this relaxing of concern about orthodoxy, there has been a great multiplication of contacts with Protestant Pentecostals. The grass roots ecumenism which many regard as the most promising factor of the ecumenical movement, is going on in the charismatic renewal with impressive results. However, the rapid growth of interdenominational prayer groups and communities has tended to foster development of a kind of piety and doctrine in which the distinctive features of Catholicism (belief in the Real Presence, sacramental confession, Marian devotion, etc.) are somewhat neglected and at times even called into question. The resulting spirituality, although often zealous and efficacious, is cut off from some of its roots and inhibited from attaining its full and balanced development.

Along with practical ecumenism have come the beginnings of forays into ecumenical theory. Although these are not yet developed enough to be appraised, some appear to be poorly informed about the program for ecumenism drawn up by Vatican II, and about the experience and critique to which their ideas have already been subjected. Ill-conceived and premature ventures in this domain could easily be counterproductive, by provoking harsh affirmations of orthodoxy that would end the gentle climate of respect, understanding and acceptance in which grass-roots ecumenism flourishes.

The last trend to be noted here has to do with the people who are doing the writing. In the early years, they were nearly all heavily involved in the renewal, sometimes to the point of total dedication, and qualified mainly by their experience in it (brief though that necessarily was) and devotion to it. They were often intelligent, articulate, and theologically literate, although few were professional theologians or ordained pastors. From about 1970 on, however, we begin to meet treatises by professional theologians, some of whom are not much involved in the renewal personally: Fathers McDonnell

and Gelpi in this country, Sullivan in Rome, Tugwell and
Hocken in England, and lately Fathers Mühlen in
Germany and Laurentin in France.

Where the early exponents were trying largely to
articulate matters of their own or their close associates'
personal experience, and to furnish guidelines for
others, the academic theologians are more preoccupied
with interpreting these experiences in the light of the
great Christian dogmas and the previous experience of
the Church. The amount of agreement, or at least of
peaceful accord, between the two groups of writers, is
impressive and suggests a fundamental realism and
wholesomeness on both sides. Nevertheless, one can
detect divergencies likely to create eventual tension. The
early literature, heavily influenced by models in the
main-line Pentecostal denominations, is oversimplified,
and not always in deep accord with the Catholic understanding of the sacraments, sanctifying grace, the ordained priesthood, and perhaps most especially the
mystery of the Church. The scholars, on the other hand,
in seeking to relate the renewal to other experiences of
the Church's history, and to set it in a broader theological
perspective, have not been fully immune to the danger of
missing or distorting its genuine originality, or of repres-
sing some of its life and spirit under a mound of
erudition.

Here, as acutely as anywhere I know of, there is need
of a plurality of approaches that listen to one another
with sincere docility. The man of practical involvement
needs to be free to express the fruits of his experience
and his insights in the language that comes spontaneously to him, without being intimidated by a theological
censorship fussing at imprecisions. But he must also
acknowledge the limited validity of what he thus has to
say, and be amenable to correction by those who have a
more professional competence. The theologian must
bring into the dialogue his concern for the far-reaching
and often not obvious implications of a stand taken on a

particular point, and his consciousness of the great doctrinal and theological principles that have been forged and tested in the experience, reflection and judgment of the Church down through the ages. But no amount of learning ever exempts him from a readiness to recognize, with humble, reverent openness, the ever-new surprises of the Spirit in the least of God's children.

While it is of course possible and desirable for personal experience and academic theology to concur in the same person, there is such diversity in the modes of thought of the one who spontaneously articulates raw experience, and the one who relates, reflects and distinguishes, that it seems reasonable to suppose that solid progress in the formation of a valid theory of the renewal will depend largely on the readiness of people with diverse gifts to cooperate with one another.

Besides those just mentioned, the dialogue needs also the contributions of the psychologist, the sociologist, and the historian. It needs the ordained pastor, with his experience of and concern for the problems, needs and reactions of the whole Christian populace, and his sacramental charism (quite different from that of the theologian) as pastor and teacher for them. However, this is not the place to elaborate on such points.

The following bibliography is intended to give the most substantial literature on the charismatic renewal in the Roman Catholic Church through December, 1974. (A few works from early 1975 have also been recorded.) It does not include material on the Pentecostal movement or charismatic renewal in other denominations, nor works by members of other denominations, except insofar as they seem relevant to the Catholic movement. Sometimes it has been hard to know where to draw the line; in such cases, I have generally tended to include rather than exclude the work in question, e.g. when Reverend Morton Kelsey, an Episcopalian priest, writes for a Catholic journal.

The selection of material for inclusion has been

guided by the purpose of giving practical help to someone making a study of the renewal. Thus, I have tried to retain only those writings of some enduring value. But it should be acknowledged that there is a great quantity of pamphlets and leaflets, often of only local circulation, which serve a useful purpose in acquainting people with the renewal, and are occasionally of real quality. It would be impossible to survey them all, and listing them here would seldom serve any useful purpose. Hence, leaflets and mimeographed material have not, as a general rule, been included (although there are exceptions); yet anyone studying this subject would do well to familiarize himself with some of this material. On the other hand, some works need to be cited, not because they are of superior quality in themselves, but because they have had in fact a notable influence. In areas that have been abundantly treated it was possible to be more selective, whereas in areas that are poor, it seemed better sometimes to cite what was available rather than nothing at all.

I have tried to examine all of the English language material,[3] although in a few cases this was impossible because a given work was inaccessible or came to my attention too late. The important French and German literature I have tried to include; but since most of it is scattered in periodicals often difficult to locate, and much appeared while this bibliography was being compiled, it is doubtless inadequately covered here. Portuguese, Dutch and Spanish literature I have made no attempt whatsoever to survey, although a few works of some importance in those languages that have come to my attention are cited. Foreign translations of works which appeared originally in English have not been listed. Articles which appeared first in journals, and were later included in a book, have not been listed separately.

After considerable hesitation, I have decided not to include a section on personal testimonies. There is an ocean of such material and anyone studying the renewal certainly ought to be acquainted with some of it. However, it is to be found everywhere; and while some of it is very inspiring and enlightening, little of it stands out in such a way as to designate it for inclusion in preference to the rest. Some writings of this genre, however, appear here in works included under other headings.

The Literature: Format

Abbreviations

As the Spirit . . . *As the Spirit Leads Us,* edited by Kevin and Dorothy Ranaghan (Paramus, N.J.: Paulist, 1971).

CRS Charismatic Renewal Services, Ann Arbor, Mich., and South Bend, Ind.

DP Dove Publications. Pamphlets published (usually without indication of date) at the Benedictine Monastery (since 1973 an abbey) of Our Lady of Guadalupe at Pecos, N. Mex., 87552.

NC *New Covenant,* Ann Arbor, Mich. (See section on periodicals)

PM *The Pentecostal Movement in the Catholic Church,* by E. D. O'Connor, C.S.C. (Notre Dame, Ind.; Ave Maria Press, 1971. Revised edition, 1974.) References are to the latter.

PN *Pastoral Newsletter,* Ann Arbor, Mich. (See section on periodicals.)

OR *L'Osservatore Romano,* Citta del Vaticano. (Daily journal of Church affairs.)

ORe *L'Osservatore Romano,* weekly edition in English (published since 1968, giving translations of the chief papal addresses of the previous week).

TPP *Talks of Pope Paul VI.* (Weekly leaflet edition of papal addresses published by the Franciscan Marytown Press, Kenosha, Wis.)

TPS *The Pope Speaks, American Quarterly of Papal Documents,* Chevy Chase, Md., (later 3622 12th St., N.E., Wash. D.C. 20017) 1954ff.

THE LITERATURE: BIBLIOGRAPHY

I. GENERAL EXPOSITIONS

1968   Osowski, Fabian. "Pentecost and Pentecostals: A Happening." *Review for Religious,* 27 (Nov. 1968): 1064–1088.

1969   Ranaghan, Kevin and Dorothy. *Catholic Pentecostals.* New York: Paulist Press.

1970   Byrne, James. *Threshold of God's Promise: An Introduction to the Catholic Pentecostal Movement.* Notre Dame: Ave Maria Press. (Pamphlet.)

1971   Gelpi, Donald, S. J. *Pentecostalism: A Theological Viewpoint.* New York: Paulist Press.

       O'Connor, Edward, C.S.C. *The Pentecostal Movement in the Catholic Church.* Notre Dame: Ave Maria Press.

1972   Magsam, Carlos. *La Renovacion Carismatica.* (Printed without indication of date or place "Sola para difusion privada.")

       Tugwell, Simon. *Did You Receive the Spirit?* New York: Paulist Press. (Many of the chapters appeared first in *New Blackfriars* and elsewhere. These have not been separately indexed in the present bibliography.)

1973   Carrillo, Alday Salvador, M.Sp. S. *Renovacion en el Espiritu Santo.* Mexico: Instituto de Sagrada Escritura.

       Pelletier, Joseph, A. A. *A New Pentecost: Renewal in the Holy Spirit.* Worcester, Mass.: Assumption publications, 500 Salisbury St., 01609. (Booklet)

       Smet, Walter. *Ik Maak Alles Nieuw. Charismatische beweging in de kerk.* Tielt en Utrecht: Lannoo.

       Tugwell, Simon, O.P. *Catholic Pentecostalism.* London: Catholic Truth Society. (Pamphlet.)

       White, T. A. *Pentecostal Catholics.* Melbourne: A.C.T.S. Publications.

1974   Grossmann, S. *Der Aufbruch: Charismatische Erneuerung in der katholischen Kirche.* Kassel.

       Magsam, Charles. *The Experience of God.* Maryknoll, New York: Orbis.

       Melancon, Oliva, C.S.C. *Renouveau charismatique, prophétisme.* Ed. Gagne. St. Justin; Canada.

       Walsh, Vincent M. *A Key to Charismatic Renewal in the Catholic Church.* St. Meinrad, Ind.: Abbey Press.

II. PARTICULAR ELEMENTS AND ASPECTS OF THE RE-NEWAL.

Most of the following topics are treated also in the general expositions listed in #1.

A. Baptism in the Spirit

1967   O'Connor, Edward, C.S.C. "Baptism of the Spirit: Emotional Therapy?" *Ave Maria* 106 (Aug. 19, 1967): 11–14.

1969   Clark, Stephen. "Confirmation and the Baptism of the Holy Spirit," Pecos, N. Mex.: DP.

1970   Clark, Stephen. "Baptized in the Spirit," Pecos, N. Mex.: DP.

Gelpi, Donald L. "Understanding 'Spirit Baptism.' " *America* 122 (May 16, 1970): 520–521.

1972   McDonnell, Kilian and Bittlinger, Arnold. *The Baptism in the Holy Spirit as an Ecumenical Problem.* Notre Dame: CRS. (Booklet)

Schneider, H. "Heiligung and Geisttaufe." *Stimmen der Zeit* 190. (Dec. 1972): 426–428.

Tugwell, Simon. "Reflections on the Pentecostal Doctrine of 'Baptism in the Holy Spirit.' " *Heythrop Journal* 13 (July): 268–281; (Oct.): 402–414. Summarized in *Theology Digest* 21, no. 3 (Autumn 1973): 223–237.

1973   Wild, Robert. "Baptism in the Holy Spirit," *Cross and Crown* 25 (June): 147–161.

1974   Carrillo Alday, Salvador, M.Sp.S. *El Bautismo en el Espiritu Santo.* Mexico City: Instituto de Sagrada Escritura. (Based on a talk given at the International Leaders' Conference of the CCR in Rome, October 9–11, 1973. An excerpt in English translation was published in NC 3 (April): 27–30.)

Fischer, Balthasar. "The Meaning of the Expression 'Baptism of the Spirit' in the Light of Catholic Baptismal Liturgy and Spirituality." *One in Christ* 10, no. 2: 172–173.

Giblet, J. "Baptism in the Spirit in the Acts of the Apostles." *Ibid.,* pp. 162–171.

Mollat, Donatien. "The Role of Experience in the New Testament Teaching on Baptism and the Coming of the Holy Spirit." *Ibid.,* pp. 129–147.

Pennington, Basil. "The Baptism in the Holy Spirit and

Christian Tradition." NC 3 (May): 28–30. (Condensation of
a paper given at the Regional Conference for American
Cistercians in June, 1973.)

Sullivan, Francis. "Baptism in the Holy Spirit: a Catholic Interpretation of the Pentecostal Experience." *Gregorianum* 55, no. 1:
49–68. (Paper read at a theological conference on the
charismatic renewal, Notre Dame, July 20–22, 1973. An
excerpt from it was reprinted in NC 3 [May]: 28–30.)

B. Charisms

*During the period of time covered by this bibliography, quite a number of
articles on charisms appeared having no particular connection with the
charismatic renewal. They are not included in the present bibliography, which
is restricted to the literature pertaining to this movement, and does not
undertake to give a general coverage of the topics as such. Some of these articles
will be found cited in my 1969 article; others in Father Rogge's bibliography,
"Charismatic renewal. . . ," listed in VI.*

1969   Clark, Stephen. *Spiritual gifts.* Pecos, New Mexico: DP.
       O'Connor, Edward D., C.S.C. "The New Theology of
          Charisms in the Church." *American Ecclesiastical Review* 161
          (Sept.): 145–159.
1973   Cazelles, H. "l'Esprit et les charismes dans l'Eglise," *Cahiers
          marials* 90 (15 Novembre): 323–332.
       Ford, J. Massyngberde.* "Ministries and Fruits of the Holy
          Spirit." Notre Dame: Catholic Action Office.
1974   Dulles, Avery. "Charisms for the whole Church," NC 3
          (April): 30–31.
       O'Connor, Edward D., C.S.C. "Charism and Institution."
          American Ecclesiastical Review 168, no. 8 (Oct.): 507–525.

C. Tongues (Glossolalia)

1969   Killian, Matthew, O.C.S.O. "Speaking in Tongues." *The Priest*
          25 (Nov.): 611–616.

*In earlier publications, Dr. Ford spelled her name "Massingberd."
In the course of 1973, she adopted the present spelling.

1970   Ford, Josephine M. "The Theology of Tongues in Relation-
        ship to the Individual." *Bible Today* (April) pp. 3314–3320.
1971   Ford, J. Massingberd. "Toward a Theology of 'Speaking in
        Tongues.' " *Theological Studies* (March) pp. 3–29. (Repub-
        lished in *Baptism of the Spirit*. Techny: Divine Word, 1971.)
        Kelsey, Morton. "Speaking in Tongues in 1971: An Assess-
        ment of Its Meaning and Value." *Review for Religious* 30
        (March): 245–255.
1972   O'Connell, Daniel C., and Bryant, Ernest T. "Some Psycholog-
        ical Reflections on Glossolalia." *Review for Religious* 31
        (1972): 974–977.
        Pickell, D. "Speaking in Tongues." *Cross and Crown* 24 (Sum-
        mer): 280–285.
1973   Tugwell, Simon. "The Gift of Tongues in the New Testa-
        ment." *Expository Times*. 84: 137–140.
        "Identified Tongues." NC 2, n. 7 (January) (Report on
        glossolalic tongues that have been identified as known
        languages.)
1974   Archer, Antony, O.P. "Teach Yourself Tongue-Speaking."
        New Blackfriars 55, no. 651 (August): 357–364. (A wholly
        negative, somewhat derisory, critique of the phenomenon.)
        Harrisville, Dr. Roy A. "Speaking in Tongues." *Sisters Today*
        (June–July) pp. 599–609.
        Wansborough, Henry. "Speaking in Tongues." *The Way* 14,
        no. 3 (July):193–201.

D. Prophecy

1973   Montague, George. "The Spirit and the Word." NC 2
        (April):24–27.
        Yocum, Bruce. "Prophecy." NC 2 (June): 26–27; 3 (July):
        12–14 and 4 (August): 19–22.
1974   Labonte, Arthur. *Exploring the Gift of Prophecy*. Pecos, N. Mex.:
        DP.

E. Healing

1972   Gelpi, Donald L. "The Ministry of Healing." *Pentecostal Piety*.
        New York: Paulist, pp. 1–58.

Scanlan, Michael, T.O.R. *The Power in Penance*. Notre Dame:
Ave Maria Press.

1973   Martin, Francis. "The Healing of Memories." *Review for
Religious* 32 (May): 498–507.

Healing. Special issue of NC 3 (November) with articles by
Agnes Sanford, Barbara Schlemon, Michael Scanlan and
Flor de Maria Ospina de Molina.

1974   MacNutt, Francis, O.P. *Healing*. Notre Dame: Ave Maria
Press.

Scanlan, Michael. *Inner healing. Ministering to the human spirit
through the power of prayer*. New York: Paulist Press.

Inner Healing. Special issue of NC 3, no. 12 (June) with articles
by Francis MacNutt, Barbara Schlemon, and Michael
Scanlan, supplemented in the following issue (July) 4, no.
1, with articles by James Brassil and George Kosicki and
testimonials.

F. Prayer meetings

1970   Ford, J. Massingberd. "Spontaneous Prayer Groups." *Sisters
Today* 46 (Feb.): 342–347.

1971   Ranaghan, Kevin. "The Nature of the Prayer Meeting." *As the
Spirit. . .* , pp. 38–59.

1974   Cavnar, Jim. *Participating in Prayer Meetings,* Ann Arbor,
Mich.: Word of Life. (This book was prepared by a series of
articles in NC 2 (Nov. and Dec. 1972, Jan., March and
April, 1973, and by a DP pamphlet in 1969.)

G. Charismatic communities

1971   Danielson, D. "A Community of Pentecostals." *Sisters Today* 43
(Dec.): 215–224. (Report on the Word of God community
in Ann Arbor.)

Ghezzi, Bertil. "Three Charismatic Communities." *As the
Spirit. . .* , pp. 164–186.

Martin, Ralph. "Life in Community," ibid., pp. 145–163.

1972   Clark, Stephen B. *Building Christian Communities. Strategy for
Renewing the Church*. Notre Dame: Ave Maria Press.

Word of God Community. "The Word of God." Ann Arbor: Word of Life.

1973 Pennington, Basil. "A Community for Today and Tomorrow." *Review for Religious* 32, n. 3 (May), 508–513. (Report on the True House community.)

1974 Ford, J. Massyngberde. "Neo-Pentecostalism within the Roman Catholic Communion." *Dialog* 13 (Winter): 45–50. (A very one-sided comparison of two types of groups.)

What is Christian Community? (The November, 1974, issue of NC with articles on this subject by Steve Clark, Jean Vanier, Bob Horning, Kerry Koller, and Jim Cavnar.

Courrier Communautaire International 9, no. 4 (1974) *Ces communautés dites charismatiques.* (Booklet.)

1975 Casey, Rick. "Whither Charismatics?" *National Catholic Reporter,* August 15ff. (A series of articles critically examining the covenant communities.)

H. The charismatic renewal in religious orders and communities

Whereas the preceding section dealt with communities coming into existence as a result of the charismatic renewal, the present one deals with the influence of the renewal on already existing communities.

1972 Amyot, Sister Florette. "What Is the Spirit Saying to Religious Today?" NC 1 (March): 6–8.

1973 Wild, Robert. " 'It is Clear That There are Serious Differences Among You' (I Cor. 1:11): The Charismatic Renewal Entering Religious Communities." *Review for Religious* 32 (Sept.): 1093–1102.

1974 Greeley, Mary Ellen, R.S.M. "Charismatic Involvement for Religious." *Review for Religious* 33 (May): 601–608.

undated Carrillo Alday, Salvador, M. Sp. S. *La Renovacion Carismatica y las Comunidades Religiosas.*

I. Spirituality

Here are included both 'works of edification,' designed to foster spiritual growth, and theoretical works discussing the spirituality developing in the renewal.

1970ff *The Life in the Spirit Seminars Team Manual.* (This is a
        pamphlet designed to guide those preparing people to
        receive and cooperate with the Baptism in the Spirit. It is
        the product chiefly of the community at Ann Arbor,
        Michigan, and has gone through a series of developments.
        It originated in a small, offset edition, prepared under the
        direction of Ralph Martin, in June, 1970. What is usually
        called the first edition, with minor revisions and additions
        by James Byrne, was published by the Communication
        Center in January, 1971. The second edition, edited by
        Stephen Clark, appeared in January, 1972. The third
        edition, without indication of editorship, was published in
        September, 1973, by CRS.)
1971   Martin, Ralph. *"Unless the Lord Build the House. . . ."* Notre
        Dame: Ave Maria Press.
1972   Clark, Stephen. *Building Christian Communities.* Notre Dame:
        Ave Maria Press.
        Clark, Stephen B. *Growing in Faith.* Notre Dame: CRS.
1973   Ivens, Michael, S. J. and Colledge, Edmund, O.S.A. "When
        You Pray . . . Pentecostal Prayer." *The Way* 13, no. 4 (Oct.):
        325–336.
1974   Clark, Stephen B. *Knowing God's Will.* Ann Arbor: Word of
        Life Press
        Hocken, Peter. "The Spirit and Charismatic Prayer." *Life and
        Worship,* 43: 1–10.
        Martin, Ralph. *Hungry for God.* Practical help in personal
        prayer. New York: Doubleday.
        McDonnell, Kilian, O.S.B. "The Distinguishing Characteris-
        tics of the Charismatic-Pentecostal Spirituality." *One in
        Christ* 10, no. 2: 117–128.
        Steindl-Rast, Brother David F. K., O.S.B. "Charismatic Re-
        newal, a Challenge to Roman Catholic Worship." *Worship*
        48, no. 7 (Sept): 382–391.

J. Ecumenism

1970   Clark, Stephen. "Renewal *in* the Catholic Church." *Pastoral
        Newsletter* (June) pp. 3–7.
1971   Ranaghan, Kevin. "Catholics and Pentecostals Meet in the
        Spirit." *As the Spirit. . . ,* pp. 114–144.
1972   Rogge, Louis, O. Carm. "Ecumenical Aspects of Catholic

Pentecostalism." *Sword* 32, no. 2 (June): 11–24. (*Sword* is a privately published review of the Canadian-Carmelite Fathers of the Canadian-American province of the Most Pure Heart of Mary at 31 North Broadway, Joliet, Ill. 60435.)

"Vatican Enters Dialogue on Pentecostalism," NC 1 (January): 6–7.

1973   Harper, Michael. "Charismatic Renewal—A New Ecumenism?" *One in Christ* 9, no. 1: 59–65.

McDonnell, Kilian, O.S.B. "The Experiential and the Social: New Models from the Pentecostal/Roman Catholic Dialogue." *One in Christ* 9, no. 1: 43–58.

"Vatican-Pentecostal Dialogue Continues." NC 3 (September): 24.

1974   Martin, Ralph. "God is Restoring His People," NC 4, no. 3 (Sept.): 1–6. (Edited text of an address given at the 1974 International Conference on the Charismatic Renewal in the Catholic Church, at Notre Dame. Published also in modified form in *Logos Journal* 4, no. 6 (Nov.–Dec.): 249–253. An amplified version is scheduled to be published by CRS in 1975, tentatively entitled *Fire on the Earth*.)

K. Social action

1972   *Christians and Social Action.* Two special issues of NC, 2. Part I (Oct.) articles by Bishop McKinney, John Randall, Larry Hogan, Paul Witte, Phil O'Mara, Joe Cuticelli, Francis Martin and Larry Christenson. Part II (Nov.) articles by James Burke, Francis MacNutt, Steve Clark, Phil O'Mara and Jerry Barker.

1974   Danielson, Dan. "The Charismatic Renewal and Social Concern." NC 3 (June): 37–39.

L. Miscellaneous

1. Works embracing several diverse topics.

1970   Ford, Josephine M. *The Pentecostal Experience.* New York: Paulist Press.

O'Connor, Edward, C.S.C. *Pentecost in the Catholic Church,*
    Pecos, N. Mex.: DP (A revised reprint of articles which
    originally appeared in 1967 and 1968 in the *Ave Maria* and
    Ecumenist.)

1971 Ford, J. Massingberd. *Baptism of the Spirit: Three Essays on the
    Pentecostal Experience.* Techny, Illinois: Divine Word Publi-
    cations.

Ford, J. Massingberd. "Tongues-Leadership-Women:
    Further Reflections on the New-Pentecostal Movement."
    Spiritual Life 17 (Fall): 186–197.

Ranaghan, Kevin and Dorothy, editors. *As the Spirit Leads Us.*
    New York: Paulist Press. (Articles by the editors and by S.
    Clark, J. Cavnar, S.B. Anthony, L. and V. Kortenkamp, R.
    Martin, B. Ghezzi, J. Byrne, J. Connelly and G. Martin.)

1972 Gelpi, Donald L., S. J. *Pentecostal Piety.* New York: Paulist
    Press.

1974 Montague, George, T., S.M. *Riding the Wind.* Notre Dame:
    CRS

Montague, George T., S.M. *The Spirit and His gifts.* New York:
    Paulist Press. (Based on the article, "Baptism in the Spirit
    and Speaking in Tongues," *Theology Digest* 21 (1973):
    342–360, supplemented with a chapter on prophecy,
    interpretation and discernment.)

Le mouvement charismatique. Special issue of *La Vie Spirituelle,*
    (Jan.–Feb.) with articles by Besmard, Riocreux, Hocken,
    Tugwell, Garrigues, Lafont and de Monléon.

1974 "Catholic Pentecostals," special issue of *New Catholic World* 207
    (Nov./Dec.) (Articles by Joseph Fichter, Ralph Martin,
    Donald Gelpi, Harold Cohen, Terry Malone, Edward
    O'Connor, James Ferry, James Empereur. Survey of recent
    books by J. Rodman Williams.) Reprinted by Paulist Press
    in 1975 as a booklet, *Pentecostal Catholics,* edited by Robert
    Heyer.

Reconnaître l'Esprit. Montréal: Editions Bellarmin (8100
    Boulevard St Laurent). (Talks given by Jacques Custeau
    and Robert Michel at a conference on the charismatic
    renewal held at Loyola College, Montréal, in the summer of
    1973.)

*Wiederentdeckung des Heiligen Geistes. Der Heilige Geist in der
    charismatischen Erfahrung und theologischen Reflexion.*
    (Oekumenische Perspektiven 6). Frankfurt am Main, J. Knecht

and O. Lembeck. (Contributions by Harding Meyer, Kilian McDonnell, Walter Hollenweger, Vilmos Vajta, and Anna Marie Aagaard.)

2. *Other miscellaneous works.*

1969   O'Connor, Edward, C.S.C. "The Laying on of Hands." Pecos, N. Mex.: DP.
1970   Clark, Stephen. " 'Saving' Catholics." PN (Oct.) pp. 4–5.
        Clark, Stephen. *Confirmation and the Baptism of the Holy Spirit.* Pecos, N. Mex.: DP. PN (August) pp. 3–6.
        Ranaghan, Kevin. "The Problem of Re-Baptism," PN (December) pp. 6–8.
1971   Byrne, James. "Charismatic Leadership," *As the Spirit. . .* , pp. 187–210.
        O'Connor, Edward, C.S.C. "Discernment of Spirits." Part I: PN (May) pp. 5–8. Part II: NC 1 (Oct.): 12–17. Part III: NC 1 (Jan. 1972): 10–11. Revised ed., NC 4 (1975), April, May, and June.
        Del Monte Sol, Teresa. "Pentecostalism and the Doctrine of Saint Teresa and Saint John of the Cross." *Spiritual Life* 17 (Spring): 21–33.
1972   O'Connor, Edward. *Pentecost in the Modern World,* Notre Dame: AveMaria Press.
        Ranaghan, Kevin. "The Lord, the Spirit, and the Church." NC 2 (August): 1–5. Republished as a pamphlet by CRS, 1973.
1973   Carr, Aidan. "A Catholic Pentecostal Parish," *Homiletic and Pastoral Review* 73 (Jan.): 67–69. (Account of the "first" Pentecostal parish in Geneva, Illinois.)
        Clark, Stephen. *Where Are We Headed? Guidelines for the Catholic Charismatic Renewal.* Notre Dame: CRS.
        Ford, J. Massingberd. "Pentecostal Poise or Docetic Charismatics?" *Spiritual Life* 19 (Spring): 32–47.
1973   Kosicki, George (editor). *The Lord is My Shepherd, Witnesses of Priests.* Ann Arbor: CRS.
        McDonnell, Kilian, O.S.B. "Eucharistic Celebrations in the Catholic Charismatic Movement." *Studia Liturgica* 9: 19–44.
        O'Connor, Edward. "Institution and Inspiration, Two Modes of God's Presence in the Church." in *Jesus, Where Are You*

Taking Us? Ed. by Norris Wogen. Carol Stream, Ill.:
Creation House, pp. 189–203.

Randall, John. *In God's Providence, The Birth of a Catholic
Charismatic Parish.* Plainfield, New Jersey: Living Flame
Press.

1974   Cirner, Randy. "Deliverance, Part I." NC 3 (April): 4–7. Part
II, *ibid.*, (May): 22–25.

Mühlen, Heribert. "Die Pfingsterfahrung und ihre Fortdauer
in Firmsakrament." *Bestellt zum Zeugnis, Festgabe fur Bischof
Dr. Johannes Pohlschneider.* Ed. by K. Delahaye, E. Gatz, H.
Jorissen. Aachen.

O'Connor, Edward, C.S.C. *The Gifts of the Spirit.* (Vol. 24 of St.
Thomas Aquinas, *Summa Theologiae*, 1a2ae, 68–70: Latin
text with translation, introduction, and notes.) London:
Eyre and Spottiswoode, and New York: McGraw-Hill.

O'Connor, Edward, C.S.C. "When the Cloud of Glory Dissi-
pates." *New Catholic World* 217 (Nov./ Dec.): 271–275.

Spohn, William C. "Charismatic Communal Discernment and
Ignatian Communities." *The Way*, Supplement no. 20
(Autumn): 38–54.

III. CRITICAL AND HISTORICAL STUDIES

A. Historical studies

*Most of the general expositions of the renewal begin with a sketch of its
history; there have been only a few properly historical studies, all of them
restricted to a very particular domain.*

1971   Connelly, James, C.S.C. "The Charismatic Movement: 1967—
1970." *As the Spirit. . .* , pp. 211–232.

International Beginnings. Special issue of NC 1, no. 5 (Nov.),
with reports on the beginnings of the Renewal in several
foreign countries.

1973   La Fay Bardi, Miguel, O. Carm. "El Movimiento Carismatico
en Lima en 1972." (Inedita disertacion teologica para optar
el grado de Licenciatura en teologia. Facultad de Teologia
Pontificia y Civil de Lima. Mimeographed; 47 pp.)

Charismatic Beginnings: Duquesne 1977. Special issue of NC 2
(February), with articles by Patti Gallagher, Jerry and

Annamarie Cafardi, Pat Bourgeois, Paul and Mary Ann Gray, Dave Mangan, and Jim Manney.

1974   Flynn, Thomas. *The Charismatic Renewal and the Irish Experience.* London: Hodder and Stoughton.

Hudsyn, Jean-Luc. *Naissance du "Renouveau charismatique" dans l'espace culturel francophone.* Mémoire présenté pour l'obtention du grade de licencie en théologie. Université Catholique de Louvain.

McCarthy, Jerome, C.S.Sp. "The Charismatic Renewal and Reconciliation in Northern Ireland." *One in Christ* 10, no. 1: 31–43.

B. Psychological and sociological studies

1967   Nouwen, Henri. "A critical analysis." *Ave Maria* 105 (June 3): 11–13, 30. (Originally published in the Notre Dame student publication, *The Scholastic,* April 21, 1967, pp. 15 ff. Republished in *Ave Maria,* June 3, 1967, and again as a chapter of the book *Intimacy,* Notre Dame Fides Press, 1969, pp. 77–90. My article, "Baptism in the Spirit: Emotional Therapy?" in the pamphlet *Pentecost in the Catholic Church,* 1970 (See p. 164) was written in reply to it.)

1970   Hine, Virginia. "Anthropological and Sociological Aspects of the Charismatic Renewal Movement within the Roman Catholic Church." (Paper read and circulated at a conference on the Charismatic Renewal movement within the Roman Catholic Church at the Bergamo Center for Christian Renewal, Dayton, Ohio, June 6, 1970. Not published.)

1971   Haglof, Anthony, O.C.D. "Psychology and the Pentecostal Experience." *Spiritual Life* 17 (Fall): 198–210.

Perrin, Steven W. "A Clanging Cymbal: Conflict among Catholic Pentecostals." Doctoral thesis in the department of anthropology at the University of Michigan State. (Not published.)

1973   Fichter, Joseph. "Pentecostals: Comfort vs. Awareness." *America* 129, no. 5 (September 1): 114–116.

Fichter, Joseph H., S. J. "Women in Charismatic Renewal." *National Catholic Reporter,* (September 28) pp. 11–13.

Greeley, Mary Ellen, R.S.M. *A Study of the Catholic "Charismatic Renewal."* (Doctoral dissertation in the Department of Sociology at the University of St. Louis, mimeographed.)

1973   Grom, B. "Die katholische charismatische Bewegung." *Stim-
        men der Zeit* 191 (Oct.): 651–671.
        McDonnell, Kilian, O.S.B. "Pentecostal Culture: Protestant
        and Catholic." *One in Christ* 7, no. 4: 310–318.
        Moore, John. "The Catholic Pentecostal Movement." *Doctrine
        and Life* 23 (April): 177–196.
1974   Fichter, Joseph H. "How It Looks to a Social Scientist." *New
        Catholic World* 207 (Nov./Dec.): 244–248.
1975   Fichter, Joseph. *The Catholic cult of the Paraclete.* New York,
        Sheed and Ward.

C. Theological interpretations and critiques

*Only works concerned with the renewal as a whole are listed here. Those
treating particular aspects are listed in #II.*

1968   O'Connor, Edward D. "Pentecost and Catholicism." *The
        Ecumenist* 6 (July–August): 161–164. Reprinted in *Pentecost
        in the Catholic Church,* (1970) DP.
        O'Connor, Edward D. "To Roman Catholic Priests Enquiring
        about the Pentecostal Movement." (Originally a mimeog-
        raphed text privately circulated. 3 pp. Revised, Pentecost,
        1970. Published in *One in Christ* 7, no. 4 (1971): 401–404.)
1970   McDonnell, Kilian. "Catholic Pentecostalism: Problems in
        Evaluation." *Dialog* 9 (1970): 35–54. Reprinted by DP, also
        in *Theology Digest* 19 (1971): 46–51.
1970   Monléon, Albert M. de, O.P. "Le 'renouveau charismatique'
        aux Etats-Unis." (Le pentecôtisme catholique américain),
        Vers L'Unité Chrétienne, (octobre–novembre) pp. 207–211.
1971   Byrne, James. "A Vision of the Charismatic Renewal." PN
        (January) p. 3.
        Clark, Stephen B. "Charismatic Renewal in the Church." *As the
        Spirit . . .* pp. 17–37.
        Eimer, Robert, O.M.I. "The Catholic Pentecostal Movement,"
        The Priest 27, no. 3 (March): 35–43.
        Ford, Josephine Massingberd. "Fly United—But Not in Too
        Close Formation: Reflections on the Neo-Pentecostal
        Movement." *Spiritual Life* 17 (Spring): 12–20.
1972   Congar, Y. "Actualité renouvellé du Saint-Esprit." *Lumen Vitae*
        (French ed.) 27: 453–460. Engl. transl.: "Renewed Actual-
        ity of the Holy Spirit." *Lumen Vitae* (English ed.) 28 (1973):
        13–30.

McDonnell, Kilian. "Catholic Charismatics." *Commonweal* 96 (May): 207–211.

Mederlet, E. and McDonnell, K. *Charismatisches Erneuerung der Katholischen Kirche.* Schloss Craheim bei Wetzhausen, Oekumensicher Schriftendienst.

Neuman, M. "The Action of the Holy Spirit in the Individual Believer: Perspectives from Christian Spirituality and Theology." *Cistercian Studies* 7, no. 1: 33–62.

Rogge, Louis, O. Carm. "Catholic Pentecostalism." *Sword* 32, no. 1 (Feb.): 6–23.

Sullivan, Emmanuel, S.A. "Can the Pentecostal Movement Renew the Churches?" *Study Encounter* 8, no. 4.

Sullivan, Francis, S.J. "The Pentecostal Movement." *Gregorianum* 53: 237–266. Cf. *Theology Digest* 21 (1973): 257.

Wild, Robert. "Is the Charismatic Renewal in the Church a New 'Montanism'?" *Homiletic and Pastoral Review* 73 (Dec.): 67–72.

1973 Caffarel, Henri. *Faut-il parler d'un Pentecôtisme catholique?* Paris: Editions du Feu Nouveau.

Fox, Robert J. "Charismatics: Their Place in the Church." *Our Sunday Visitor* (August 19) p. 1 ff.

Gelpi, Donald, S.J. "American Pentecostalism." *Spiritual Revivals.* Ed. by Christian Duquoc and Casiano Floristan. (*Concilium*, New Series 9, no. 9.) New York: Herder and Herder.

Gelpi, Donald, S.J. "Charismatic Renewal: Problems, Possibilities." *National Catholic Reporter* (Aug. 3) pp. 7 and 14.

Giblet, J. "Le mouvement pentecôtiste dans l'église catholique aux USA." *Revue Théologique de Louvain* 4: 469–490.

McDonnell, Kilian. "Statement of the Theological Basis of the Catholic Charismatic Renewal." Grand Rapids Michigan Diocesan Publications. Reprinted by DP, by NC (vol. 3, Jan. 1974, pp. 21–23) and by *Review for Religious* (Vol. 32:2, 1974, pp. 344–352). (Text composed in collaboration with Salvador Carrillo, Albert de Monleon, Francis Martin, Donatien Mollat, Heribert Mühlen and Francis Sullivan in connection with the International Leaders' Conference on the Charismatic Renewal in the Catholic Church, Rome, Oct. 9–11, 1973.)

McHale, John V. "The Charismatic Renewal Movement." *The Furrow.* 24 (May): 259–271.

1974 Congar, Y. "Charismatiques ou quoi?" *La Croix.* (Jan. 19) Reprinted in *La Chambre Haute* 7: 27–29.

Fox, Robert J. "Pentecostals: Are They Becoming 'Too Respectable'?" *Our Sunday Visitor* (August 25)

Gelpi, Donald L., S.J. "Can You Institutionalize the Spirit?" *New Catholic World* 217 (Nov./Dec.): 254–258.

Hocken, Peter. "Catholic Pentecostalism: Some Key Questions." *The Heythrop Journal* 15 April and July): 131–145, 271–204.

Laurentin, René. *Pentecôtisme chez les catholiques: Risques et avenir*. Paris: Beauchesne.

Mühlen, Heribert. *Geisterfahrung und Erneuerung*. München, Don-Bosco. (This book was prepared by articles published in the course of this same year in *Geist und Leben* (pp. 246–256), *Theologie und Glaube* (pp. 28–45), *Catholica* (3:1 ff.), and *Rheinische Merkur* (May 31, p. 21).

Mühlen, Heribert. *Einleitung* to *Spontaner Glaube* by E. D. O'Connor (German translation of *The Pentecostal Movement in the Catholic Church*), Freiburg: Herder, pp. 11–27.

Mühlen, Heribert. "An Interview with Fr. Heribert Mühlen: Theologian of the Holy Spirit." NC 4 (July): 3–6.

McDonnell, Kilian, and others. *Theological and Pastoral Orientations on the Catholic Charismatic Renewal*. Prepared at Malines, Belgium, May 21–26, 1974. Ann Arbor: Word of Life.

Ranaghan, Kevin. "Catholic Charismatic Renewal: The First Seven Years." NC 3 (March): 3–6.

Uribe Jaramillo, Alfonso, Obispo de Sanson-Rionegro. *El actual Pentecostes del Espíritu Santo*. Medellin: Editorial Granamerica, Colombia.

Suenens, Cardinal L. J. *Une nouvelle Pentecôte?* Desclée de Brouwer.

The Roman Catholic-Pentecostal Dialogue. (One in Christ 10, no. 2. A resume of the meetings between the Secretariat for promoting Christian unity, and representatives of various Pentecostal groups, held at Zürich-Horgen in 1972 and Rome in 1973. Includes most of the papers presented at these meetings, and the lists of points of agreement reached by the participants.)

"Libérer l'esprit: le renouveau charismatique." *Prêtre et Pasteur* 77 (4450 rue St. Hubert, Montréal, Canada) n. 5: 225–288.

1975   Storey, William. "Reform or Suppression. Alternatives Seen for Catholic Charismatic Renewal." *A. D. Correspondence*

10, no. 11 (May 24). (Report of an interview by John Reedy in the biweekly bulletin published at Notre Dame, Indiana 46556.)

D. Denunciations

I have taken the unusual step of separating 'denunciations' from simple critiques because, in the case of the present subject, they clearly constitute a distinct body of literature. A critique may be very biased or negative; nevertheless, it aims at giving an objective account of the good as well as the bad in its subject. A denunciation takes off from the settled judgment that its subject is evil, and aims to prove this, and to arouse people against it. There are, of course, borderline cases which could be put in either category. If some of them are included here, it is because of the usefulness of grouping together the attacks which have been made on the renewal.

1969 Barbarie, T. "Tongues, si, Latin, no." *Triumph* 4 (April): 20–22. (Reply by E.D. O'Connor, ibid., (July) p. 5; response by Barbarie, ibid., p. 40)

1970 Greeley, Andrew. "Glossolalia: 'It's Rooted in Emotional Disturbance'." *National Catholic Reporter* (October 2) p. 17. (Letters in response to the above article by E.D. O'Connor and Frank Manning, ibid., October 16; Louis J. Broussard, ibid., October 23; Kilian McDonnell, ibid., October 30.)

1971 Hardon, John A. "Pentecostalism: Evaluating a Phenomenon." Lecture given at the Annual Conference for the Clergy, Archdiocese of New York, April 20–21. (Dittoed, not printed).

Most, William. "The New Pentecost?" *Our Sunday Visitor* (April 25) p. 7ff

1972 Crehan, Joseph, S.J. "Charismatics and Pentecostals." *Christian Order* 13 (October and November): 582–593, 678–689. (Perhaps the most erudite and clever of the attacks made from a Catholic standpoint; but grossly misrepresenting and discrediting it by means of sarcastic jibes, allusions to irrelevant religious frauds and even obscenities.)

Docherty, Jerome, O.S.B. "Pentecostals—Who Are They?" *The Wanderer,* July 27.

Duff, Frank. "Fiddling While Rome Burns." *Maria Legionis* 20, no. 4: 1–5.

Dwyer, Robert J. Archbishop of Portland. "False Promises, Searing Disillusionments." *Catholic Sentinel* (Portland),* January 21.

Rumble, Rev. L., M.S.C. "Pentecostal Revivalism." *The Australasian Catholic Record* 49 (Jan.): 26–39.

Slade, Jack A. "The 'Pentecostal' Movement and the Jesus Revolution." *Present Truth* (April) pp. 17–21. (See note on the following entry.)

"Pentecostalism and the Jesus Revolution Challenged and Refuted." Transcript of three forums held in Brisbane, Australia, by a panel consisting of Messrs. Robert and John Brinsmead, John Slade, Geoffrey Paxton, and Jack Zwemer. Published in *Australiam Forum*, Topics no. 1, 2 and 3, by *Present Truth*, P.O.B. 1311, Fallbrook, Cal. 92028. Topic no. 3, "Is the Charismatic Movement Catholic or Protestant?" was reprinted in the review, *Present Truth*, June 1972, 5–11. (These and the other articles cited from this review are concerned mainly to show that the charismatic renewal in the Protestant world is an incursion of Roman Catholicism.)

Anon. "On the Religious Front." *Present Truth* (July–August).

Justification by Faith and the Charismatic Movement. Special issue of *Present Truth.* (September–October) containing a series of unsigned articles, notably, "Protestant Revivalism, Pentecostalism and the Drift Back to Rome," pp. 19–25. (This article was reprinted as a separate pamphlet. Likewise the whole issue was reprinted without a date, and with different pagination.)

Anon. "Pentecostalism, a Natural Fruit of Teilhardism." *Vers Demain,* (April) p. 29.

1973   Dwyer, Archbishop Robert J. "Pentecostalism Plays with an Old Heresy." *The Twin Circle,* (August 31) p. 2ff.

Likoudis, James. "The Pentecostal Controversy." *Social Justice Review,* (Sept.) (Reprinted by Central Bureau Press, 2835 Westminster Place, St. Louis, MO, 63108.)

O'Meara, Frank. "Pentecostalism is Not the Answer." *U.S. Catholic,* (Dec.).

*Each of the articles by Archbishop Dwyer appeared in several different Catholic papers at about the same date, with the title varying from paper to paper.

Paxton, Geoffrey J. "Pentecostalism and the Australian Forum." *Present Truth* 2, no. 3 (June): 17–21.

Thibeault, Guy. " 'Catholic' Pentecostalism: The Masonic Ecumenism of Tomorrow," *Vers Demain* (English language ed.) (July, August, September) pp. 22–23. (French translation, "Le mouvement Pentecotiste chez les catholiques," in the French language edition of the same review, (Nov.—Dec.) p. 24 ff.)

Zwemer, Jack D. "The Nature and Extent of the Pentecostal Movement." *Present Truth* 2, no. 3 (June): 28–29.

1974   Burns, Robert, Fr., C.S.P. "The Charismatic Movement." *The Wanderer.* p. 20.

Dwyer, Archbishop Robert J. "Charismatic Renewal." *The National Catholic Register.** (July 21) (Replies *ibid.* by E. O'Connor and R. Kryzanski, August 4, p. 8, T. Curley and R. [De] Grandis, Sept. 1, p. 8.)

Dwyer, Archbishop Robert J. "The Bishops and the Charismatics." *The National Catholic Register.* (Dec. 15) (editorial).

Present Truth 3, no. 1 (February). Issue concerned largely with Pentecostalism under two headings, "The Current Religious Scene and the Gospel," by Robert D. Brinsmead, and "The Current Religious Scene and the Bible," by Geoffrey Paxton.

Villeurbane, Eugène de, capucin. *Illuminisme "67": Un faux renouveau: Le pentecôtisme dit "catholique."* Verjon, 01270, Coligny, France.

E. Appraisals of the renewal in the Roman Catholic Church by outsiders

The following list embraces only works of a sustained theological character. It does not include journalistic reports, autobiographical accounts, or personal impressions, although note should at least be made of two delightful books in this last category by Douglas Wead, Father McCarthy Smokes a Pipe and Speaks in Tongues *(Norfolk: Wisdom, 1972) and* Catholic Charismatics: Are They for Real? *(Carol Stream, Illinois: Creation House, 1973). Neither does it include general surveys of the charismatic renewal giving merely superficial reports on what has happened in the Catholic Church.*

1969   Harper, Michael. "Reports from North America." *Renewal* 23 (Nov.): 5–8.

1970   Harper, Michael. "Catholic Pentecostals." *Renewal* 25 (Mar.):
        1–4.

        Hollenweger, Walter J. "Das Charisma in der Oekumene. Der
        Beitrag der Pfingstbewegung an die allgemeine Kirche,"
        Una Sancta 25: 150–159. Summary, "Pentecostalism's Con-
        tribution to the World Church," *Theology Digest* 19, no. 1:
        54–57.

1971   Le Cossec, Charles (editor). "Que faut-il penser des
        'Catholiques Pentecôtistes'?" Documents "Experiences",
        no. 2 (quarterly published by the Centre Missionaire,
        29270 Carhaix, France).

        Plowman, Edward E. "Catholics Get the Spirit." *Christianity
        Today.* 15 (July 16): 31–32.

1972   Mouw, Richard. "Catholic Pentecostalism Today." *The Re-
        formed Journal.* (July–August) pp. 8–15.

1973   Hollenweger, Walter. *New Wine in Old Wineskins: Protestant and
        Catholic Neo-Pentecostalism.* Glouscester, England: Fellow-
        ship Press.

1974   Jones, James W. *Filled with New Wine: The Charismatic Renewal
        of the Church.* New York: Harper and Row. (Touches on the
        Catholic experience incidentally to a discussion of a theory
        of the renewal in the Christian churches generally.)

        "Non! Monsieur le Cardinal Suenens. Nous ne sommes pas
        d'accord!" *Documents "Expériences,"* no. 16. (Articles by Y.
        Charles, J.-M. Thobois, C. Le Cossec and E. Louédin).

F. The charismatic renewal, or Pentecostal movement, in the non-Catholic world, appraised by Catholics

*Before the charismatic renewal made its appearance within the Catholic
Church, a number of Catholic scholars had already begun to interest themselves
in the Pentecostal movement in the non-Catholic world. Although their
research does not seem to have contributed significantly to engendering the
Catholic movement, it does belong surely to the prehistory of the latter, and
hence is included here.*

1963   O'Hanlon, Daniel J. "The Pentecostals and Pope John's 'New
        Pentecost!' " *America* 108 (May 4): 634–636.

1966   Lepargneur, Francisco, O.P. "Reflexões católicas em face do
        Movimento Pentecostal no Brasil." *O Espírito Santo e o
        Movimento Pentecostal.* (Symposium presented by the As-

sociaçãó de Seminarios Teológicos Evangélicos) S. Paulo, pp. 46–67.

1966 McDonnell, Kilian. "The Ecumenical Significance of the Pentecostal Movement." *Worship* 40 (December): 608–629.

1967 Baxendale, Richard, S. J. "The Pentecostal Movement: Does it matter?" *The Clergy Review* 52 (Jan.): 9–19.

1968 McDonnell, Kilian. "Holy Spirit and Pentecostalism." *Commonweal* 89 (November): 198–204.

McDonnell, Kilian. "The Ideology of Pentecostal Conversion." *Journal of Ecumenical Studies* 5: 105–126.

1969 Damboriena, Prudencio, S. J. *Tongues as of Fire.* Cleveland, Ohio: Corpus Publications.

1971 Moura, Abdalaziz de. "O Pentecostalismo como fenômeno religioso popular no Brasil," *Revista Eclesiástica Brasileira* 31: 78–94. Summarized in *Theology Digest* 20 (1972): 44–48.

1972 McDonnell, Kilian, O.S.B. "The Classical Pentecostal Movement." NC 1 (May): 1–3.

1973 Gelpi, Donald, S. J. "Pneuma '72: A Personal Theological Reflection." NC, 2 (April): 3 and 27–28. (Report on the meeting of the Society for Pentecostal Studies).

undated Moura, Abdalazis de. "Importancia des Igfejas Pentecostais para a Igreja Catholica," Recife (Brazil).

IV. PRONOUNCEMENTS BY THE HIERARCHY

A. Pope Paul VI

Of the many statements by Pope Paul on the charismatic (and pseudo-charismatic) elements of the Christian life, the more important are listed below. The majority of them were talks given by the Pope at his weekly public audience. Since most of them have no official titles, and the titles assigned by editors vary from journal to journal, only the dates are given here. A much more complete presentation of this material, citing the important texts in full, is in preparation by the present editor.

May 21, 1964. OR, May 21.
Sept. 14, 1964. OR, Sept. 14–15. TPS 10: 106–109.
June 6, 1965. OR, June 7–8.
May 18, 1966. OR, May 19.
Oct. 12, 1966. OR, Oct. 15. TPS 12: 79–81.

May 17, 1967. OR, May 18.
May 25, 1969. OR, May 26–27. ORe, June 5.
May 26, 1971. OR, May 27. ORe, June 3.
Feb. 13, 1972. OR, Feb. 14–15. ORe, Feb. 17, 1972. TPS 17:
    39–42.
May 21, 1972. OR, May 22–23. ORe, June 1.
May 24, 1972. OR, May 25. ORe, June 1, 1972. TPS 17:
    144–147.
Oct. 25, 1972. OR, Oct. 26. ORe, Nov. 5, 1972. TPP 7, no. 47.
Nov. 29, 1972. OR, Nov. 30. ORe, Dec. 7, 1972. TPP 8, no. 2.
May 23, 1973. OR, May 24. ORe, May 31.
June 6, 1973. OR, June 7. ORe, June 14.
Oct. 10, 1973. OR, Oct. 11. ORe, Oct. 18.
June 2, 1974. OR, June 3–4, 1974. ORe, June 13.
June 26, 1974. OR, June 27. ORe, July 4.
Oct. 16, 1974. OR, Oct. 17. ORe, Oct. 24.
Jan. 11, 1975. OR, Jan. 12–13. ORe, Jan. 23.
June 19, 1975. OR, May 19–20. OR, May 29, NC, July, 1975.

Only three of the above addresses can be taken as referring specifically to the charismatic renewal movement which sprang up in 1967 at Duquesne, Notre Dame, Ann Arbor, etc., and two are very discreet. One is that of October 10, 1973, addressed to representatives of an International Leaders' Conference on the Charismatic Renewal, meeting at Grottaferrata, near Rome. Without explicitly naming the charismatic renewal, the Pope rejoices at the renewal of spiritual life manifested in many forms in the Church today, in which he recognizes the work of the Holy Spirit. The original text in L'Osservatore Romano, *Oct. 11, 1973, is in French. The English translation in the English language edition of the* Osservatore *for Oct. 18, 1973 is reprinted in NC 3, no. 5 (Dec. 1973).*

The Pope's second allusion to the charismatic renewal came in his public audience of October 16, 1974. At one point in his address, discarding his prepared text (that which was printed in L'Osservatore Romano *for the following day), the Pope spoke impromptu. A translation of his actual words, taken from a tape recording made by the Vatican Radio Station, has been published in* New *Covenant, 4, no. 7 (January, 1975), on p. 20. It includes the following remarks: ". . . we can but hope that these gifts will come and with abundance, that in addition to grace there are charisms that the Church of today can also possess and obtain. . . . How wonderful it would be if the Lord should still increase an outpouring of charisms in order to make the Church fruitful, beautiful, and marvelous, and capable of establishing itself even to the attention and astonishment of the profane world, of the secularized world. We will mention a book which has been written precisely at this time by Cardinal Suenens, called* Une Nouvelle Pentecôte?. *In it he describes and justifies this new expectation which can really be a historical providence in the Church and based upon an outpouring of supernatural graces called charisms."*

On May 19, 1975, Pope Paul held a special audience for the International Conference on Charismatic Renewal meeting in Rome, May 16–19. He declared that "nothing is more necessary for . . . a world more and more secularized, than the testimony of this 'spiritual renewal,' which we see the Holy Spirit bringing about today in the most diverse environments." After describing its manifestations, he asked, "How then could this 'spiritual renewal' be other than a blessing for the Church and for the world?" and went on to lay down three principles to help ensure that this would be the case: 1) faithfulness to the authentic teaching of the faith; 2) grateful reception of all gifts, with primacy to the higher; 3) the supremacy of love over all other gifts.

B. Bishops, major superiors, etc.

Since many of these statements occur in pastoral letters of only limited circulation, a brief indication of the contents of each is given. This list includes all such texts known to me, but there are very likely others that I have missed. It is noteworthy that the tone of these documents is overwhelmingly favorable. Even though most are cautious and reserved, and some express criticisms of particular points, practically all make a favorable evaluation of the renewal, and not a single one condemns it or pronounces it to be fundamentally wrong. This collective testimony of the pastors of the Church is a very weighty one.

There have been several reports of religious superiors prohibiting or restricting participation by members of their communities in the renewal; but so far as my research has been able to determine, no official document has issued from any bishop or major superior condemning the renewal in itself. If there are any, they must be very few. The one apparent exception would be some newspaper articles published by Archbishop Robert Dwyer of Portland, Oregon. However, these were written in his capacity as a private commentator on the religious scene, not as ordinary. (It is significant that Archbishop Dwyer allowed Catholic charismatic prayer groups to function openly in his diocese, without taking steps toward prohibiting them, although their priest leaders spontaneously kept him fully informed about them. This is at least an impressive testimony to the integrity with which the Archbishop observed the distinction between his personal opinions and decisions made in function of his office.) They are not classified here, but under the heading Denunciations, p. 171. *A few other newspaper reports of episcopal statements are retained here simply because it would complicate things uselessly to make a special category for them.*

1963   Suenens, Léon-Josef, Cardinal. "The Charismatic Dimension
        of the Church." speech addressed to the Second Session of
        the Second Vatican Council, Oct. 22, 1963; published in
        Council Speeches of Vatican II, edited by Y. Congar, H. Küng,
        and D. O'Hanlon, New Jersey: Paulist Press, 1964, pp.
        29–34; also in *Furrow* 15 (Fall 1964): 72–74. (The French
        original is reproduced also in an appendix to the Cardinal's
        pastoral letter for Pentecost, 1973.)
1969   Committee on Doctrine of the National Conference of
        Catholic Bishops of the United States of America. "Report
        on the Pentecostal Movement in the Catholic Church."
        (Nov. 14). (Reprinted in many places, e.g., *Theology Digest*
        19 [1971]: 52.)
1970   Bishops of the United States of America, "Christians in our
        Time." National Pastoral Letter issued at the semi-annual
        meeting of the National Conference of Catholic Bishops in
        San Francisco (April). (This letter, insisting strongly on the
        presence of the Holy Spirit in the Church during these
        times of turmoil, does not formally address itself to the
        charismatic renewal. But coming just five months after the
        November 1969 meeting, in which the Bishops received a
        formal report on the renewal, it is presumably not unre-
        lated to it.)
        Carter, Emmett, Bishop of London (Ontario). Circular letter
        no. 8, (March 20) to the priests of his diocese. The relevant
        passage is reproduced in PM (2nd ed. p. 20) and in *One in
        Christ* 7–4 (1971): 400–401. (Pentecostals use Scripture with
        the inspiration and movement of the Holy Spirit to develop
        a deep sense of the presence of God and of His effective
        action.)
1971   Hannan, Philip, Archbishop of New Orleans. Statement on
        the charismatic renewal published in the *Clarion Herald,*
        newspaper for the archdiocese of New Orleans, October
        28. Reprinted in NC 1 (Jan. 1972): 11. (The renewal means
        to renew faith, stimulate prayer, encourage participation at
        Mass, unite Christians, increase fervor.)
        Hogan, Joseph, Bishop of Rochester. "The Spirit of the Lord
        Fills our World." Radio broadcast of June 5 over station

WSAY and affiliates. Revised text published as "Charismatic Renewal in the Catholic Church: an Evaluation." NC 1 (Sept.): 2–4, and as a series of four articles in the Rochester *Courier Journal*, Aug. 11, 18, 25, and Sept. 1. (The meaning of baptism in the Spirit; effects renewal of faith and life; why in our time?; danger of spiritual pride; need of theological guidance.)

1971 Manning, Timothy, Archbishop of Los Angeles, "On Devotion to the Holy Spirit." Pastoral letter to his diocese, June. (Briefly situates "Pentecostal Activity" in the general outlines of the action of the Holy Spirit; gives some pastoral cautions.)

McKinney, Joseph, Auxiliary Bishop of Grand Rapids. Interview in NC 1 (Sept.): 10–16. (Effects on his personal life; baptism in the Spirit; reactions of bishops; emotional aspects; soundness of the national leaders; reactions of priests; fruits.)

"Bishops and the Charismatic Renewal," special issue of NC 1 (Sept.) containing the statements of Bishops Carter and Hogan, and the interview with Bishop McKinney, cited above, reports on Cardinals Dearden, Miranda and Casariego, and Archbishop Hannan as well as the 1969 statement of the American Bishops.

1972 Committee on Pastoral Research and Practices of the National Conference of Catholic Bishops of the United States of America. (An informal, oral report on an enquiry made during the preceding winter was given to the Bishops at their meeting in Atlanta, Georgia, April 13 by Bishop John Quinn. No official report was published, but a summary of Bishop Quinn's remarks was published by Bishop Joseph McKinney in NC (June) pp. 10–11.)

Declaración de la Conferencia de Obispos Católicos de Puerto Rico sobre el Movimiento Pentecostal en la Iglesia Católica. (A statement published by the Puerto Rican bishops, June 13 adopting on the whole the 1969 report of the Committee on Doctrine of the American Bishops, but calling attention to dangers and abuses noted in their own country.) Text in *Mensajes de la CEP* (Conferencia Episcopal Puertorriqueña) 1, no. 2 (Junio, 1973).

The Sacred Congregation for the Doctrine of the Faith. Letter of July 28 (Prot. N. 219/70), signed by Cardinal Seper, to

Father Jose Guzmán Ponce de León (see the following entry) referring him to the 1969 report of the American Bishops.

Guzmán, Ponce de León, Rev. José, Superior General of the Misioneros del Espíritu Santo. "Movimiento de Renovación Cristiana en el Espíritu Santo." Circular Letter n. 11/VIII, Nov. (Reports on his enquiry to the Sacred Congregation for the Doctrine of the Faith about this controversial movement, its reply to him, and the good fruits of this movement in members of the Congregation. Summons the missionaries to "receive with joy and enthusiasm the grace which heaven sends us." Cf. the preceding entry.)

Hayes, James M., Archbishop of Halifax. "A report on the Catholic charismatic renewal conference," sent to his priests, June 20. (Account of the International Conference at Notre Dame, June 2–4, endorsing and encouraging the formation of Pentecostal prayer groups in his diocese.)

Hayes, Archbishop James. "Reflections on the Charismatic Renewal." NC 2 (Aug.): 6–7.

McKinney, Joseph, Auxiliary Bishop of Grand Rapids. "An Open Letter to Priests." NC 1 (June): 8–9.

Suenens, Leo J., Cardinal. "A New Charismatic Age." *America* 126, no. 19 (May 13): 503–505. (An excerpt, giving his first impressions of the charismatic renewal, was reprinted in NC 2 (July): 6–7.)

Vath, Joseph, Bishop of Birmingham, Alabama. Pastoral letter of February 16. An excerpt encouraging "groups of Christians who have begun to meet for prayer together in the Holy Spirit" was reprinted in *The Catholic Mind* 70 (May): 5–6 and in NC 1 (June 1970): 11.

1973   Baum, William W., Archbishop of Washington, D.C. Letter to his priests, dated October 15. (Recommends the charismatic renewal to them, and urges them to give it their assistance.)

Martínez Martínez, Bishop Jorge, Auxiliary and Vicar General of the Archdiocese of Mexico." Alguñas Orientaciones sobra el llamado 'Movimiento de Renovación Cristiana en el Espíritu Santo," Circular letter no. 5 to the priests and faithful of the Archdiocese, February 16. Published in *Señal* (diocesan weekly of Mexico City), March 14. English translation, *Catholic Mind* LXXII, No. 1284 (June, 1974): 26–28.

McCarthy, Edward A., Bishop of Phoenix. "On the Holy Spirit," pastoral letter of June 2, published in the June issue of the diocesan review, *Alive,* 400 East Monroe, Phoenix, Arizona, 85004. (The work of the Holy Spirit in Christ and in the Christian. The charismatic renewal, characterized by a cultivation of the gifts of the Spirit, especially the prayer gifts, is one of several spiritual movements that have been leading in the renewal of the spiritual life of the people of the diocese.)

McKinney, Bishop Joseph. "An Open Letter to Catholic Charismatics." NC 3 (Sept.): 10–11.

O'Rourke, Edward, Bishop of Peoria. "Interview with Bishop O'Rourke." NC 3 (October): 15–16. (Deficiencies and dangers of the charismatic renewal.)

Suenens, Léon-Josef, Cardinal. "An interview with Cardinal Suenens." NC 3 (June): 1–5. (Charismatic renewal, corresponsibility, and institutional reform in the Church; the Cardinal's intervention on charisms at the Council; his relationship with Pope Paul.)

Suenens, Leon-Josef, Cardinal. "Mission for Tomorrow." NC 3 (July): 10–11. (Text of homily given at the concluding Mass of the International Charismatic Conference at Notre Dame, June 1–3.)

Suenens, Cardinal Leo Josef. "Come, Holy Spirit." NC 3 (Oct.): 7–8. (Excerpt from a talk given in Milwaukee: the importance of the charismatic renewal in the Church today.)

Suenens, Leon-Josef, Cardinal. "Redecouvrir le Saint-Esprit." Pastoral letter for Pentecost. (Brief exposition of the Charismatic Renewal against the background of the action and gifts of the Spirit.)

1974 Baum, William W., Archbishop of Washington. "The Holy Spirit and Prayer." Pastoral letter of July 14, 1974. (On the occasion of a Charismatic Day of Renewal held at the Catholic University of America. The role of the Holy Spirit and of community in Christian prayer.)

Dearden, John Cardinal, Archbishop of Detroit. "A Living Church." NC 4 (Nov.): 24–25. (Excerpts from homily on Pentecost Sunday at a Mass for charismatic Catholics.)

Suenens, Léon-Josef, Cardinal. "Charismatics at Notre Dame." *The National Catholic Register* (Sept. 1) p. 7. (Impressions of the Eighth International Conference of the

Charismatic Renewal in the Catholic Church, June 14–16, 1974.)

Uribe Jaramillo, Alfonso, Bishop of Sonson-Rionegro (Columbia). *El actual Pentecostes del Espíritu Santo.* Medellin, Columbia. (Booklet reviewing the doctrine of the Holy Spirit in the light of Vatican II, the teaching of recent Popes and the charismatic renewal.)

Watson, Alfred M., Bishop of Erie. Letter to his priests, July 22 urging them to cooperate with the renewal movement, and appointing a diocesan moderator for it.

1975   Committee for Pastoral Research and Practices, of the National Conference of Catholic Bishops. *Statement on Catholic Charismatic Renewal.* Publications Office, USCC, 1312 Massachusetts Avenue N.W., Washington, D.C. 20005.

Bishops of Canada. *Charismatic Renewal.* Message of the Canadian Bishops addressed to all Canadian Catholics. (Statement approved at the Bishops' meeting in Ottawa, April 14–18.) Canadian Catholic Conference, 90 Parent Ave., Ottawa Ontario K1N 7B1. (Published simultaneously in French.)

Lucey, Cornelius, Bishop of Cork and of Ross (Ireland). (Lenten letter to his diocese on new religious movements. Catholics are free to join the Renewal, but should not pin too much faith on it.)

V. PERIODICALS

New Covenant, edited by Ralph Martin, published at Ann Arbor, Mich., monthly since July, 1971.

The Pastoral Newsletter, edited by Ralph Martin, published at Ann Arbor, Mich., from June, 1970 until June, 1971, after which it was replaced by *New Covenant.*

New Creation: Journal of the Charismatic renewal movement in Ireland. Edited by Kay Donnelly, 2 Longford Terrace, Monkstown, Co. Dublin, Ireland.

Newsletter Serving the Charismatic Renewal Throughout Australia and the Pacific. Published at Red Hill, Q., Australia, beginning in October 1973.

One in Christ, edited by Dom Benedict Heron O.S.B. and R. M. Slade, at the Benedictine Convent, Priory Close, London N14 4AT

England. While devoted properly to the work of ecumenism, this journal frequently carries noteworthy articles on the charismatic renewal.

Alabare, a Spanish language equivalent of *New Covenant,* published at Box 1, Aguas Buenas, Puerto Rico, 00607.

La Chambre Haute, edited by Henri Caffarel (Bayard-Presse, 5 rue Bayard, 75380 Paris), bulletin appearing bi-monthly since January, 1973.

Magnificat, 2 Byzonder Weg, 3042 Lovenjoel, Belgium.

The Logos, edited by Rev. Eusebius Stephanou, at 2133 Embassy Drive, Fort Wayne, Ind. 46806. This periodical, founded in 1968, has the declared intention of "serving the charismatic renewal in the Orthodox Church". While it is not of course Roman Catholic, its affinity with Catholicism makes it worth being noted here.

Directory of Catholic Prayer Groups. A list of charismatic prayer groups of Catholic orientation compiled annually since 1969 at the Communication Center, P.O. Drawer A, Notre Dame, Indiana, 46556.

(A number of other newsletters serving local charismatic groups are listed in Father Louis P. Rogge's bibliography.)

VI. PREVIOUS BIBLIOGRAPHIES

(Only bibliographies which give material not retained here are listed.)

1971   Melton, John Gordon. *The Catholic Pentecostal Movement: a Bibliography,* Evanston, Ill., Garrett Theological Seminary Library; The Institute for the Study of American Religion, 1971. 20p. (Garrett bibliographical lectures, no. 7. A nearly exhaustive list of everything published on the subject to that date, including newspaper articles, mimeographed tracts, and leaflets of only local circulation. Classified and annotated. Marred by numerous misspellings of authors' names.)

O'Connor, Edward D., C.S.C. *The Pentecostal Movement in the Catholic Church,* Notre Dame, Ave Maria Press, 1971, pp. 295–301.

1973   Lambert, M. *Catholiques Pentecôtistes: Essai bibliographique de langue française.* I (Jan.) II (Dec.) Bureau de documentation pastorale (Chausée de Wayre 216, 1040 Bruxelles), Bulletins no. 6 and 9 (mimeographed).

Seguy, Jean. *Les conflits du dialogue*. Paris: Cerf. (Contains a bibliography on the Pentecostal movement, which, however, I have not had the opportunity to examine.)

1974   Hocken, Peter. "Pentecostals on Paper." *The Clergy Review*. Part I: Character and History. LIX, no. 11 (Nov.): 750–767 (a survey of some recent literature on Pentecostalism in all denominations); Part II: Baptism in the Spirit and Speaking in Tongues. LX, no. 3 (March 1975): 161–183; Part III: The Gifts of the Spirit and Distinctive Catholic Features. LX, no. 6 (June 1975): 344–367.

Laurentin, René. "Bibliographue sur le néo-Pentecôtisme catholique." *Pentecôtisme chez les catholiques* (Paris: Beauchesne) pp. 253–260. (Select, classified list of the chief works, mainly in English and French.)

Mühlen, Heribert gives a brief bibliography of the chief German literature in note 2 of his introduction to *Spontaner Glaube* (the German translation of my book, *The Pentecostal Movement...*), Herder, Freiburg etc., 1974, p. 255. It is repeated with slight modifications in his article, "Charismatisches und sakramentales Verstandnis der Kirche," *Catholica* 28: Heft 3.

Rogge, Louis P., O. Carm. "Charismatic Renewal and Traditional Pneumatology." (Mimeographed bibliography designed to accompany a course, classified according to topics.)

Rogge, Louis P., O. Carm. (A judicious and helpfully annotated bibliography of select material, compiled in conjunction with the preparation of a thesis. Mimeographed, but untitled.)

Anon. "Pentecostals." *Review for Religious* 33, no. 6 (Nov.): 1468.

NOTES

Introduction

1. Of course this movement had many historical roots, but if any one moment could be assigned as its birth, it would have to be January 1, 1901 in Topeka, Kansas.
2. Neils Bloch-Hoell, *The Pentecostal Movement: Its Origin, Development and Character* (Copenhagen, 1964).
3. Articles submitted for possible inclusion in future volumes will be welcomed.
4. The 1974 Synod of Roman Catholic Bishops spoke of "the Holy Spirit's action which overflows the bounds of the Christian community." (Declaration approved in the final general session, October 26, 1974, para. 11; *Osservatore Romano,* English ed., (Nov. 7, 1974): 3.)
5. Gerard M. Hopkins, "God's Grandeur," *Poems* (Oxford: Oxford University Press, 1948).
6. In the times foretold by Joel and announced by Peter, all are prophets in the sense that all are filled with the Spirit. For a Hebrew, to be filled with the Spirit meant, in effect, to be a prophet, to see visions and the like. The diversity of gifts in the New Covenant made it possible for St. Paul to distinguish between prophecy in the strict sense of acting as God's spokesman, and other gifts equally bestowed by the Holy Spirit (I Cor. 12:4). But prophecy remains, according to St. Thomas Aquinas, the chief of the *gratiae gratis datae* (*Summa Theologiae* II-II, 171ff).
7. Thus, St. Thomas Aquinas, *Summa Theologiae* I,32,I. But there have been serious Christian theologians who thought that reason could demonstrate the trinity of persons in God; thus St. Anselm and Abailard, to cite only the two classic examples.
8. Cf. S. Morenz, "Geist. I. Religionsgeschichtlich," *Religion und in Geschichte und Gegenwart* II (Tübingen: Mohr, 1958).

I. Prophecy in Israel

1. B. Duhm, *Israels Propheten* (1916; reprinted with a few changes, Tübingen: 1922).

2. K. Baltzer, "Considerations Regarding the Office and Calling of the Prophet," *Harvard Theological Review* 61 (1968): 567.

3. R. Rendtorff, "prophētēs; B. *nābî* in the Old Testament," *Theological Dictionary of the New Testament* VI (Grand Rapids: Eerdmans, 1968): 796. (Hereafter cited as *TDNT.*)

4. I. Engnell, *A Rigid Scrutiny* (Nashville: Vanderbilt University Press, 1969): 123.

5. Amaziah used one of the accepted names for prophet, *ḥōzeh,* literally "seer", the title given to Amos by the final editor of the book in 1:1.

6. The term "classical prophet" seems to have been standardized by W. Eichrodt, *Theology of the Old Testament* (Philadelphia: Westminster Press, 1961): 338–391—translated from the 6th German ed. 1959; the 1st ed. appeared in 1933. Eichrodt's discussion of Israel's charismatic leadership—seers, nazirites, judges, nabism and classical prophecy—remains the best in any language for an overall comparative study (pages 289–391).

7. In the Hebrew canon, Daniel is placed among the *Writings,* which include smaller collections like the psalms or the five liturgical *megilloth* (Ruth, Song of Songs, etc.) and end with Daniel, Ezra, Nehemiah and I-II Chronicles. Daniel seldom enters a discussion of prophecy, unless a very late apocalyptic form of it.

8. We discussed this aspect in our article, "A Community Assesses Its Prophets," *Sisters Today* 45 (January 1974): 243–259.

9. The necessary relationship of prophets to Israel's covenantal or traditional religion is vigorously presented by R. E. Clements, "Prophecy and Covenant," *Studies in Biblical Theology,* no. 43 (Naperville: Allenson, 1965) and Walter Brueggemann, *Tradition for Crisis: A Study in Hosea* (Richmond: John Knox Press, 1968); W. G. Williams, "Tension and Harmony Between Classical Prophecy and Classical Law," *Transitions in Biblical Scholarship: Essays in Divinity* VI (Chicago: University of Chicago Press: 1968): 71–91.

10. Jesus' image as prophet is underlined by Luke. See the classic study of Felix Gils, *Jésus Prophète* (Louvain: Publications Universitaires, 1957); Joachim Jeremias, *New Testament Theology: The Proclamation of Jesus* (New York: Scribner's, 1971): 76ff; and the extensive bibliography in John Reumann, *Jesus in the Church's Gospels* (Philadelphia: Fortress, 1968): 398, fn 3, accompanying pages 219–222.

11. Cf. J. Lindblom, *Prophecy in Ancient Israel* (Philadelphia: Fortress, 1973, reprint from Blackwell ed. of 1962): 48, "Of the beginnings of prophecy in Israel we know nothing," that is, in detail, about the way Israel absorbed this institution from the Canaanites (cf. Lindblom, p. 97) or about Israel's connections with earlier Mesopotamian forms of prophecy.

12. Cf. J. A. Wilcoxen, "Narrative Structure and Cult Legend: A Study of Joshua 1–6," *Transitions in Biblical Scholarship* (see fn. 9)

43–70; J. Harvey, "La Typologie de l'Exode dans les Psaumes," *Sciences Ecclésiastiques* 15 (1963): 383–405; L. Sabourin, *The Psalms: Their Origin and Meaning.* 2 ed (New York: Alba House, 1974): 138–9; in the earlier two volume edition (1969) I: 142–3.

13. The seventy elders who received the spirit in the days of Moses remained in ecstasy only a very short while (Num. 11:14–17, 24–30). Lindblom, p. 102 fn. 11, thinks that this section of the Pentateuch is an attempt to justify the more permanent form of ecstasy at a later date. M. Noth, *Numbers* (Philadelphia: Westminster Press, 1968): 87–90 indicates how these verses are a later addition to the earlier form of "J" or "E". J. DeVaulx, *Les Nombres: Sources Bibliques* (Paris: Gabalda, 1972): 153–5, recognizes later prophetic forms inserted into the earlier text of "E".

14. Only here in I Sam. 10:5 is Gibeah given the double name *Gibeath-elohim.*

15. F. Brown, S. R. Driver, & C. A. Briggs, *A Hebrew and English Lexicon of the Old Testament* (Oxford: Clarendon Press, 1953): 29.

16. Cf. A. Gelin, "The Latter Prophets," *Introduction to the Old Testament,* A. Robert & A. Feuillet, ed. (New York: Desclée, 1968): 232; R. Rendtorff in *TDNT* VI: 796–7 gives further references.

17. Normally in Semitic languages like Hebrew, nouns are derived from a verb form. Just the opposite happened in the case of *nābî'*, an indication how Israel's *active* performance of prophesying gradually changed the meaning of the noun, borrowed from non-Israelite sources. Amos rejected the noun but applied the verb to himself, thus changing the sense of the former.

18. In the account of the burning bush (Exod. chap. 3) the verb *rā'āh* ("to see") occurs six times in the first four verses and leads up to the great revelation of the divine name *Yahweh* and the commissioning of Moses.

19. Cf. R. Rendtorff, "The Concept of Revelation in Ancient Israel," *Revelation as History,* ed. W. Pannenberg (New York: Macmillan, 1968): 29.

20. A. Heschel, *The Prophets* (New York: Harper & Row, 1962): 444.

21. Samuel combined several of these offices with charismatic prophecy, but his case was rare.

22. I Kings 20:35ff; II Kings 1:8; Isa. 20:2; Zech. 13:4–6.

23. I Kings 22:1–6, 10–12, II Kings 4:38–44.

24. Num. 22:7; Mic. 3:11; Ezek. 13:19.

25. i.e., the ax is borrowed in II Kings 6:5.

26. I Kings 20:35ff; II Kings 2:9; 6:1ff.

27. II Kings 4:1ff; also Samuel was married (I Sam. 8:1–5).

28. There is no indication that Elijah or Elisha were married. Cf. I Kings 17–II Kings 18.

29. For a long description, see Lindblom pp. 65–82, fn. 11.

30. Although Bible translations in this article generally reproduce what I consider the best all-purpose rendition into English, the *New American Bible (NAB)*, prepared by members of the Catholic Biblical Association of America and sponsored by the Bishops' Committee of the Confraternity of Christian Doctrine (Paterson, NJ: St. Anthony Guild Press, 1970), in a few instances I prefer a variation, as here in the tense of the verbs. *NAB* reads: "I *was* no prophet..."

31. "The Lord *took* me" translates the Hebrew *lāqaḥ* which implies a strong initiative on God's part. This verb is employed in the Hebrew Bible, for instance, in Gen. 5:24 and II Kings 2:3 of the Lord's taking Enoch and Elijah to himself. Cf. K. Baltzer, cited in note 2.

32. A study of the *word* in the book of Amos reveals a profound psychological transition. Ecstatic prophets announced God's word in an evidently wondrous way, with melody, dance and unrecognizable sounds. Amos spoke the people's language so well and laid bare the sordid realities of life so clearly that he usually prefaced his remarks with "Hear this word [*of mine*]" and his book is introduced with "The words of Amos," in Hebrew *dibrê Amos,* the plural of *dābār.* The final editor in 7:16 calls this wide range of human reactions on Amos' part "the word of the Lord," in Hebrew, *debar yahweh.* See our study, "The Creative Word of Yahweh," *Creative Redemption in Deutero-Isaiah* (Rome: Biblical Institute Press, 1970) chap. 7.

33. A. Heschel, *The Prophets,* p. 360.

34. Against the position of such authors as J. Vollmer, *Geschichte Rückblicke und Motive in der Prophetie des Amos, Hosea und Jesaja.* BZAW, 119 (Berlin-New York: de Gruyter, 1967), who claim that Amos advocated an abrupt break in Israel's institutions and a final judgment at hand, ending Israelite history and tradition. This question has already been touched upon in this article.

35. Cf. W. Brueggemann, "Amos IV 4–13: Israel's Covenant Worship," *Vetus Testamentum* 15 (1965): 1–15.

36. Cf. H. W. Wolff, *Dodekapropheton Amos: Biblischer Kommentar AT XIV:6* (Neukirchen-Vluyn, 1967): 109–117. See also the popular monograph of Wolff, *Amos the Prophet* (Philadelphia: Fortress, 1973), better entitled in its German original, "Amos' Spiritual Homeland"; C. Westermann, *Basic Forms of Prophetic Speech* (Philadelphia: Westminister Press, 1968).

37. Not only did Amos reject the title *nābî'* but the majority of the classical prophets seldom if ever applied the title to themselves. It occurs only in the biographical parts, written about Jeremiah (*i.e.,* Jer. 20:2), and is frequently employed only by the prophet Ezekiel who reversed the whole classical movement and redirected its attention back to temple and priesthood as the major source of salvation.

38. Cf. C. Stuhlmueller, *The Prophets and the Word of God.* 2 ed. (Notre Dame: Fides, 1966) chap. 1.

39. Cf. G. Montague, *The Biblical Theology of the Secular* (Milwaukee:

Bruce, 1968); W. Brueggemann, *In Man We Trust: The Neglected Side of Biblical Faith* (Richmond: John Knox Press, 1972); and the classic work of G. von Rad, *Wisdom In Israel* (Nashville: Abingdon, 1972).

40. This humanization and control of the divine are clearly brought out in the symposium of essays by H. Frankfort and others, *The Intellectual Adventure of Ancient Man* (Chicago: University of Chicago Press, 1946), reprinted in paperback under a less felicitous title *Before Philosophy* (Penguin Books, 1949).

41. Cf. J. F. Ross, "The Prophet as Yahweh's Messenger," *Israel's Prophetic Heritage.* J. Muilenburg Festschrift (New York: 1962): 98–107; N. Habel, "The Form and Significance of the Call Narrative," *Zeitschrift für Alttestamentliche Wissenschaft* 77 (1965) 297–323.

42. J. D. G. Dunn, "New Wine in Old Wine-Skins: VI. Prophets," *Expository Times* 85 no. 1 (Oct. 1973): 7. Dunn rightly stresses the continuous way the classical prophet referred to a divine compulsion or to an extraordinary experience of God. Cf. our own article, "The Theology of Vocation according to Jeremiah the Prophet," *The Bible Today Reader* (Collegeville: Liturgical Press, 1973): 224–230, reprinted from *The Bible Today* 58 (Feb. 1972): 609–615.

43. One of the latest, comprehensive studies is W. E. March, "Prophecy," *Old Testament Form Criticism,* ed. J. H. Hayes (San Antonio: Trinity University Press, 1974) chap. 4, 141–177. To discern how the classical prophets are comparable to the prophets at Mari in Mesopotamia, yet much less reliant upon superstitious counter-checks in haruspex, and so seemingly less sacred and more secular, see W. L. Moran, "New Evidence from Mari on the History of Prophecy," *Biblica* 50, no. 1 (1969): 15–56.

44. Cf. C. Stuhlmueller, "Amos, Desert-Trained Prophet," *The Bible Today Reader,* 194–200, (see fn. 42); or A. Gelin's conclusion that "Like St. Paul and Teresa of Avila, Ezekiel was perhaps afflicted with epilepsy, but (by way of a backhand compliment) he was certainly not a deranged person," *Introduction to the Old Testament,* 322 (see fn. 16).

45. For these human factors in the lowly origin and diffusion of such an extraordinary invention, see the informative article of P. Kyle McCarter, "The Early Diffusion of the Alphabet," *The Biblical Archaeologist* 37 no. 3 (Sept. 1974): 54–68.

46. Little wonder then that Elijah and Elisha became symbolic of mysterious characters in Mal. 3:1 and 23 (cf. Matt. 17:10–23). Cf. *Elie le prophète.* 2 vols. (Paris: Desclée de Brouwer, 1956).

47. A. Heschel, *The Prophets* p. 257 (see fn. 20).

48. R. E. Clements, *Prophecy and Covenant,* pp. 12–13 (fn. 9).

49. C. Stuhlmueller, "The New Exodus," *Creative Redemption,* chap. 4, (fn. 32).

50. Therefore, Jesus permitted most details about the future organization of the Church to be worked out in the future. Jesus' main legacy was the thrust of ideals and choice of disciples.

51. Cf. A. Heschel, *The Prophets,* p. 185 (fn. 20). "History is not a blind alley, and guilt is not an abyss. There is always a way that leads out of guilt: repentance or turning to God. The prophet is a person who, living in dismay, has the power to transcend his dismay. Over all the darkness of experience hovers the vision of a different day."

52. I. Engnell, *A Rigid Scrutiny,* p. 170, exaggerates but is not totally wrong: "the predictions of the false prophets were sometimes fulfilled and . . . to a great extent, the predictions of the genuine prophets were not fulfilled."

53. Here would be the place to discuss further the criterion for true and false prophets. If fulfillment of prophecy, at least according to the understanding of its first speaker, is not sufficient, other criteria enter: perseverance within Israel and continuous fidelity to Yahweh, personal disinterestedness, fidelity and honesty. Cf. Rendtorff, *Prophètes,* pp. 804–7, and the controversial book of J. L. Crenshaw, *Prophetic Conflict: Its Effect Upon Israelite Religion,* BZAW (Berlin-New York: de Gruyter, 1971) p. 124. Even when Second-Isaiah discussed prophecy-fulfillment in a series of passages on "First and Last," many questions remained unanswered, and the future can always take one by surprise (cf. Isa. 48:3, 6b–7). See also *Creative Redemption,* chap. 6, fn. 32.

II: Inspiration

1. Sextus Empiricus, *Adversus Mathematicos* IX.20–24 (*Adversus Physicos* I. 20–24).

2. Cicero, *De Divinatione* I.30.62ff., and II.53.119; Diogenes Laertius VIII.24.

3. "Full of the god" or *entheos* means that a god has entered the human person and uses his or her vocal organs as if they were his own. See Cicero, *De Devinatione* I.67ff.; Plato, *Apology,* 22C; Plato, *Meno* 99C; Plato (?), *Ion* 534C.

4. Plato, (?) *Ion* 534C.

5. Plato, *Menexenus* 99C ff.

6. Plato, *Phaedrus* 244A ff.

7. According to Plato, *Timaeus* 71E, sickness is one of the conditions which favor the emergence of supernatural powers. See also Aristotle, *Divinatio per Somnium* 646a. 24.

8. Xenophon, *Apology of Socrates* 30 and *Cyropaedia* VIII.7.19ff.

9. Plato, *Apology* 39C and the *Republic* 571D ff.

10. Cicero, *De Divinatione* I.50, 113–114.

11. *Ibid.* I. 30.63.

12. Plato, *Republic* 571D ff.

13. Herodotus I. 30.
14. Homer, *Iliad* II.5ff, IV. 795ff., VI. 13ff., *et passim.*
15. Herodotus, V.56., VII.12, *et passim.*
16. Plato, *Crito* 44A ff.
17. Tertullian, *De Anima* 44.1.
18. Al-Kindi, *Cod. Taimuriyye Falsafa* 55.
19. Al-Kindi, *loc. cit.*
20. Plato, *Apology* 39C; Xenophon, *Defence of Socrates* 30; Plato, *Phaedo* 84E.
21. Homer, *Iliad* XVI. 851.
22. Homer, *Iliad* XXII. 356.
23. Michael Psellus, *Scholion ad Johannem Climacum* 6.171.
24. Dio Chrysostom (Dio of Prusa), *Olympic Discourse or On Man's First Conceptions of God,* Oratio XII 27ff.
25. Plutarch, *Moralia (De Tranquillitate Animi)* 447C ff.
26. Aristotle, *Eudemian Ethics* 1248 a 23 ff.
27. See note 29, *infra.*
28. Homer, *Odyssey* VIII. 44, and VIII. 498.
29. According to Homer, *Odyssey* XXII. 347 ff., Phemius declares: "I am self-taught. . . . It was a god who implanted all sorts of lays in my mind." Here speaks the creative poet whose verses suddenly and spontaneously well up out of some unknown and uncontrollable depth as he needs them. "He "sings out of the gods," as the best minstrels always do. See here also Homer, *Odyssey* VIII. 487 ff., *et passim;* Hesiod, *Theogony* 94 ff.
30. Plato, *Phaedrus* 244A ff.: "Our greatest blessings come to us by way of madness. . . , provided it is given to us by divine gift." According to Greek tradition, there are four forms of "divine madness," namely, prophetic madness, sent by Apollo; ritual madness, sent by Dionysius; poetic madness, inspired by the Muses; and erotic madness, a gift of Aphrodite and Eros. See Plato, *loc. cit supra,* this note., and *ibid.,* 265B. —*Ate* (sense of guilt), according to Homer, *Iliad* IX. 505 ff., and *ibid.,* XIX. 91 ff.; XIX. 270 ff., *et passim,* is actually a state of mind and, as a matter of fact, a sort of "temporary insanity" due to some daemonic force or agency. It is not necessarily an act of revenge or, perhaps, the punishment for some wrong committed, but an "abnormal state of mind." It is, in the final analysis, a supernatural interference with human behavior. In *Odyssey* XVIII. 327, and *ibid.,* XX. 377, Homer seems to imply that insanity or mental disease is of supernatural origin.
31. Plato, *Phaedrus* 265B.
32. Homer, *Iliad* I. 69 ff.
33. Plato, *Meno* 98D ff.
34. Plato, *Meno* 100A.
35. Pythagoras founded a sort of religious community which included both men and women. The rules of this community were

determined by the expectation of lives yet to come. Pythagoras himself seems to have combined in his person the indifferentiated functions of a wonderworker, magician, poet, philosopher, sage, preacher, prophet, healer and public councellor. It is fairly safe to assume that Pythagoras and the Pythagoreans taught (1) that the body is the prison of the soul (a notion also adopted by Plato); (2) that vegetarianism is an essential rule of life; and (3) that the unpleasant consequences of sin, both in this world and in the next world, can be "washed away" by religious rituals. See also Plato, *Cratylus* 400C; and *Republic* 364E ff.—The "guardians" in Plato's *Republic* may possibly be nothing else than "westernized shamans." These "guardians," like the Asiatic shamans, are trained for their high office by a special kind of discipline and instruction. Both must be dedicated to a way of life which cuts them off from average men. They both, the Platonic "guardian" and the shaman, renew their contact with the ultimate source of wisdom by periodic retreats; and they both will be rewarded after death by receiving a special status in the "world beyond." It is possible that this sort of "elitism," which becomes manifest in Plato's *Republic*, already was propagated by Pythagoras and the Pythagoreans and, ultimately, by the Asiatic shamans.

36. In a certain way this is also true as regards the Platonic Academy during the scholarchate of Plato.

37. Plato, *Phaedo* 67B, and *ibid.*, 82D.

38. Plato, *Sophist* 226D ff.; Plato, *Laws* 735B ff., and *ibid.*, 815C; 831A; 865A ff.; 868A ff.; 869A ff.; 871B; 881B ff.; 916C.

39. Plato, *Republic* 500Bff.

40. Parmenides, frag. B 1. 2, Diels-Kranz.

41. Diogenes Laertius IX. 2 and 5.

42. Herclitus, frag. B 50, Diels-Kranz.

43. Lucretius, *De Rerum Natura* I. 731ff.

44. Plato, *Apology* 22B.

45. Plato, *Phaedrus* 245A.

46. Democritus, frag. B 17; frag. B 18, Diels-Kranz.

47. Plato (?) *Ion* 534C.

48. Aeschylus, *Eumenides* 62.

49. Plato, *Laws* 682A.

50. Hesiod, *Theogony* 94ff., states that by the grace of the Muses, some men are poets. In other words, the art of the poet is a divine gift. See also Homer, *Iliad* I.1; III, 65ff; Homer, *Odyssey* I.1.

51. Amos 1:1.

52. Obadiah 1:1.

53. Micah 1:1.

54. *Adversus Mathematicos* IX. 20–24, or, *Adversus Physicos* I. 20–24.

55. IX. 26–27, or, *Adversus Physicos* I. 26–27.

56. Philo of Alexandria, *Legum Allegoriarum Libri Tres* III. 32.97—99.

57. Philo of Alexandria, *De Praemiis et Poenis* VII. 40–46.
58. Philo of Alexandria, *De Specialibus Legibus* I. 35, 185–36.194.
59. Cicero, *De Natura Deorum* II. 37. 95–96.
60. Sextus Empiricus, *Adversus Mathematicos* IX.20–24 (*Adversus Physicos* I. 20–24), is frag. 12, Rose²; frag. 10, Rose³; frag. 12a, Walzer; frag. 12a, Ross; frag. 14, Untersteiner, of Aristotle's lost dialogue *On Philosophy*. Sextus Empiricus, *Adversus Mathematicos* IX. 26–27 (*Adversus Physicos* I. 26–27), is frag. 13, Rose², frag. 11, Rose³; frag. 12b, Walzer; frag. 12b, Ross; frag. 26, Untersteiner, of Aristotle's *On Philosophy*. Philo of Alexandria, *Legum Allegoriarm Libri Tres* III. 32. 97–99, is frag. 14, Rose²; frag. 12, Rose³; frag. 13, Walzer; frag. 13, Ross; frag. 15, Untersteiner, of Aristotle's *On Philosophy*. Philo of Alexandria, *De Praemiis et Poenis* VI. 40–46, is frag. 13, Walzer; frag. 13, Ross; frag. 16, Untersteiner, of Aristotle's *On Philosophy*. Philo of Alexandria, *De˙ Specialibus Legibus* I. 35. 185–36. 194, is frag. 13, Walzer; frag. 13, Ross; frag. 16, Untersteiner, of Aristotle's *On Philosophy*. Cicero, *De Natura Deorum* II. 37. 95–96, is frag. 14, Rose²; frag. 12, Rose³; frag. 13, Walzer; frag. 13, Ross; frag. 18, Untersteiner, of Aristotle's *On Philosophy*.
61. Plato, *Laws* 966D.
62. Sextus Empiricus, *Adversus Mathematicos* IX. 20–24 (*Adversus Physicos* I. 20–24.)
63. Philo of Alexandria, *De Praemiis et Poenis* VII. 41–43.
64. Philo of Alexandria, *De Specialibus Legibus* III. 35. 185ff. In the *De Opificio Mundi* II. 7, Philo of Alexandria insists that "there are people who are awed more by the universe than by the Creator of this universe and, hence, insist that this universe is without beginning and everlasting . . . whereas on the contrary we ought to be astonished by His powers as the Creator and Father, and not to assign to the universe a disproportionate majesty."

III: Source of Life

1. H. B. Swete, *The Holy Spirit in the Ancient Church* (London, 1912) 430 pp.; Hugo Rahner, *Earth Spirit and Divine Spirit in Patristic Theology*, Eranos Yearbook Series XXX, no. 1; G. Kretschmar, *Le développment de la doctrine du St. Esprit du N.T. à Nicée* (Vigil, Christmas 1963), pp. 5–51; G. Verbeke, *L'Evolution de la doctrine du Pneuma du Stoicisme à Augustin* (Paris, 1945), 570 pp. among others.
2. Basil, *On the Spirit* 19, *Library of Nicene and Post-Nicene Fathers* VIII (Grand Rapids: Eerdmans Publishing Co.): 31–31 (hereafter cited as LNPF); Gregory Nazianzen, *Fifth Theological Oration* 29, the names of the Holy Spirit; Augustine, *De Trinitate* XV, 19.

3. For this inquiry I rely on a limited number of sources, namely, *Ascension of Isaiah* (hereafter cited as *Ascension*), *Apostolic Tradition, Didascalia Apostolorum, Hermas,* Ignatius of Antioch, the apologists (except for Athenagoras *On the Resurrection* and *The Epistle to Diognetus*), *Odes of Solomon,* Irenaeus (except for books I and II Melito Tertullian, Cyprian, Clement of Alexandria, Origen's *First Principles* (hereafter cited as *First Princ.*), *Dialogue with Heraclides* (hereafter cited as *Dial. Hera.*), *Contra Celsum, Commentary on Song of Songs* (hereafter cited as *Com. Song.*), *On Prayer, On Martyrdom*; among the post-Nicene fathers, *The Life of Antony,* Ambrose (*De sacramentis* and *De mysteriis*). Cyril of Jerusalem (*Catecheses* and *Mystagogical Homilies*). I quote preferably English translations, because of the destination of the present book, but often I change the wording of these translations when it is obsolete.

4. Athenagoras, *A Plea for the Christians* 4–6, The Ante-Nicene Fathers II (Grand Rapids: Eerdmans Publishing Co.):131 (hereafter cited as ANF).

5. Tatian, *Adress to the Greeks* 4, ANF II, 66–70.

6. Tertullian, *Adversus Praxeas* 7 (hereafter cited as *Adv. Prax.*). Demons are material, and, living in the heavy atmosphere, they feed on the heavy smoke of sacrifices. Cf. Origen, *On Martyrdom* 45, Ancient Christian Writers (Westminster: The Newman Press):188 (hereafter cited as ACW).

7. Theophilus of Antioch, *Ad Autolycus* II, 15, ANF II:101 (hereafter cited as *Ad. Autol.*).

8. Justin *Apology* I, 13, ANF I:166–167; cf. ibid. 59–60: 182–183.

9. Athenagoras, *A Plea for the Christians* 24, ANF II.

10. Irenaeus, *Adv. Haer.* V, 5:1.

11. Tertullian, *Adv. Prax.* 2, ANF III:598.

12. For Clement, cf. *Exhortation,* ANF II:171ff; for Origen, cf. *First. Princ.,* English trans. by G. W. Butterworth, Harper Torchbooks, 1966. Origen, *First Princ.* 1:3.

13. Verbeke, *op. cit.* p. 1–374, explains the various notions of spirit in Stoicism, the medical schools, religious syncretism and magic, and Neoplatonism. Then, p. 387–489, he explains the influence of these schools, especially of Stoicism, upon the Apologists, Clement of Alexandria, Tertullian, Origen, Lactantius, Apollinaris, and Augustine. He notices the presence of a biblical notion of the *pneuma* (cf. *Wisdom of Solomon,* Philo of Alexandria, Paul) in these authors. In fact, however, he is not interested in a thorough investigation of the specifically biblical and Christian notion of the spirit of God and its implications in Christian anthropology, sacramental theology, and charismatic life. His contribution is a study of the Greek notion of spirit in the Fathers, especially the influence of Stoicism and the medical schools. It is not without interest to notice in the apologists that Stoic cosmology, with the *pneuma* as a power of cohesion and

unity, is completed by the affirmation of the transcendance of God and even of the Spirit of God. It is still more interesting to know that their anthropology, even that of Clement (*Strom.* VI, 16) and of Origen (*Contra Celsum* VII, 32; IV, 22–23; *First Princ.* II, 10:3, Butterworth p. 141) includes a kind of spirit, typical of Stoicism and of the medical schools, located between the soul and the body, and distinguished from the Spirit of God and even from the divine spirit in man (*Contra Celsum* II, 72; VI, 70). Among the Gnostics, who make a large use of the notion of spirit, let us mention the *Excerpts of Theodotus* found in Clement of Alexandria (cf. F. Sagnard, *Clément d'Alexandrie. Extraits de Thédote, Sources Chrétiennes*, Paris 1948).

14. In Paul, *Rom.* 2:28; 5:5; 5:21; 7:6; 8:1; 12:6; I *Cor.* 2:10; 3:1; 3:16; 10:3; 10:14; 12:27; 15:44; II *Cor.* 1:21; 2:15; 3:17; 4:13; 5:2; 7:14; 12:7; *Gal.* 5:17; 6:1; *Eph.* 1:13; 1:18; 4:4; 4:22; 6:16; *Phil.* 3:3; *Col.* 3:10; I *Thes.* 5:19; 5:23; II *Tim.* 2:18; 3:16; *Titus* 3:4.

15. *Ascension* (E. Tisserand, Paris 1909), the Angel of the Spirit, III, 16; VIII, 14; IX, 36, 39; XI, 4.

16. *Hermas, Vision* 5, for the Son; cf. J. Daniélou, *The Theology of the Jewish Christianity*, London 1964, p. 199 ff; for the Holy Spirit, *Mandatum* 11, cf. Daniélou, *ibid.* p. 142–144.

17. *Ascension* III, 23–31; IV, 17: XI, 40.

18. Irenaeus, *Adv. Haer.* VI, 36, ANF I.

19. *Wisdom of Solomon* 1:7; 8:22ff.

20. *Contra Celsum* III, 3, 5; IV, 7; VIII, 48 (cf. English tr. by H. Chadwick, Cambridge Univ. Press, 1965); Cyril of Jerusalem, *Catechesis* 16:17, LNPF VII.

21. M. J. Weaver, '*Pneuma*' *in Philo of Alexandria*, Ph.D. Thesis, Notre Dame Univ. 1973.

22. Theophilus of Antioch, *Ad Autol.* I, 2; Irenaeus, *Demonstration of the Gospel* 97; Origen, *Com. Song* II (ACW): 1–2; Athanasius, *De Incarnatione* 14; Gregory of Nyssa, *On the Making of Man* 16, ACW: 91–118.

23. Gregory Nazianzen, *Theological Orations* V, 29; Clement, *Strom.* IV, 23, 26.

24. Clement, *Pedagogue* I, 6, 35–36 (hereafter cited as *Ped.*); *Strom.* V, 11–13; Cyril of Jerusalem *Catecheses* 16:12–17.

25. Ignatius of Antioch, *To Romans*, 7:2–3; 9:3, "My spirit greets you."

26. Clement. *Strom.* III 93; IV, 26.

27. *Didascalia Apostolorum* ch. 26 (Connolly p. 242ff, Oxford: Clarendon Press, 1969).

28. *Eph.* 4:22; *Col.* 3:10.

29. Tatian, *Address to the Greeks*, 13–14.

30. In spite of M. Richard; cf. A. Grillmeier, *Christ in Christian Tradition*, London 1965, ch. 2, p. 193–219.

31. Tertullian, *Adversus Marcionem* IV, 10, ANF III.
32. Tertullian, *De anima* 14.
33. *ibid.* 11.
34. *Ad Valentinianos* 26.
35. *ibid.* 10.
36. *Adv. Prax.* 7; cf. Verbeke, *op. cit.* p. 445.
37. Irenaeus, *Adv. Haer.* V, 9.
38. *ibid.* V, 12. An excellent theology of the operations of the Holy Spirit is found in Novatian, *On the Trinity*, chap. 29, ANF 5: 640–641.
39. Origen, *Homily I On Genesis (Sources Chrétiennes);* cf. Clement of Alexandria, *Strom.* III, 93, LCC vol. II.
40. Origen, *First Princ.* II, 8 (Butterworth p. 127–128); cf. *Contra Celsum* VII, 32 for another kind of spirit in the irrational part of the soul.
41. Origen, *Dialogue with Heraclides* 136–140, LCC II, p. 442–443.
42. Philo, *Legum Allegoriae* I, 31–42; cf. J. Laporte, "La chute chez Philon et Origène," *Kyriakon*, Festschrift J. Quasten, 1 (Münster 1971): 323ff.
43. Irenaeus, *Demonstration* 42.
44. *Didascalia* XX, Connolly p. 174.
45. *ibid.* XX, p. 167.
46. *Dialogue* 132, LCC II, p. 440.
47. *ibid.* 144–167, LCC II, p. 444–453.
48. *First Princ.* II, 2, 3, 10; *Contra Celsum* III, 41–42 (for the body of Jesus); V, 22–23; VII, 32.
49. Tertullian, *De Carne Christi* 33; Irenaeus, *Adv. Haer.* V, 7.
50. For the resurrection of the body in Augustine, see *City of God* XIII, 17–24; XXI, 1–11; XXII, 11–30. We have the same organs, without using them because there is no need for it, and the law of gravity is suspended, which makes the heavenly journey possible. The body is spiritual, because the soul is itself under the life-giving influence of the Spirit of God. But there is no change in the structure of the body in order to fit the conditions of another world. For Athanasius, see *On the Incarnation:* Christ in his earthly body was liable to suffering and death, but not to disease and corruption, therefore, the resurrection of his body was only the return of his soul. Our resurrected body, similarly, will be the same as before the fall, i.e., not liable to disease and death. Christ restored in his own body as in a pattern the primitive condition of the human body. The Word of God, which is the pattern for man, came into the flesh in order to restore in every regard man, or mankind, created in the beginning according to the divine image. The intervention of the Holy Spirit does not appear; the Word of God, by His divine power, achieves everything, including the Incarnation.
51. Gregory of Nyssa is closer to Origen on the subject of the resurrection of the body. The latter teaches both the resurrection and

the transformation of the body by the power of the Spirit of God. In *On the Making of Man* 16 (LNPF V, p. 404–406), Gregory teaches the resurrection of the body, according to the pattern which it was supposed to have had, if the expectation of sin had not led Divine Providence to substitute the body of the brute for it. In this present body, man cannot sin with an absolute will, like demons, but he finds an opportunity either to indulge the passions or to develop the virtues corresponding to these passions (*ibid.* chap. 11, p. 396); he can also take advantage of Christ and the sacraments. As for the body of the resurrection, which is our genuine body, it is vain to make conjectures regarding its shape and detail.

    52. *Didascalia* 20 (Connolly p. 168); Cyril of Jer., *Catecheses* 18:11.

    53. Irenaeus, *Adv. Haer.* V, 15:1.

    54. *ibid.* V, 15:1.

    55. Basil, *On the Spirit* 19, LNPF VIII, p. 31.

    56. Ps. 51:10–12 :Basil, *ibid.* 19, p. 30; Clement, *Strom.* I, 8:4; Ps. 39:7. Basil, *ibid.* 23, p. 35; Ps. 33:6 Basil, *ibid.* 19, p. 31.

    57. Irenaeus, *Adv. Haer.* V, 7:1.

    58. Eusebius, *Ecclesiastical History,* V, 24:4–6.

    59. *ibid.* III, 31.

    60. Irenaeus, *Adv. Haer.* V, 11:1; Origen, *On Prayer* 9–10.

    61. *Dial. Hera.* 152–160, LCC II: 447–450.

    62. Origen, *First Princ. Preface.*

    63. *De Trinitate,* books II, III. Augustine ascribes the theophanies, or interventions of the Word of God in the Old Testament, to the operations of the essence of God directly, and indirectly to the whole Trinity, thus putting an end to the old biblical tradition of the Living Word of God directly efficient, prophetic, creator, and to a similar, though less monopolysing tradition on the Spirit of God.

    64. Justin, *Dialogue* 87, ANF I, p. 243 (hereafter cited as *Dial*).

    65. Justin, *Dial* 87; Origen, *Com. on Song,* pr. 3.

    66. Tertullian, *De cultu feminarum* I, 3. For the notion of the prophetic spirit in antiquity and in Philo, see Hans Lewy, *Sobria ebrietas, Untersuchungen zur Geschichte der antiken Mystik*, Giessen Toepelmann 1929, 175p. The Christians, following Philo, adopted the Greek notion of inspiration and ecstasy, but they regularly ascribe their prophetic inspiration to the Spirit of God, who uses the prophet like a musical instrument (Athenagoras, *A Plea for the Christians,* 7–10; Justin, *Dial.* 24; 77; Clement, *Ped.* II, 6; *Odes of Solomon* 6; 14; 28). They contrast it with the demonic inspiration of the pagans, especially of the Pythia of Delphi (Athenagoras, *A Plea for the Christians,* 26–27; *Contra Celsum* II, 25; VIII, 48). According to the Christians the prophets, though inspired in ecstasy, are not without any activity of their mind—at least as they understood what they were told by the Spirit, including the deeper meaning of the Redemption through Christ and the Church. Likewise moral dispositions are required of

them, since "prophets are reliable witnesses who are ready to give up their own life for the truth" (*Contra Celsum* VII, 3–4). The gift of prophecy seems to include the gift of knowledge and wisdom, according to Origen (*Contra Celsum* III, 18; cf. *Odes* 36). According to the Christians, inspiration among the pagans, except for the poets (Theophilus, *Ad Autol.* II, 7–8 and Clement *Strom.* I, 17), comes from demons who send visions and live on sacrifices. It is either devoid of any moral connotation, or occurs in the case of the weak or the wicked.

67. Justin, *Apology* I, 31; Clement, *Strom.* I, 22:1; 149:3.

68. Tertullian, *Adv. Prax.* 27, ANF III, p. 624.

69. Clement, *Strom.* III, 83–84. Origen, *First Princ.*, Preface; *Contra Celsum* V, 33; VI, 68.

70. Origen, *Dial.* 2; *Contra Celsum* I, 32; Cyril, *Catecheses* 12:22; Ambrose, *De sacramentis* IV, 12.

71. Tertullian, *Adv. Prax.* 26.

72. *ibid.* 27.

73. Irenaeus, *Adv. Haer.* V, 12:3.

74. Irenaeus, *Adv. Haer,* V, 3; IIII, 16:1.

75. *ibid.* III, 17 ANF I, p. 444.

76. Justin, *Dial.* 87; Irenaeus, *Adv. Haer.* III, 18:3; *Demonstration* 9; *Didascalia* 23 (Connolly, p. 198–199).

77. Origen, *Contra Celsum* VII, 44.

78. *First Princ.* I, 3, Butterworth, p. 38–39.

79. *ibid.* II, 10:5, Butterworth p. 141–143.

80. *ibid.* II, 10, 7, Butterworth p. 144–145.

81. Origen, *Homilies on Numbers,* for instance, Hom. 27; *Homilies on Matthew,* Book XI, 5, ANF X, p. 434.

82. *Dial.* 163, LCC II, p. 453.

83. *First Princ.* I, 6; II, 3, 11.

84. *Contra Celsum,* VI, 81.

85. *Dial. Hera.,* 144ff, especially p. 150, LCC II, p. 446.

86. *Ped.* I, 6, ANF II, p. 217.

87. *Adv. Haer.* III, 24, ANF I, p. 458.

88. *De Praescriptione* 37.

89. *Didascalia* 9, (Connolly p. 93).

90. Ambrose, *De sacramentis* I, 14; VI, 5.

91. *Contra Celsum* I, 46.

92. *Apostolic Tradition* 19:1 (Dix p. 30, SPCK).

93. *ibid.* 20:2 (Dix p. 31).

94. Exorcism, *ibid.* 20:3, 8; unction, *ibid.* 21:10.

95. *ibid.* 22:1–3 (Dix p. 38–39).

96. Tertullian, *De baptismo* 4, ANF III.

97. cf. J. Daniélou, *From Shadows to Realities,* London: Burns & Oates, 1960; P. Lundberg, *La typologie baptismale dans l'Ancienne Eglise,* Lund 1942.

98. Cyril, *Catechetical Lectures,* LNPF VII; *Procatechesis* 1:16.

99. *Sermon for the Feast of Lights,* Hamman, *Baptism,* p. 124.

100. Theodore of Mopsuestia, *Catechetical Homilies* IV, Woodbroke Studies by Cambridge: Mingana, 1933, p. 20, 51.

101. Chrysostom, *Homily* 25 *On John 3:5;* Hamman, *Baptism,* p. 177–78.

102. Ambrose, *De mysteriis* 4:21, LNPF X, p. 319–320.

103. Basil, *Protreptic on Holy Baptism,* Hamman, *Baptism,* p. 76.

104. Cyril, *Catecheses* III, *On Baptism* 3, LCC IV, p. 90.

105. Cyril of Jer., *Myst. Hom.* II, *On Chrism* 1–3, LNPF VII, p. 149–150; Origen, *Com. Song.,* I, 3 (ACW p. 70ff).

106. Cyril of Jer., *Myst. Hom.* V, *On the Eucharistic Rite* 7, LNPF VII, p. 154.

107. Ambrose, *De sacramentis* I, 15.

108. *Apostolic Tradition* IV, 12 (Dix, p. 9).

109. L. Bouyer, *The Eucharist,* Univ. of Notre Dame Press, 1968; J. Laporte, *La doctrine eucharistique chez Philon d'Alexandrie,* Paris 1972.

110. *Odes of Solomon* 6, 11, 14, 28, 36; cf. A. Jaubert, *La notion d'Alliance dans le Judaisme aux approches de l'ère chrétienne,* Paris 1963, where the author deals with priesthood or sacrifice.

111. *Apostolic Tradition* XXVIII, 6–7 (Dix p. 54–55); *Didascalia* IX (Connolly p. 96); *Apostolic Constitutions* VII, 29 (ANF VII, p. 471).

112. *Didascalia* XVIII (Connolly p. 156–160).

113. *Sermo* 71.

114. *Homily on Ephesians* XI, LNPF XIII, p. 105; cf. D. Greeley, *The Church as Body of Christ According to the Teachings of St. J. Chrysostom,* Thesis, Notre Dame University 1971, especially chap. 8, p. 125–136.

115. Ignatius, *To Smyrnians* 5–6, LCC I: 114–115.

116. Cyprian, *On the Unity of the Church* 6, 10, 11, 13, 14.

117. Cyprian, *Ephesians* 68–75, the dispute with Stephen about baptism given by heretics.

118. Augustine, *De baptismo contra Donatistas Libri VII.*

119. *ibid.*

120. Each party denies the other the right to be a church, to have valid or working sacraments, to possess the Holy Spirit. The Donatists refuse it to Catholics, *Contra Literas Petiliani* 33–46 (hereafter cited as *Contra Lit. Pet.*); and Augustine refuses it to the Donatists, though acknowledging the validity (not the spiritual efficacy) of Donatist baptism, *Contra Lit. Pet.* 104–108; *De baptismo contra Donatistas* I, 15; VII, 13–19.

121. Augustine refutes Cyprian (or rather the Donatists who rely on the error of Cyprian) with regard to the validity of baptism conferred by heretics, in *De baptismo contra Donatistas,* but he maintains that their baptism is 'dead,' and leads to condemnation unless they enter the Catholic Church, which alone possesses the Holy Spirit. Augustine appeals to the unity of the Church, which is found in the Universal Church, the heir of Christ's promise. This argument is

right. However, since the manifestations of the Holy Spirit are seen as well in severed Churches or denominations, and in sects, we may assume, on a phenomenological basis, that the Holy Spirit is there too, without probably contradicting Augustine's argument of the unity of the Church.

122. For Bishops, *Apostolic Tradition* III, 1–6 (Dix. p. 4–6); for presbyters, *ibid.* VIII, 2–5 (Dix. p. 13–14); for deacons, *ibid.* IX, 2–11 (Dix. p. 15–18).

123. *Didascalia* X, (Connolly, p. 104).

124. Cyprian, *Ephesians* 57 (Bude).

125. Basil, *On the Spirit* 19; Origen, *On Prayer* 28:8 (ACW p. 111–112).

126. *Didascalia* I.

127. *Apost. Const.* VIII, 8–9, ANF VII, p. 484–485.

128. Clement, *Strom.* 1, 8:4.

129. Augustine, *Enarr. in Psalmos* L, P.L. 36:485; Sermo 71.

130. Tertullian, *On Modesty* 21, ANF IV, p. 98–100.

131. Origen, *On Prayer* 8 (ACW p. 111).

132. For instance, E. Schweitzer, *Church Order in the N.T.*, London 1961, ch. 15–17.

133. Cf. Eusebius, *Ecclesiastical History* V, 14–19 (LNPF I, p. 229–237) for the ancient Church, and other testimonies in Pierre de Labriolle, *La Crise montaniste*, and *Les sources*, Paris 1913.

134. *ibid.* p. 538–547; Cf. G. Kretschmar, *La doctrine du St. Esprit du N.T. à Nicée*, Vig. Chr. 22, 1963, p. 28ff, favorable to Montanism.

135. Labriolle, *op. cit.* p. 34–105, Montanist oracles; p. 23ff, prophetesses.

136. *ibid.* ch. IV, p. 144–181: Origen, *First Princ.* II, ch. 7.

137. Tertullian, *De velandis virginibus* 1; *De monogamia* 2–4; 14.

138. Tertullian, *De pudicitia* 21.

139. Labriolle, *op. cit.* p. 162–174.

140. Visions, cf. *Oracle* 17; prophecy, cf. *Oracles* 1–4; 11; inspirations, cf. *Oracle* 5 (Labriolle, *op. cit.* p. 34–105.).

141. *ibid.* p. 168–174; Behm, *Glossolalia*, in TDNT I, p. 722–727. (English).

142. Ignatius, *Ad Rom.* 7:2; cf. *Ad Eph.* 5:3; *Ad Philad.* 1:1; *Ad Magn.* 8:2.

143. Clement, *Strom.* I, 21; 143:1.

144. Labriolle, *op. cit.* p. 122ff.

145. Clement, *Strom.* II, 52, LCC II, p. 64; Cf. Eusebius, *Ecclesiastical History* II, 31, where, according to *Act.* 21:8–9, they are virgins.

146. *Hermas, Visions.*

147. *Passion of Polycarp* 12:2; 16:2 ("Apostolic and prophetic teacher, Bishop of the Catholic Church in Smyrna").

148. *ibid.* 5:2 (the burning pillow); 9:1 (the divine voice in the stadium).

149. *Passio Perpetuae,* ANF III, p. 699–706, especially 4, 7, 8, 10, 11, 12, 13, 14.
150. *Epistle of the Gallican Churches, The Vision of Attalus,* Eusebius, *Ecclesiastical History* V, 3:2–3.
151. *Passion of Polycarp* XII; Clement, *Strom.* IV, 9; Cyril, *Catecheses* 16:21.
152. *Passion of Polycarp* I-III; XIV.
153. *Passion of Perpetua* XV.
154. *ibid.* XX.
155. Clement, *Strom.* IV, 7.
156. Tertullian, *Apologeticum,* end.
157. *Contra Celsum,* I, 46, 68; III, 24 (physical and moral miracles).
158. *ibid.* VII, 8.
159. *On Prayer* 12, 13.
160. I *Tim.* 5:3–16.
161. *Didascalia,* XV (Connolly p. 132–140).
162 J. P. Arendzen, *An Entire Text of the 'Apostolic Church Order'* J.T.S. 3, 1902, p. 71.
163. *Didascalia,* Ch. XIV, XVII.
164. *Hermas,* The Parable of the Vine and the Elm, Similitude II, ANF II, p. 32.
165. *Epistle of Polycarp to Philippians* IV, 3; *Didascalia* XV, (Connolly p. 133).
166. *Didascalia* XVII (Connolly p. 156–158).
167. Clement, *Strom.* II, 2, LCC II, p. 41.
168. Clement, *Quis dives salvetur?* 34, ANF II, p. 601.
169. *ibid.* 35, p. 601.
170. *Didascalia* V (Connolly p. 38).
171. *Contra literas petiliani* I, 12, 28–29, 53.
172. *Apostolic Tradition* XXVI (Dix p. 48).
173. *ibid.* XV (Dix p. 22).
174. *Apostolic Constitutions* VIII, 26, ANF VII, p. 493.
175. Justin, *Dial.* 82, 88; Irenaeus, *Adv. Haer.* V, 6:1.
176. Justin, *Dial.* 76.
177. Justin, II *Apology* 6, ANF I, p. 190.
178. Irenaeus, *Adv. Haer.* V, 18:2.
179. *Life of Antony* 13, 35; Tertullian, *Ad Uxorem* II, 5, ANF IV, p. 46.
180. *Apostolic Tradition* XXXVII (Dix p. 68).
181. Justin, *Dial.* 8, ANF I, p. 198.
182. *Contra Celsum* I, 6 (Chadwick p. 9).
183. *Ad uxorem* II, 5, ANF IV, p. 46.
184. *Didache* X, 7; XI, 3 to XIII, 7; XV, 1–2.
185. J. P. Audet, *La Didaché,* Etudes Bibliques, Paris 1958, chap. I, and p. 432–458.
186. *Didache* X, 7.

187. Cyprian, Ep. 10; *Didascalia* XX (Connolly p. 168).
188. Origen, *On Martyrdom*, 42 (ACW p. 186).
189. Clement, *Strom.* II, 20; *Didascalia* Ch. 19.
190. Cyprian, *Ep.* 38, 39, 40.
191. *ibid.* 15, 19, 32.
192. *Life of Antony*, 22, 23, 36–43.
193. The message of Hermas is destined for all, *Vision* 2 (end), and a branch of olive tree is given to everyone, *Similitude* 8.
194. In *Hermas*, the spirit of patience and the spirit of anger (5:33) are paralleled with the angel of justice and the angel of evil (6:36; 12:49), with a holy spirit and a spirit of sadness (10:40), with the good and false prophet (11:43), with good and bad desire (12:44), with virgins in black clothes (vices) and virgins in bright clothes (virtues) (*Sim.* 9:13–15). In the *Life of Antony*, there are devils and a satan (41), but the spirits themselves seem to be some kind of personification of vices, which exercise both a power of temptation, e.g. the spirit of lust (41) and of harrassment, e.g. through visions, voices, and blows (28). They are opposed by faith in God, prayer, fasting, the Sign of the Cross, and the awareness that they are clever but not powerful, since they can only take advantage of the passions in man. See also Clement, *Strom.* II, 20.
195. *Life of Antony* 14, LNPF IV, p. 200.
196. *ibid.* 20, p. 201.
197. *Sayings* I, 11, 15, II, 1, 2, 9, III, 22, IV, 49, 51, 61, 62 V, 4, VI, 6, VII, 5, 32, VIII, 19, IX, 2, 6, X, 40, 55, 110, 114, XI, 2, 43, XII, 2, XIII, 7, XV, 28, 29, 68, XVI, 19, XVII, 1, 2.
198. Clement, *Strom.*, I, 4 to 12; *Contra Celsum* VII, 23.
199. *ibid. Strom.* II, 69, *Strom.* V, 4, *Strom.* VI, 13, *Strom.* VII, especially 44, 62, 68, 80, 87, 88, 104, 105.
200. Clement, *Strom.* VII, 80, LCC II, p. 144.
201. *ibid.* 80.
202. Origen, *First Princ.* II, ch. 7, *The Holy Spirit; Contra Celsum* III, 18–46.
203. Cf. F. Bertrand, *Mystique de Jésus chez Origène*, Aubier, Paris 1951.
204. *First Princ.* II, 7:2 (Butterworth p. 117).
205. *Contra Celsum* VI, 13–14 (Chadwick p. 327).
206. *First Princ.* II, 11:5 (Butterworth p. 150).
207. *Com. Song* II, 4, ACW: 123.

IV: Islam

1. The classic study of this subject is D. B. Macdonald, "The Development of the Idea of Spirit in Islam," *Acta Orientalia* IX (1931):

307–351, reprinted in *The Moslem World* XX, no. 1 (1932): 25–42, II: 153–168 (from which the citations are taken), completed by Thomas O'Shaughnessy, S.J., *The Development of the Meaning of Spirit in the Koran* (Rome: Pontificum Institutum Orientalium Studiorum, Orientalia Christiana Analecta 139, 1953). Louis Massignon, "L'idée de l'esprit dans l'Islam," *Eranos-Jahrbuch* XIII (1945; Zürich: Rhein-Verlag, 1946): 277–282, is a brief but provocative treatment, and the subject comes up repeatedly in his *Essai sur les Origines du Lexique Technique de la Mystique Musulmane* (Paris: J. Vrin, 1954), and in his monumental chef-d'oeuvre *La Passion d'al-Hosayn Ibn Manṣour al-Hallj, Martyr mystique de l'Islam,*, 2 vols. (Paris, 1922).

 2. Louis Gardet and M.-M. Anawati, *Introduction à la Théologie Musulmane* (Paris: J. Vrin, 1948) is still the best general introduction to the subject. F. M. Pareja, *Islamologie* (Beyrouth: Imprimerie Catholique, 1964), the latest of many editions in many languages, is a giant history and bibliography. A novice might prefer to begin with H. A. R. Gibb, *Mohammedanism: An Historical Survey,* 2nd ed. (London: Oxford University Press, 1971) and W. Montgomery Watt, *Muhammad: Prophet and Statesman* (London: Oxford University Press, 1969). The author's own *Anthology of Islamic Literature* (New York: Holt, Rinehart and Winston, 1964) and *Modern Islamic Literature* (New York: Holt, Rinehart and Winston, 1970) might prove to have some value.

 3. Note the different preference in H. A. R. Gibb and J. H. Kramers, *Shorter Encyclopaedia of Islam* (Ithaca: Cornell University Press, n.d.) *s.v.* "Nafs," pages 433–436, which may only reflect editorial parsimony. Of course Macdonald and O'Shaughnessy, *opera cit.,* have much to say about the matter.

 4. Edward W. Lane, *An Arabic-English Lexicon* (London, 1863—1885), *s.v.* "*Rūḥ,*" Book I, part 3, page 1180.

 5. The author accepts, on this fundamentally important question, the conclusions of O'Shaughnessy, *op. cit.,* especially pages 42–68. The four "anomalous texts" do not appear to constitute a "fifth" sense-group; nor is the analysis in the *Shorter Encyclopaedia of Islam,* pages 433–434, on this matter satisfactory.

 6. Nöldeke *et al., Geschichte des Qor'āns,* 3 vols. (Leipzig: Dietrich, 1909–1938); Blachère, *Introduction au Coran, Le Coran,* 3 vols. (Paris, 1947–1950). In a later edition, (Paris, 1957) Blachère returned to the traditional order without comment. The best English translation of the Koran is that of A. J. Arberry, *The Koran Interpreted* (New York: Macmillan, 1955).

 7. O'Shaughnessy, *op. cit.,* uses the translation of Richard Bell, *The Qur'ān* (Edinburgh, 1937–1939), for a deliberate purpose, and so it is this translation which the author follows hereafter, except for his own of one Sura; *vid.* note 27, *infra.* K = Koran throughout.

 8. O'Shaughnessy, *op. cit.,* pages 25–33; Macdonald, *op. cit.,* II, pages 157–159.

9. *Rasūl* ("messenger" or "ambassador") is carefully distinguished in Arabic from *nabi* ("prophet"); and it is, of course, *rasūl* which found its way into the *shahādah* (profession of faith in Islam): "There is no god but *Allāh*, and Mohammed is His messenger." The dating of this *āyah*, "relegating" Jesus to Mohammed's own status while freely granting Him to be God's "word" and "a spirit from Him," is an important matter, in light of later developments. Cf. Wilfred Cantwell Smith, "Some Similarities and Differences between Christianity and Islam," in *The World of Islam,* edited by James Kritzeck and R. Bayly Winder (London: Macmillan, 1959), pages 47–59.

10. On this stage of development, see especially M. M. Bravmann, *The Spiritual Background of Early Islam: Studies in Ancient Arab Concepts* (Leiden: E. J. Brill, 1972), pages 39–122; O'Shaughnessy, *op. cit.,* pages 33–42, penetrating in analysis but lacking the benefit of Bravmann's longer concentration.

11. The reference is to an early Christian story which found its way into countless apocryphal collections, notably Coptic Ethiopian, wherein Our Lord's first miracle was speaking from the cradle; see the author's *Sons of Abraham* (Baltimore and Dublin: Helicon, 1965), pages 57–71. "The representing of the spirit in the earlier suras (chapters of the Koran) as a mysterious being set above the angels reflects the Gnostic coloring that runs throughout the Koran. In suras composed at a later date, when the Prophet had come into closer contact with Christianity and Judaism, he adapted to his own use the Biblical concepts of spirit—breath of life, inspirer of revelation, strengthening force—but even then Gnostic traces are rarely absent . . . The Prophet (Mohammed), however, combined the information drawn from such sources in no mere mechanical fashion. Rather, he refashioned his material, suiting it to his own purposes and to what he regarded as the religious needs of his countrymen. If, then, 'spirit' in the Koran approximates any of the meanings attached to the term in Scripture and the ecclesiastical writers of the early centuries, such similarity would appear merely accidental. Mohammed, probably with the aid of mentors, evolved his own theories concerning the spirit and other doctrinal points proposed for his explanation. Throughout his career as a religious reformer, but especially in Medina, his opinions, legal and dogmatic, constituted a rule of faith for his followers, some of whom had come to Islam from the heretical Christian sects and would desire to know the teaching of their new faith regarding the spirit, Jesus, and other concepts and personages familiar to them . . . (The Koran's) teachings on the spirit are expressed in stereotyped phrases possessed of a certain dignity and sufficiently vague in meaning to keep their author from being involved in discussions on theology, in which his knowledge was extremely limited." O'Shaughnessy, *op. cit.,* pages 67–68.

12. The reference is, of course, to the work of Thomas

O'Shaughnessy, S.J., again, who was killed tragically in an automobile accident in 1956.

13. There are countless references, already cited throughout Macdonald, *op. cit.*, but certainly placed in best order by Massignon in *La Passion . . .* (ref. note 1).

14. The literature on Sufism grows steadily. The best general introduction for the novice is A. J. Arberry, *Sufism* (London: George Allen & Unwin, 1950). J. Spencer Trimingham, *The Sufi Orders in Islam* (Oxford: Clarendon, 1971) is an invaluable study, as is Louis Gardet, *La Mystique Musulmane* (Paris, 1968).

15. Gardet, *op. cit.*, pages 84–102.

16. James Kritzeck and William H. Lewis, eds., *Islam in Africa* (New York: Van Nostrand, 1969), pages 87–109.

17. Macdonald, *op. cit.*, I, page 159.

18. They are more striking, clearly, when set next to the Semitic and Hellenic confrontations on Christology.

19. See R. C. Zaehner, *Hindu and Muslim Mysticism* (London: The Athlone Press, 1960); but cf. the (possibly extreme) position taken by Massignon in *Essai sur les Origines du Lexique . . .* against the Hindu influence, and the author's review of Zaehner's book in *Speculum* XXXVI, no. 4 (October, 1961): 698–700.

20. W. Montgomery Watt, *Muslim Intellectual: Al-Ghazali* (London: George Allen & Unwin, 1969); George F. Hourani, "The Chronology of Ghazāli's Writings," *Journal of the American Oriental Society* 79, no. 4 (Oct.–Dec., 1959): 225–233. A comprehensive bibliography of Al-Ghazāli's works, taking into account new manuscript discoveries and all recent scholarship on them—and him, is long overdue.

21. Macdonald, *op. cit.*, II, pages 153–162.

22. On 'Attār, see the many works of Hellmut Ritter; but Fritz Meier, "Der Geistmensch bei dem Persichen Dichter 'Attār," *Eranos-Jahrbuch* XIII (cit., note 1): 281–353, is one of the finest and best-documented studies of a major Sufi poet. On Ibn al-Fāriḍ, R. A. Nicholson, *Studies in Islamic Mysticism* (Cambridge, 1921), is probably the best source in English, although many of the other sources cited in this chapter refer to him *passim*.

23. Macdonald, *op. cit.*, II, page 163.

24. *Ibid.*, II, pages 165–166. The question of possible Hindu influence on these ideas is treated by Zaehner, *op. cit.* Clearly the lexicon of "varieties" of "Holy Spirit" was swelled by many outside influences.

25. Massignon, "L'idée de l'esprit . . .", page 281; Macdonald, *op. cit.*, pages 161–162.

26. The notion of Jesus as "the Perfect Man" had been native within Islam, even outside Sufism, for many centuries before this occurrence. It seems to have caused far less difficulty than its

transference to the person of Mohammed; cf. Massignon, *La Passion...*, pages 174–186.

27. The author's translation, adopting A. J. Arberry's decision on the meaning of *ṣamad*.

28. Macdonald, *op. cit.*, I, pages 3–40, defines the position of Ibn Qayim al-Jawziyya (d. 1350), in his *Kitab al-Ruḥ*, as the normal Sunni, "ordinary" position of Muslims on the subject. The author tends to doubt that this was or is so. Cf. Massignon, "L'idée de l'Esprit...", page 232.

29. On Sufi literature in general, see the bibliography in Pareja, *op. cit.*, pages 744–789.

30. Massignon, *La Passion...* and *Essai sur les Origines...*, once again, provide ample proof and references.

31. Trimingham, *op. cit.*, especially pages 200–207.

32. *Ibid.*, ref. on page 302. Massignon describes a *dhikr* in "L'idée l'Esprit...", pages 278–280, and Vincent Monteil another in Kritzeck and Lewis, *op. cit.*, pages 87–109.

33. As a typical example, see *Sufi Studies: East and West*, edited by L. F. Rushbook Williams (New York: E. P. Dutton, 1973), and the innumerable books of Idries Shah, published by Penguin Books in England.

34. On this dolorous period of the decline of Sufism, *vid.* H. A. R. Gibb and Harold Bowen, *Islamic Society and the West* I, Part II, (London: Oxford University Press, 1957): 179–206.

35. They had been off to a good start with the complicated patterns of the *tafsīr* literature; cf. the tables in O'Shaughnessy, *op. cit.*, pages 24, 32, 43, 52, 65. Al-Ghazāli certainly added to it; cf. Macdonald, *op. cit.*, II, pages 154–156.

36. This point is frequently made and substantiated in detail by J. Spencer Trimingham in his various books on Islam in Africa; see also Kritzeck and Lewis, *op. cit.*, especially pages 88–109.

37. See Martin Lings, *A Sufi Saint of the Twentieth Century: Shaikh Ahmad al-'Alawi: His Spiritual Heritage and Legacy,* 2nd ed. (Berkeley and Los Angeles: University of California Press, 1971). Note the striking resemblance of the photographs of the Shaykh's face to the face on the Holy Shroud of Turin.

V: Movements

1. This paper was presented originally at the Roman Catholic-Pentecostal dialogue in Rome, June 18–22, 1973, and then in a theological conference on the charismatic renewal at the University of Notre Dame, July 20–22, 1973. In its original form it was published in

the ecumenical quarterly, *One in Christ* 2 (London: 1974). It has been annotated and revised for the present publication.

2. Gottfried Arnold (1666–1714): *Unpartheyische Kirchen-und Ketzerhistorie vom Anfang des Neuen Testaments bis auf Jahr 1860* (Frankfurt: 1699). *Fortsetzung und Erlaüterung der unpartheiische Kirchen- und Ketzerhistorie bestehend in Beschreibung der noch übrigen Streitigkeiten im siebzehnden Jahrhundert* (Frankfurt: 1700); *Historia et descriptio theologiae mysticae, seu theosophiae arcanae et reconditae itemque veterum et novorum mysticorum* (Frankfurt: 1702).

3. Cf. Apoc. 1.

4. Cf. Rom. 12:6–8.

5. I Cor. 13.

6. Rom. 5:8.

7. *The Mysticism of Paul the Apostle* (New York: Macmillan, 1955).

8. *The Christian in the Theology of St. Paul* (London: G. Chapman, 1967).

9. Handley Carr Glyn Moule (1841–1920), Bishop of Durham.

10. Text and translation in *The Apostolic Fathers* II ed. by G. R. Cake (Harvard: 1913): 307–345. Polycarp, Bishop of Smyrna, was martyred ca. 155.

11. Critical edition of the English translation of the *Passio* by J. A. Robinson *Texts and Studies* 1, #2 (Cambridge: University Press, 1891).

12. Montanus began his prophesying some time during the latter half of the third century in Phrygia (modern Asia Minor).

13. Karl Holl, *Enthusiasmus und Bussgewalt beim griechischen Mönchtums* VI (Leipzig: J. C. Hinrichs, 1898): 331.

14. English translation by Robert Meyer, *Ancient Christian Writers* #107, Westminster, MD.: Newman Press, 1950).

15. *Apophtegmata Patrum*, a collection of sayings from Egyptian monks dating from the fourth and fifth centuries. Migne *P.G.* 65:71–440.

16. Athanasius to Dracontius, Migne PG 25:521–534; *The Nicene and Post-Nicene Fathers* 2, Vol. IV, Letter 49, p. 557.

17. Macarius was a great monk of Egypt (ca. 300–ca. 390). The fifty homilies traditionally attributed to him are of uncertain authorship. They appear in volume 34 of Migne's *Patrologia Graeca*.

18. Cf. *Homily* 1:12; *Homily* 49:1.

19. An unknown writer whose works are first heard of about 518. He adopted the pen name of Dionysius (i.e., the famous convert of St. Paul at Athens; cf. Acts 17:34).

20. See the beginning of the *Mystical Theology*, English trans. C. E. Rolt (New York: Macmillan, 1940).

21. Cf. *Vision*, 14th and 15th answers; also *One Hundred Chapters on Spiritual Perfection*, chapter 25. (Text and French translations in *Sources Chrétiennes* 5, Paris: Cerf, 1955).

22. See his 29th catechetical sermon in *Catéchèse* III, ed. B. Krivocheine *Sources Chrétiennes* 113, (Paris: Cerf, 1965).

23. See his 34th catechetical sermon *ibid.*

24. *The Prayer of Jesus,* by a Monk of the Eastern Church (New York: Desclée, 1967).

25. Migne PG 150, 771–1372 and 151, 1–678.

26. The Blacherna Synod of 1351. In 1368, another synod of Constantinople canonized Gregory as a "Father and Doctor of the Church."

27. Selections from this enormous work have been translated into English by E. Kadlouboysky and G. E. H. Palmer in the volumes *Writings from the Philokalia on prayer of the heart,* (London: Faber and Faber, 1951) and *Early Fathers from the Philokalia,* ibid., 1954.

28. St. Nil or Nilus was born in 1433. His biography has never been written. Cf. *History of Christian Spirituality* 3 by Bouyer, Leclercq, Vanden and Cognes, (New York: Desclée, 1963 ff.): 19ff.

29. English translation, *The Fire of Love,* ed. by R. Harvey, *Orchard Series* 106 (London 1896).

30. *The Melos Amoris of R. R. Hampole,* edited by E. Arnold, Oxford, 1957.

31. This fourteenth century work seems to have been written after Rolle's works, but before those of Walter Hilton. A critical text has been edited by P. Hodgson (Early English Text Society. Original Series 218, 1944); modernized versions by E. Underhill (London, 1924), J. McCann (London, 1944) and H. Brinton (New York and London, 1948).

32. Ruysbroeck's works, written in Flemish, have been published by J. van Mierlo and others at Antwerp, 1932–1934. English translations are available for *The Twelve Beguines* by J. Francis, (London, 1913, *The Adornment of the Spiritual Marriage, The Sparkling Stone,* and *The Book of Supreme Truth* by C. Dom, (London, 1916), *The Seven Steps of the Ladder of Spiritual Love* by P. Taylor, (London, 1944) and of *The Kingdom of the Lovers of God* by T. Hyde, (London, 1919).

33. Works in Migne, *Patrologia latina* 180: 201–726; see also vol. 182: 531–33 and 184: 307–436 for other writings of his wrongly attributed to St. Bernard. English translation of his *Works* 19 (Cistercian Publications: Spencer, Mass. 1970.)

34. *Summa theologiae* I-II, Question 68. This text has been translated and annotated in *The Gifts of the Spirit* by E. D. O'Connor, (= vol. 24 of the bilingual edition of the *Summa* published by Blackfriars: Oxford, and McGraw Hill: New York, 1974). On each of the seven gifts in particular, see *Summa* II-II, questions 8, 9, 15, 16, 19, 22/2, 45, 46, 52, 121, 139, and 140.

VI: Mysticism

1. None of what follows is mere speculation; it is all based on the testimony of serious witnesses. Where appropriate, I have cited recognized authorities in the field of spirituality. For some of the points put forward here, I am doing little more than articulating the experience and insights of others who, however, must remain anonymous. Of course, even when an experience is sure, the interpretation placed upon it will inevitably remain more or less debatable.

2. In using such language, we must not, of course, lose sight of the terrible discontinuity of this life which normally passes through alternating phases of light and shadow, joy and sorrow, peace and tension. Nevertheless a fundamental permanence remains beneath this variety of modes.

3. See the *Way of Perfection,* chapter 33. In *The Interior Castle,* this prayer is treated in the Fourth Dwelling (mansion), chapter 3, under the name, 'prayer of recollection.' In the famous comparison of prayer to the watering of a garden, the grace of quiet is represented by the second way, i.e., by the use of a machine which brings water more easily and abundantly than the gardener can do by hauling it in buckets. Further stages of the prayer of union are represented by the aqueduct which brings a stream of water to the garden, and finally by the abundant rainfall. See the saint's *Life,* chapters 13 and following.

4. To call God an object in this sense is not to demean Him to the level of a thing, but simply to suppose that it is possible really, albeit inadequately, to know Him and worship Him (to say nothing of loving Him, which belongs more properly to the Jewish and especially Christian religions).

5. Several texts illustrative of this point are cited by Poulain, *The Graces of Interior Prayer* (London, 6th ed. 1912), in appendix to chapter 6 (p. 108 ff.).

6. Cf. Poulain, ibid.

7. Garrigou-Lagrange seems to be loyal to the witness of the mystics when he explains "the contact of the divine essence with the substance of our soul" by a "profound action (in French: *"motion"*) (of God) upon the basis of the intellect and will, where they are rooted in the substance of the soul . . . bearing them towards Himself." *Les trois âges de la vie intérieure* 2 (Paris: Cerf, 1951): 703. The translation of this passage in *The Three Ages of the Interior Life* 2 (St. Louis and London: Herder, 1948): 592f seems to miss some important nuances.

8. Cf. F. X. Durrwell, *The Resurrection* (New York: Sheed and Ward, 1960): 289.

9. Cf. St. Teresa of Avila: "This heavenly water spreads through all the room in the castle, and through all the powers of the soul, until finally it reaches even the body." *Interior Castle,* Fourth Dwelling, ch. 2.

10. A brief, systematic survey of the doctrine, with examples from the lives of the mystics, is given by Poulain, op. cit., chapter 6. Many supplementary examples can be found in Johann Goerres, *Christliche Mystik* (Regensburg and Landshut, 1836 ff.), book 3. In the latter case, however, besides the uncritical credulity of the author, which makes it necessary to use his material with caution, the classifications are inconsistent and the systematic interpretations given to them often seem forced and imaginary, so that it is not easy to get to the true sense of the examples.

11. *Op. cit.* Poulain, appendix to chapter 6.

12. The analogy with yoga is only too evident; but it is wise to be cautious about assuming an identical significance in the two cases.

13. Cf. Johann Goerres, *Christliche Mystik,* as cited in note 10. Book III, ch. 2, is devoted to "supernatural and mystical movements," caused by the Holy Spirit taking possession of the motive powers. Auguste Saudreau, in *The Mystical state* (New York: Benziger, 1924): 163 ff. gives several texts which, especially when taken together, suggest the same thing.

14. Cf. *Dark Night of the Spirit,* chapters 5 and 9.

VII: Literature

1. These early reports are not retained in the present bibliography. For references, see E. D. O'Connor, C.S.C., *The Pentecostal Movement in the Catholic Church* (Notre Dame: Ave Maria Press, 1971), pp. 297–298.

2. *New Covenant,* September 1974, p. 5.

3. Most of the work of searching out and recording this material was done by Sister Amata Fabbro, O.P., to whom I am deeply grateful.

INDEX

Only the text and the bibliography have been indexed.
Authors merely cited in the footnotes are not noted here.